Moral Realism

BLOOMSBURY ETHICS SERIES

Bloomsbury Ethics is a series of books written to help students explore, engage with, and master key topics in contemporary ethics and moral philosophy.

Series Editors: Thom Brooks, Reader in Law, Durham Law School, UK and Simon Kirchin, Department of Philosophy, University of Kent, UK.

Available now:

Intuitionism, David Kaspar
Reasons, Eric Wiland
Virtue Ethics, Nafsika Athanassoulis

Forthcoming in the series:

Autonomy, Andrew Sneddon
Moral Motivation, Leonard Kahn
Trust, Ethics and Human Reason, Olli Lagerspetz

BLOOMSBURY ETHICS

Moral Realism

KEVIN DELAPP

BLOOMSBURY

LONDON · NEW DELHI · NEW YORK · SYDNEY

Bloomsbury Academic
An imprint of Bloomsbury Publishing Plc

50 Bedford Square	175 Fifth Avenue
London	New York
WC1B 3DP	NY 10010
UK	USA

www.bloomsbury.com

First published 2013

British Library Cataloguing-in-Publication Data
A catalogue record for this book is available from the British Library.

ISBN: HB: 978-1-4411-2691-7
PB: 978-1-4411-6118-5
ePub: 978-1-4411-4828-5
ePDF: 978-1-4411-6418-6

Library of Congress Cataloging-in-Publication Data
DeLapp, Kevin Michael, 1978–
Moral realism/Kevin DeLapp.
p. cm. – (Bloomsbury ethics)
Includes bibliographical references (p.) and index.
ISBN 978-1-4411-2691-7 (hardcover: alk. paper) –
ISBN 978-1-4411-6118-5(pbk.: alk. paper) –
ISBN 978-1-4411-4828-5 (ebook epub: alk. paper) –
ISBN 978-1-4411-6418-6 (ebook epub: alk. paper)
1. Moral realism. 2. Ethics. 3. Realism. I. Title.
BJ1500.M67D45 2013
171'.2–dc23
2012024338

Typeset by Deanta Global Publishing Services, Chennai, India
Printed and bound in India

CONTENTS

PREFACE

This book introduces readers to the topic of "moral realism." The first chapter articulates why moral realism *matters* and the subsequent chapters expand the scope of the discussion beyond the usual disciplinary comfort zones of philosophy (metaphysics, epistemology, semantics) and into the realms of cultural anthropology, social psychology, and political science. While the focus throughout is on canvassing the various possible formulations of moral realism, a new specific type of realism is also presented which has its own theoretical advantages and which can also serve heuristically as a guiding thread through different debates. The reader should gain from this book a better sense of not only the resources and diversity of moral realism as a theory, but also its embedded political, cultural, and psychological significance.

My fascination with moral realism began during my first exposure to philosophy, and I extend deep appreciation to my undergraduate professors Ellen Suckiel and John Isbister, who patiently mentored me at a time when I had more enthusiasm than accuracy. Moral realism was also the topic of my doctoral dissertation, and I owe great intellectual and personal debts to my advisors David Wong and Owen Flanagan; it was their masterful interdisciplinary scholarship that inspired in me the conviction that moral realism must address real-life concerns for it to be worth defending. I should also like to thank the rest of my graduate evaluating committee – Elizabeth Kiss, Tad Schmaltz, and Michael Ferejohn – for their many constructive comments over the years.

Part of Section 3.4 first appeared as "The merits of dispositional moral realism," in *The Journal of Value Inquiry* 43 (2009): 1–18. Part of Sections 5.3 and 7.1 are adapted from "Giving responsibility a guilt-trip: virtue, tragedy, and privilege," in *Philosophica* 85 (2012): 1–32. And elements of Sections 6.2–6.4 were published as "Moral perception and moral realism: an 'intuitive' account of epistemic justification," in *The Review Journal of Political Philosophy* 5 (2007): 43–64. My thanks to the editors and publishers of these journals for their kind permission to reprint this material.

I am grateful to Thom Brooks and Simon Kirchin for their vision in organizing this series, to the editorial staff (Sarah Campbell, Rachel Eisenhauer, and Laura Murray) at Bloomsbury for their helpful guidance and suggestions, and to three anonymous referees who commented on an early proposal for this project. Any remaining errors are my own. Finally, I thank my family (Tom, Jan, and Kathryn) for their never-ending encouragement (even when discussions of metaethics somehow always pop up at holiday dinners), and my wife, Sarah Tignor – my own source of "re-enchantment".

CHAPTER ONE

Values in a disenchanted world

1.1 Disenchantment

This book is about morality in the broadest, most fundamental sense. The philosophical study of such a topic is called "metaethics," reminding us that we are not so much searching for particular answers to everyday ethical questions (e.g. is it okay to tell a small lie to bring about a greater good? do the ends justify the means?), but instead are seeking an understanding of the very idea of morality in the first place. What do we mean by moral words such as "good," "right," and "evil"? Do these words correspond to any objective facts, or are they merely (perhaps useful) artificial creations? The general position of this book is to defend a metaethical view commonly called "Moral Realism." This view will not necessarily tell us what to do in actual, concrete situations (although we will consider some possible concrete applications in Chapter 7); rather, it is designed to help shed light on what morality itself is. Specifically, moral realists believe that something about our ethical beliefs, actions, and concepts is "real" in some sense—that a core aspect of morality is "not up to us" or is "independent" from us in some way. Moral realists believe that there are "moral truths" in the world and that an individual or even an entire culture might be "wrong" about moral matters.

On the one hand, some may find this sort of moral realism highly intuitive, if not downright obvious. After all, humans are constantly making moral claims about what "should" or "should not" be done, about what is "right" and "wrong," about things or people which are "good" or "bad." Morality is a ubiquitous and foundational dimension of our lives: our moral ideals and behavior are part of how we define ourselves as both individuals and groups. Indeed, morality is deeply intertwined with our sense that our lives and actions "have value" or "mean something" (cf. Wiggins 1976). Yet, on the other hand, the claim that "morality" is somehow "real" may strike others as naive and unhelpful. After all, "morality" is a broad domain of human experience and thought, and saying that "it" is real is rather like saying "biology" or "art" is real—either trivial or else a category mistake. Furthermore, even a cursory philosophical reflection is sufficient to recognize that there are formidable challenges facing moral realism: *Where* are these alleged moral facts, and why do people constantly (and often brutally) disagree about them? For morality to affect us in the alleged existential way that it does, must it not be at least partially subjective? Those who find this second line of reasoning more attractive may be called *moral antirealists*.[1]

The very existence of this debate tells us something about the contemporary position in which morality finds itself. Metaethics as a domain of philosophical inquiry is by and large a uniquely modern phenomenon. This is not to say that earlier cultures or people never reflected on the foundations of morality, or did not have commitments to particular views which have analogs in modern metaethics. Even though the word "metaethics" wasn't coined until well into the twentieth century, we can still, for instance, speak perfectly sensibly about Plato's or Aquinas's or Zhuangzi's metaethical outlooks. But there are features of the modern world that undergird our approach to morality in fundamentally different ways than these earlier thinkers may have appreciated. Most notably, the specific terms of the contemporary realist/antirealist debate have arisen in response to what we might call a modern "disenchantment" with traditional substitutes for metaethics. The idea that modernity has been "disenchanting" in certain ways was popularized by Max Weber, "the father of sociology," who famously remarked that, "The fate of our times is characterized by rationalization and intellectualization and, above all, by 'the disenchantment of the world'" (1948: 155). Since Weber's time, the theme of "modernist dissatisfaction" has almost assumed the status of a truism. Rather than evaluate this theme in its generality, however, let's look at three particular features of modern "disenchantment" that have been thought to generate unique challenges for moral realism.

First, organized religion has lost much of its uncontested status in the modern world. This is certainly not to say that individuals or cultures are necessarily becoming "less religious." For example, while an increasing number of young Americans might be leaving the organized churches, mosques, or temples of their parents, their "spirituality" and the degree to which they see religion as important in their lives seems to be on the rise.[2] So-called mega churches are getting more mega, mission trips are on the rise, and far from Nietzsche's provocative prognosis that, under conditions of modernity, "God is dead," globalization instead seems to have generated *more* religious zeal and influence in political affairs worldwide (cf. Shah and Toft 2006). However, even if people are not necessarily becoming less religious, nonetheless the *authority* of religion is becoming more contestable. Theology can no longer be assumed as the "queen of the sciences" as it was for centuries, for theology is relative to a specific religious tradition which provides its starting assumptions, and modernity has confronted us with a variety of different, potentially competing religious traditions, and thus potentially divergent theologies. Choice of membership within different religious affiliations is more open, and atheism as a social-political identity is an explicitly articulated (if still controversial) alternative in a way that would have largely been a nonstarter two centuries ago.[3] Religiousness has become more of a self-conscious phenomenon than an enthymematic constituent of identity: even for religious individuals, there is more of an awareness of religion qua religion (i.e. as something against alternatives). Sectarian fissures within historic religious traditions highlight the "open question" that confronts a particular faith. It is not obvious that we all live within the same Christendom, or Dar al-Islam, or under the same Heaven, mainly because, from a religious perspective, it is not clear that there is a monolithic "we" any longer. (Of course, there probably never was such monism; the point, though, is just that this plurality is harder to deny in the modern world.) Thus, even religious *fundamentalism* must be seen as a uniquely modernist phenomenon, that is, as a counter-culture response that only makes sense as opposition to (perceived) developments in mainstream modern cultures.

These modern religious trends have interesting implications for metaethics. If people traditionally associate morality with religion—that is, if religion is often the vehicle or context through which values are communicated, codified, celebrated, and enforced—then fragmentation in the authority of one may affect confidence in the other. We shall have much more to say about the relationship between moral realism and religion in subsequent chapters (see §§2.2 and 3.3), but at a minimum, uncertainty regarding religious truths subtracts one of the possible models for the sort of uncontested moral objectivity to which realists are attracted.

A second potential source of disenchantment can be a heightened awareness of cross-cultural differences. Some of these differences might be religious, but modernity has also presented myriad instances of cultural diversity that are more directly moral in nature. As we shall see in subsequent chapters (see §4.1), a tempting reason in favor of moral *anti*realism is that it not only seems to better explain and accommodate moral diversity, but it also might support more tolerant responses to such diversity (see §7.2). As with the modernist confrontation of religious diversity, sensitivity to cultural pluralism also problematizes a traditional source of moral authority.

Finally, for some, a third potential source of disenchantment is the elevation of modern science to a position of epistemological and cultural authority. "Science" here does not mean merely the experimental investigation of natural facts, but rather the wholesale cosmological outlook we can call the "naturalistic conception" of humans and the world. According to such a conception, both physical phenomena and "human nature" alike may be satisfactorily understood in purely materialistic, if not mechanistic, terms. Despite the apparent explanatory and pragmatic successes of such a program, it seems *prima facie* difficult to account for "values" in a plenum of pure "facts." This is particularly challenging for moral realism. Can morality be "scientized" without sacrificing its objectivity or without reducing it to something nonmoral? What confidence can realists have in the existence of invisible "moral properties" that cannot be quantitatively measured, predicted, or understood through scientific models? We shall have much more to say about the relationship between science and realism in the ensuing chapters (see §§3.3 and 6.1), but the need for moral realism to respond to science as a worldview highlights something unique about modern metaethics.

These three sources of potential disenchantment—religious contestation, cultural pluralism, and the naturalistic conception of the world—are obviously intertwined. It has been by turning the scientific method of observation and measurement toward other cultures (whence the birth of modern disciplines such as anthropology, sociology, etc.) that cultural pluralism has been showcased. And insofar as religion is a dimension of culture, pluralism in the one goes hand in hand with pluralism in the other. Science and religion have also been viewed as linked in especially intimate ways vis-à-vis modernist disenchantment. Leveraging Weber's thesis, Charles Taylor also reflects a prevalent sentiment when he places secularism at the heart of disenchantment, diagnosing what he describes as,

> a fundamentally different existential predicament from that which dominated most previous cultures and still defines the lives of other people today. That alternative is a predicament in which an unchallengeable framework makes imperious demands that we fear being unable to meet. We face the prospect of irretrievable condemnation or exile, of being marked down in obloquy forever, or of being sent to damnation irrevocably . . . the form of danger here is utterly different from that which threatens the modern seeker, which is something close to the opposite: the world loses altogether its spiritual contour, nothing is worth doing, the fear is of a terrifying emptiness, a kind of vertigo, or even a fracturing of our world and body-space. (1989: 18)[4]

It is not necessary to agree fully with Taylor's specifically religious diagnosis of disenchantment in order to recognize that a metaethical view such as moral realism faces serious challenges. And the focus of this book is certainly not to defend religion *per se* (indeed, we shall see in the coming chapters that there are deep incompatibilities between religion and moral realism), nor to nostalgically lament the rise of cultural diversity or scientific paradigms. After all, these three sources of potential disenchantment are not *bad* things: the freedom of (and from) religion, increased sensitivity to and celebration of cultural diversity, and the explanatory power and practical benefits of modern science can all be wonderful aspects of modern life. The point is not to lament the "loss" of blindly monolithic religions, ethnocentric assumptions, or nonscientific mysteriousness. But in their absence, we do have to confront hard questions about the foundations of morality which religious, cultural, and nonscientific frameworks naively obscured. In this way, modern metaethics arises as an opportunity to think about morality in a "de-mythologized" way (to borrow Rudolf Bultmann's term). Modernist disenchantment, then, is a precondition for metaethics as an inquiry distinguishable from theology, casuistry, or social science. In a disenchanted world, moral realism cannot be blithely taken for granted—it must be actively *argued* for. The question this book seeks to address, then, is this: can morality survive the modernist gauntlet of secularism, scientism, and pluralism and emerge as a distinctive sphere of meaning with some anchorage in our conception of "reality"?

1.2 Meta-metaethics

Using the sort of "disenchantment" we discussed above as a starting point for a theory of moral realism differentiates this book from most other defenses of realism. Usually, realism is assumed—whether implicitly or explicitly—to be a default position in "commonsense" phenomenology. This alleged status of realism being "innocent until proven guilty" means that realists only primarily need defensive strategies against attackers, rather than needing to articulate their own positive arguments. If we take disenchantment seriously, however, this will not do. A satisfactory theory of moral realism will need not merely to poke holes in the theories of its rivals, but to articulate proactively a way in which morality can be "real" even in the face of cultural pluralism and a scientific conception of the world.

Yet, a defense of any metaethical position must ultimately be answerable to the experiences and perspectives which generated the questions to which it is a response. If morality is one of the things that give meaning to our lives, then a metaethical conclusion that takes us so far away from the needs and values with which we started as to be unrecognizable to us will have missed the whole point of metaethical theorizing in the first place. This is not an argument that metaethics can never tell us anything new or surprising, or that it can never call for sometimes drastic revisions in our understanding of morality. Nor is this an argument that there is any "default" consensus—whether realist or antirealist—which can settle debates preemptively. It is rather a metaphilosophical axiom—or, to coin a term, a "meta-metaethics"—which this book shall presume.

One meta-metaethical axiom we shall assume going into our discussion of moral realism is that morality (whatever that might mean and regardless of whether it turns out to be "real" or not) is *important* in some sense. William James makes the observation that moral (or metaethical) theorizing not only always begins from some starting point (which provides the *explananda* for the metaethical theory), but that this starting point is itself intrinsically moral.

> What is the position of him who seeks an ethical philosophy? To begin with, he must be distinguished from all those who are satisfied to be ethical sceptics. He *will* not be a sceptic; therefore so far from ethical scepticism being one possible fruit of ethical philosophizing, it can only be regarded as that residual alternative to all philosophy which from the outset menaces every would-be philosopher who may give up the quest discouraged, and renounce his original aim. That aim is to find an account of the moral relations that obtain among things, which will weave them into the unity of a stable system, and make of the world what one may call a genuine universe from the ethical point of view. (1891: 184–5)

In James's terminology, quietism, nonchalance, or nihilism (in the sense of thinking that there are *no* values, not even antirealist ones) are simply not "live options."

In this way, we can see that metaethical theory cannot be wholly divorced from ethical practice, let alone from first-order normative theorizing. As Matthew Kramer has argued, moral realism is itself a (first-order) moral doctrine, and "most of the reasons for insisting on the objectivity of ethics are ethical reasons" (2009: 2). This does not mean that there will be any isomorphic or necessary relation between a metaethical position and a particular normative framework. Both realism and antirealism may be compatible with any number of normative frameworks (and vice versa), just as normative frameworks may underdetermine specific judgments on applied ethical issues. Despite this underdetermination, however, James provides a transcendental argument that we need *some* sort of starting point for metaethical theorizing, and that it makes good sense to use as a starting point the very fact that morality itself is deemed significant enough to warrant theorizing in the first place.

This does not absolve the would-be realist from the burden of offering substantive and proactive arguments in favor of her position. But it does prevent realism from being ruled out *a priori*, and it reminds us that antirealism faces its own burdens of accommodating the humanist, existentialist, and pragmatic concerns we bring to the metaethical table in the first place. In this way, realism has a metaphilosophical advantage over antirealism—not because it is more firmly grounded in "commonsense folk morality" (I am skeptical that there is any such stable thing), but because it saves the phenomenon of its *explanandum*.

1.3 Re-enchantment

So far, we have seen that modernist disenchantment—that is, the contestation of traditional candidates (such as religion) for the "objective authority" of morality—presents a *prima facie* challenge for moral realism. On the other hand, we have also seen that realism has a "transcendental" advantage by being answerable to the meta-metaethical motives that pull us into the business of theorizing in the first place. Using this advantage as a starting point, this book will attempt to articulate how moral realism can "re-enchant" morality as a distinctive sphere of meaning. The criteria for "re-enchantment" will involve satisfactorily addressing the three sources of disenchantment we have noted, namely, religious contestation, cultural pluralism, and naturalistic conceptions of the world.

I believe that realism can successfully meet these challenges in a variety of ways, the combinations of which will yield different formulations of realism. In each of the chapters that follow, we shall examine a particular challenge that the sources of disenchantment level against morality, and explore ways in which realists might respond. Chapter 2 sets the stage by trying to get clearer on the core commitments of moral realism. Previously, we spoke about realists believing that "morality" is "objective" or "real," and that there can be moral "truths." In specifying each of these terms, we shall articulate a bare-bones framework which any bona fide moral realism must accept. In the subsequent chapters, however, we shall consider ways in which different subtypes of realism might diverge along varying ontological, psychological, epistemological, anthropological, and normative fault lines. The focus throughout these chapters will be to present realism in all its rich variety and to defend it from antirealist alternatives.

My own view, however, is that not all realisms fare equally well at re-enchanting morality. Furthermore, the internal debates within realist circles can be dizzying in their complexity and scope. Thus, partially because I think it is the strongest version of realism and partially as a heuristic or "guiding thread" through the various dimensions of the debate, I will present an original formulation which I call "pluralistic moral realism." This new type of realism is characterized by the following commitments:

- *Semantically*, it is cognitivist and committed to a correspondence theory of truth;

- *Metaphysically*, it is naturalistic in the sense of coextensive property reduction, without being naturalistic in the sense of cointensive reduction;

- *Ontologically*, it is characterized by plural dispositional properties that are stance-independent without being thereby "objective";

- *Anthropologically*, it embraces incommensurable cross-cultural differences and insoluble moral dilemmas;

- *Psychologically*, it allows for cases in which true moral beliefs fail to motivate concomitant action, even while always providing reasons that would justify such action; and

- *Epistemologically*, it is complemented by a perceptual version of ethical intuitionism.

While I will offer reasons in each chapter for why I believe pluralistic moral realism to be the best form of moral realism, even readers of different persuasions will hopefully find it a helpful touchstone as they progress through the chapters.

Equipped with an arsenal of realist metaphysical, psychological, epistemological, and anthropological tools and distinctions, the final chapter returns to the meta-metaethical task of making moral realism answerable to some of the first-order, normative, and humanistic motives from which it arose as a theory. Specifically, I articulate examples of what I will call "applied metaethics," that is, the application of a metaethical thesis such as realism to actual, concrete cases of moral experience and disagreement. Metaethics in general, and realism especially, is often disconnected from such concrete issues, and, conversely, applied philosophy concerning such issues is often agnostic or quietistic about more abstract metaethical commitments. But success of realism's goal of "re-enchantment" requires addressing embodied moral experiences. Toward this end, attention is given to examples of the applications which moral realism (especially *pluralistic* moral realism) might have in the real world.

1.4 Summary

Metaethics is the abstract study of the meaning and foundations of morality, broadly construed. Moral realism is a particular metaethical position which maintains that some fundamental aspects of morality are (in some sense still to be analyzed) "real," "objective," or "true." Precisely what this might mean, however, becomes problematic in light of the putative "disenchantment" generated by the decline of religious authority, the awareness of cultural pluralism, and the rise of a naturalistic conception of the world. Yet, despite the challenges that modernist disenchantment presents, realism still has initial "meta-metaethical" appeal in virtue of the alleged status of morality as a "sphere of meaning" and an *explanandum* for moral theorizing in the first place. The prospects of moral realism, therefore, hinge on the successful "re-enchantment" of morality as a sphere of meaning within a "disenchanted" secular, scientific, and pluralistic world. The chapters that follow will seek to define moral realism more precisely and develop it in ways that can satisfy the goal of re-enchantment. Specifically, as a guiding thread throughout these subsidiary debates, we will consider a unique formulation of "pluralistic moral realism."

CHAPTER TWO

The definition of realism

Moral realism comes in many different shapes and sizes, and the term will obviously vary a great deal depending on how the constituent domains of "morality" and "reality" are each cashed out. Part of the obfuscation surrounding moral realism seems to be a schizophrenic love/hate relationship with the idea that moral values or properties could be "real." On the one hand, as we discussed in Section 1.1, morality can be one of the most meaningful dimensions of human experience.[1] Yet, on the other hand, it seems philosophically naive to simply invoke the "reality" of morality without working through the complexities of what this entails. Dogmatic sermonizing about morality may bring some psychological comfort, but efforts to articulate more precisely what we mean underneath the platitudes can quickly produce sheepishness of the sort humorously illustrated in the following parody by Geoffrey Sayre-McCord (1988: 1). In a mock reality-television confessional, a member of "Realists Anonymous" (Hilary) confesses to the host (Don Philahue) in front of a live audience:

DP: What kinds of realism were you into, Hilary?
H: The whole bag, Don. I was a realist about logical terms, abstract entities, theoretical postulates – you name it.
DP: And causality, what about causality?
H: That too, Don. (Audience gasps.)
DP: I'm going to press you here, Hilary. Did you at any time accept moral realism?
H: (staring at feet): Yes.
DP: What effect did all this realism have on your life?

H: I would spend hours aimlessly wandering the streets, kicking large stones and shouting, 'I refute you thus!' It's embarrassing to recall.

DP: There was worse, wasn't there Hilary?

H: I can't deny it, Don. (Audience gasps.) Instead of going to work I would sit at home fondling ashtrays and reading voraciously about converging scientific theories. I kept a copy of 'Hitler: A Study in Tyranny' hidden in the icebox, and when no one was around I would take it out and chant 'The Nazis were bad. The Nazis were *really* bad.'

Hilary's awkwardness is something to which many moral realists can relate. How can we persist in believing that our values track something "objective" in an era when objectivity itself seems suspicious? As normatively and existentially comforting as moral realism might be, realists need to offer something more substantive than merely chanting alleged moral certainties. Indeed, in the absence of less circular expressions, moral realism has been prone to easy caricatures.

One thing at least that nearly all moral realists seem to agree on is that moral values have a certain autonomy or independence from us. Morality obviously affects us in important ways, but the "reality" which moral realists are attracted to is intended to somehow anchor at least part of morality outside the sphere of human control. Yet, how is this "independence" envisioned specifically? And from what particular aspects of human control and experience are moral values supposed to be independent? After all, morality cannot be *totally* independent from us; if it were, how could we ever come into contact with it? This chapter will try to draw a tighter conceptual circle around "realism" in an effort to identify more clearly what is at stake. Thus, this chapter is intended less as an argument for or against moral realism, but rather as an examination of what the view is committed to in its bare-bones formulation.

2.1 "Mind-independence"

To what kind of independence—and from what—is moral realism committed? A canonical answer is that moral realism recognizes specifically the *mind*-independence of moral values. This, however, seems to raise more issues than it settles, for consider the variation within canonical lists of the functions and capacities of the "mind," which includes everything from beliefs, reasons, perceptions, concepts, feelings, desires, etc. Radically different types of "realism" can be generated depending on which of these items is envisioned by the independence relation. For example, if realism requires the independence of values from feelings, emotions, and desires, then rationalists in the Kantian tradition would automatically be realists. By contrast, if realism requires the independence of values from perception, then intuitionists would be barred from realism by definition. Furthermore, making realism hinge on the independence of values from reasons or conceptions would seem to sacrifice the practical and meaning-granting nature of morality itself, which is one of the powerful attractions to realism in the first place.

Because of this, many realists restrict claims concerning the autonomy of morality specifically to the independence of values from *beliefs*. Belief-independence may be even further differentiated into what we can call (a) *causal* independence, (b) *evidential* independence, and (c) *metaphysical* independence (Brink 1989: 14–36). The moral realist who requires the causal independence of values from the human mind insists that if moral values are ever known, it is through a kind of "discovery" about something that already exists, rather than an invention of something new. The evidential-independence realist will envision values as being distinct from our standards of discovery and justification, that is, the standards or process of discovery may be invented by us, but the objects of the discovery are not. By contrast, the realist who adopts the view that moral values are metaphysically independent will require values to be separable from human conception in such a way that the values can obtain in the absence of anyone's ability to think about them.

While any of these specifications can be and have been associated with moral realism, a realism which affirms something as strong as the total conceptual independence of values seems unlikely. For, it does not seem coherent to talk about a value without referencing a perspective for whom that thing is valuable, that is, a valu*er*. In this way, we are reminded that "value" is both a verb and a noun. The moral realist wishes to defend values as real things, but this should not be at the expense of sacrificing human connectivity to those things (cf. §1.2). Views concerning the causal and evidential independence of morality, by contrast, respect the verb-sense of "value," and thus yield a much more attractive specification for moral realism. Whereas metaphysical independence would incoherently place the existence of values outside *any* conceptual scheme, evidential and causal senses of independence only require that values exist in a way distinct from what Russ Shafer-Landau has called, broadly, a "stance." Realists who acknowledge the evidential and causal independence of morality, thus, believe that, "the moral standards that fix the moral facts are not made true by virtue of their ratification from within any given actual or hypothetical perspective" (2003: 15).

This notion of stance-independence, thus, raises questions about from *whose* evidence and invention morality is allegedly independent: morality could be independent of an *individual's* beliefs, of *every* actual agent's beliefs, or of even epistemically *idealized* agents' beliefs. Certainly, moral realism must involve more than just a commitment to the independence of morality from a single individual's beliefs. You are not necessarily a realist about morality just because you think some particular person (e.g. that guy who cut me off in traffic yesterday) has gotten it wrong. A more robust position for realists is to require the independence of values from the stances of all agents. Just because something is believed, it does not follow that it is true; and vice versa, presumably there are true propositions that are not believed. If realism is a thesis about anything, it is that what is morally right or wrong is not up to us, even if we all agree.[2]

In fact, moral realism is best characterized as maintaining even the last and strongest sort of stance-independence, namely, independence from what even an ideally situated, maximally informed agent would believe. Of course, it is not clear that such an agency would ever be possible for creatures like us. Were such an agent to exist, however, the moral realist would need to maintain that the truth of moral judgments is independent of even her perfect knowledge. To say that moral truth is independent of ideal beliefs means that such beliefs do not determine or constitute moral truth. This is not to say that such beliefs (if we could ever actually get them) would not be reliable guides to moral truth. There could be a perfect isomorphism between the beliefs of an ideal agent and moral truth, such that if we wanted to know what the right thing to do really is, we could with confidence ask the ideal agent what she believes is the right thing to do. The point for the realist is just that what the ideal agent believes is at best a reflection or representation of moral truth. Moral truth may be attained by consulting beliefs, but it is not true in virtue of these beliefs: agents may be *authorities* on morality without thereby being *authors* of it.

It is important to note that, in defining moral realism in a way that requires its independence from even idealized stances, we are ruling out so-called constructivist theories as robustly realist. Constructivism is the view that moral values are generated by stances—either collective or hypothetical, and whether deliberately or implicitly. A majority of constructivist accounts are unapologetically *anti*realist. For example, Gilbert Harman (1975), J. L. Mackie (1977), and David Wong (1984) reject realism precisely because they find a cultural-constructivist account more plausible (see §4.1). Some articulations of constructivism, however, want to affirm the stance *dependence* of morality while retaining the nomenclature of "realism." Similar views may be found in the constructivist theories of:

- Roderick Firth's (1952) Ideal Observer account;

- John Rawls's (1971) Kantian commitments to the authority of "overlapping consensuses";

- Sabina Lovibond's (1983) Wittgensteinian "imaginative realism" as constructed by social and historical consensus;

- Jürgen Habermas's (1990) view that meaning and value arise out of "communicative rationality";

- Christine Korsgaard's (1996) Kantian view of rational consensus as constituting a Kingdom of Ends;

- Patricia Greenspan's (1995) "social artifact realism"; and

- Thomas Scanlon's (1998) contractualism.

Most formulations of the so-called divine command theory which seek to outsource the foundations of moral obligation to theistic sources are also constructivist for this reason (Adams 1979). Instead of an idealized collective agency which constructs and constitutes moral values, however, divine command theory appeals to the omniscient agency of a divine being. According to its proponents, the basic attraction to such constructivism is that it anchors moral constraints to a source that is independent not merely from actual and hypothetical humans, but from humanity altogether. Kant (1788: 103–10), indeed, went so far as to argue for the existence of God by appeal to what he took as a brute, transcendental need to believe that there is some transhuman force maintaining the desired linkage between moral duty and emotional happiness.

This is not the place to examine every one of these constructivist accounts in detail, and elements of them will arise when we consider various challenges to moral realism in later chapters. However, it is possible to make several observations about constructivism in general that should suffice to exclude it from moral realism proper. The inspiration behind realist-leaning versions of constructivism is to provide some sort of "objective" constraint on potentially idiosyncratic judgments. Yet, the constructivist insists, this constraint must itself be internal to some process of informed consensus. This means that it is not independent *reality* which adjudicates moral truths, but something socially or rationally emergent. Of course, certain proponents of constructivism may wish to broaden the concept of "reality" to accommodate these derivative senses; but whatever "realism" results will be importantly different than versions of moral realism which restrict themselves to full stance-independence.

Seen in this light, constructivist realism faces several *prima facie* objections. First, it will have to respond convincingly to the famous challenge issued in Plato's *Euthyphro* regarding the conceptual stability of attributing morality to fiat. Even if rational consensus generates identifiable and discrete values, the same constraint upon morality which constructivists themselves recognize seems to demand an independent constraint on the consensus in the first place: if something is morally good only because rational consensus *makes* it good, then what in turn adjudicates rational consensus in a noncircular way? Rational consensus might provide sufficient motivational, psychological, or social authority, but it does not provide the same metaethical stability which the robust moral realist seeks.

Second, constructivists (particularly in the divine command tradition) sometimes argue that the authority of morality requires a source, in the way that laws allegedly imply lawgivers. But this would seem to saddle realism with too strong a commitment to teleology, even outside the moral sphere. Must moral realists also believe that design in nature transcendentally necessitates a divine designer instead of a nonagential principle of natural selection? Furthermore, does respecting the "reality" of the laws of physics require believing that, say, the gravitation or entropy is *created* through rational consensus?[3] Third, given the constraints upon individual judgment which constructivists want to hold onto, constructivism is less parsimonious than fully stance-independent realism: constructivism must articulate and defend an additional mechanism for how moral constraint arises to replace what realists can attribute simply to reality itself (cf. Shafer-Landau 2003: 46). None of this is to say that constructivism is false. That could only be accomplished by taking each constructivist theory in its turn. Nor is the goal at present to defend moral realism against constructivism. The point is simply that the two—realism and constructivism—are not "real" in the same way.

In summary, the following definition of moral realism has emerged from our analysis so far:

> **Moral Realism** = the view that moral values exist in a way that is causally and evidentially (though not conceptually) independent from the beliefs of anyone and everyone (including idealized agents) such that evidence and beliefs do not determine or constitute those values, though they may adequately and reliably measure or reflect them.

Of course, as Joseph Butler famously noted, "every one is at liberty to use words as he pleases." This definition may not satisfy all positions which adopt the realist nomenclature, but we must stipulate some starting point. Furthermore, this definition has the virtue of embodying a "robust" specification of the otherwise generic independence advocated by most realists, while remaining flexible with respect to further metaphysical and epistemological commitments, which we will explore in the subsequent chapters.[4]

Note that our definition of moral realism does not by itself beg any questions regarding specific metaphysical, epistemological, psychological, or normative commitments. As we shall see in subsequent chapters, these are debates which occur *internal* to realism—one's position with respect to them will sort one into a specific *type* of realism, not determine whether one is a realist to begin with. Furthermore, our definition nicely makes our conception of moral reality continuous with how "reality" is used in other philosophical and nonmoral domains (Brock and Mares 2007). For instance, when someone says she is a "realist" about the external world, she does not mean that the existence of the external world is constituted by any beliefs anyone might have about it. The scientific realist thinks that the truths of science are not determined by what even perfectly informed scientists think.

2.2 Moral truth(s)

So far, we have seen how moral realism is committed to a specific version of the thesis of mind-independence. One of the reasons why we were so concerned to unpack "independence" in the preceding section has to do with the seeming link between reality and *truth*. That is, the reason why moral realists want to insist that morality is a feature of a mind-independent reality is because they also want to insist that morality can be true, and to say that something is true seems on the surface to require saying that it is also real or part of the world. Statements about unicorns are not true because unicorns are not part of the world. Statements about the tallest mountain in the world can be true because such a mountain is part of the world. Moral realists want to distinguish moral propositions from mythological propositions; they want moral predicates to be part of the world more in the way that geological predicates are part of the world. The traditional way of expressing truth is the familiar *correspondence theory*, according to which discourse contains propositional content which describes facts in the world.[5] On this view, truth is not ultimately in the "eye of the beholder": it is determined by the world, not by us, and since the world is not of our making, truth is not of our making.

There are, however, several well-known problems facing the correspondence theory of truth. For one, realists have typically failed to say to which specific parts of the world true moral propositions correspond. Not to mention the fact that it has seemed implausible to many philosophers that moral propositions are the types of utterances that could be true in the first place, either because they do not express beliefs (stay tuned for §2.3) or because they only express false beliefs (see §4.1). Partially in response to these problems, alternate "minimalist" accounts of truth have proliferated in recent years which reject the traditional correspondence model.

An ancestor of such minimalism can be found in Wittgenstein, who famously held that the meaning of any term is given by how that term is used in a language. Subsequently, Frank Ramsey (1927) offered an analogous theory about *truth*, such that the truth of a proposition is simply determined by how that proposition is used or expressed. That is, Ramsey suggested that to utter the proposition "Grass is green" is to say the same thing as "The sentence 'grass is green' is true." The phrase "is true" in the second utterance adds nothing to what is expressed in the first, since in uttering the first, the speaker is already affirming that grass is green. This is an instance of the so-called disquotational schema, that is, that truth is already implicit in a sentence without the unnecessary addition of the phrase "is true." Ramsey wielded this principle to defend a *deflationary* theory of truth, wherein truth predicates are stripped of any metaphysically substantial property, and reduced instead merely to the ability to be formally represented in a language. This is not to say that truth is thereby determined by usage in an *arbitrary* way, for there are always syntactic rules which a language must follow. The grammar of a language, thus, constrains what can be properly expressed in that language and therefore what can be true. Deflationary truth is in this way constrained by "warranted assertibility," and since deflationary truth just is what can be expressed by the grammar of a language, we can say more strongly that truth *is* warranted assertibility.

Hilary Putnam (1981) has articulated an influential challenge to the deflationary account. He argues that deflationary truth is unable to accommodate the fact that we normally think of truth as eternal and stable. But if truth is just warranted assertibility (what Putnam calls "rational acceptability"), then it becomes mutable, since warranted assertibility varies depending on what information is available. For instance, the proposition "the Earth is flat" could have been asserted with warrant (i.e. accepted rationally) a thousand years ago in a way that it could not be today because we now have more information available about the Earth. But, though warranted assertibility changed in this case, we wouldn't want to say that the *truth* of the proposition "the Earth is flat" changed.[6] Based on these problems, Putnam refines the deflationary theory by substituting a condition of *ideal* justification, that is, where warranted assertibility is not relative to what specific information a speaker may have at a specific moment, but to what information would be accessible to an ideal epistemic agent. The ideal epistemic situation is then envisioned as involving information that is both complete (i.e. involving everything relevant) and consistent (i.e. not logically contradictory). These two conditions combine to create a *convergence* of information for the ideal agent which Putnam refers to as "internal realism."

Deflationary or minimalist theories of truth have also received careful exposition by Crispin Wright (1992). Though indebted in fundamental ways to the tradition tracing back to Wittgenstein, Wright's position differs importantly from Putnam's. Wright agrees with Putnam's criticism of traditional deflationary theories of truth, namely that they make truth too variable by identifying it with something as mutable as warranted assertibility. However, Wright disagrees with Putnam that truth is constrained by the convergence of information that would be available to an epistemically ideal agent. This is because Wright thinks that it is apparent to speakers of a language that something may be true even if it is not justified in ideal epistemic conditions. Wright calls this apparentness a "platitude." Platitudes, says Wright, are what ordinary language users pretheoretically mean. Platitudes serve the same purpose of checking and balancing truth that warranted assertibility or ideal convergence serve in the theories of Ramsey and Putnam.

Assertions of truth are not chaotic or random (see the discussion of the so-called Frege-Geach problem in §2.3). If truth is measured by correspondence of sentences to the world, then the *world* can do the job of adjudicating our truth-assertions. But if truth is measured by something else—if it is reduced, "deflated," or "internal" to its usage—then something else needs to carry the burden of systematizing our truth claims. For deflationary theorists, this "something else" was the grammar of a language itself; for Putnam, the information in idealized epistemic conditions determines truth; and for Wright, truth is determined by the extent to which it satisfies the platitudes we have about it. In particular, Wright identifies four platitudes we have concerning truth: (1) we think that to assert is to present as true, (2) we think that any truth-apt content has a significant negation that is also truth-apt, (3) we think that to be true is to correspond to the facts, and (4) we think that a statement can be true without being justified (this is the platitude that Putnam's internal realism violates). Wright writes, "If an interpretation of 'true' satisfies these platitudes, there is, for minimalism, no further, metaphysical question whether it captures a concept worth regarding as truth" (1992: 34).

Even though Wright did not offer this theory as specific to *moral* truth, it has been extraordinarily influential in metaethics. It is fair to say that some version of minimalism or deflationary theory undergirds Simon Blackburn's (1993) "quasi-realism," Terence Horgan's and Mark Timmons's (1991) "cognitive descriptivism," and Allan Gibbard's (2003) "norm-expressivism." All these theories are attracted to the "realism" that minimalism seems to offer—a realism that, by defining truth in a noncorrespondent way, can accommodate and explain actual moral language without appealing to standards of stance-independence. However, we shall see that antirealists cannot have it both ways: they cannot call themselves (robust) realists unless they pay the full metaphysical price of stance-independence.

First, how can minimalism be faithful to our platitudes if one of our platitudes—namely, Wright's third platitude—is that truth involves *correspondence*? Wright seems to anticipate this criticism and responds by stressing that his account is only supposed to be a theory of what truth *is*, not of what truth *means*. Thus, says Wright, correspondence could be correct as a theory of the *meaning* of truth, even though it fails as a theory of what truth *is* (1992: 37). The problem, however, is that what truth is, on the minimalist account, is supposed to be determined by what truth means, that is, by our platitudes about truth. By grounding truth in the satisfaction of our platitudes, Wright makes his theory unable to accommodate any sharp distinction between the nature and the meaning of truth. But neither can Wright ignore the platitudinous fact that truth *means* correspondence. Furthermore, even if we do have platitudes committed to use theories of meaning, it seems likely that we have strong platitudes which tell us that truth is *not* determined by use. The problem for minimalism is that if truth is nothing more than the satisfaction of our platitudes, then truth must not be determined by usage since our platitudes tell us that truth is independent of usage.

Regardless of how Wright might respond to these objections, minimalism must admit a very close relationship between the nature and the meaning of truth. The objections we have just considered argue that this relationship must be so close as to collapse. But even if the nature and the meaning of truth could be adequately distinguished, minimalism as a theory of only the former must depend on a use-theory of the latter: recall that Wright's theory grew out of Putnam's, which grew out of Ramsey's, which in turn grew out of Wittgenstein's use-theory, which was a theory of *meaning*. However, the use-theory of meaning is itself highly controversial. Consider some common objections to it.

First, while the use-theory is in many ways intuitive, it might be thought to make meaning too external. Recall that Wittgenstein emphasized the primacy of "public language" and Putnam (1975) famously opined that "meaning just ain't in the head." If the meaning of a word is determined by how we use it, then we cannot have secret, private meanings any more than we can have secret, private usages, and we cannot have such usages because if we did, we would never be able to communicate. Understanding one another's words requires understanding how we use those words. This would be impossible if we each used words in radically different ways. This view seems correct as an analysis of how we communicate with others. But others have drawn attention to a kind of meaning that can be more intimately personal, for example, Paul Grice's (1957) "ideational" theory allows for the meaning of a term to be determined not by how it is used, but by the idea to which it corresponds. Since ideas may be private—they *are* "inside the head"—the ideational theory yields a unique "speaker meaning." Speaker meaning is the intension that a speaker has in mind with an utterance, and so may differ from the "standard meaning" determined by public usage. This is not really an objection to the use-theory, but a supplement that public meaning might not be the only relevant type of meaning.

Second, as Wittgenstein envisioned it, language on the use theory, becomes tantamount to a *game*. That is, when we speak, we are not simply reporting subjective ideas (as ideational theory would have it) nor are we merely speaking abstractly about the formal or grammatical relationships of a language; we are instead using language in a way that follows rules and conventions much as games like chess or basketball do. There are appropriate ways to use words and expressions just as there are appropriate ways to move pawns or shoot free-throws. This game analogy is at the heart of use-theories of meaning, but it threatens to break down in several intuitive instances. For example, we want to say that at least a good chunk of language is meaningful in the sense that it reflects the world around us—many of our words designate objects and properties. But games like chess are *not* meaningful in this way: the expression "a pawn captures another pawn whenever an *en passant* situation arises" reflects something only about the game of chess, whereas the expression "something will fall downward whenever it is thrown upward" reflects something about the world. Thus, use-theorists need some way of distinguishing language from other games vis-à-vis differences in meaning. Furthermore, if meaning is determined by the rules of a game or a language, then how are the rules *themselves*—which are also meaningful—to be articulated? More specifically, which rules guide the use of proper names? There does not seem to be any finite set of rules, obeyed universally by speakers, that tells us how to use proper names. Rather, the use of such names seems often vague, contextual, or otherwise inexpressible.

In addition, if the meaning of expressions and words is determined by their usage, then how is it that we find *new* expressions and words, that is, ones which have never been used before, but are nonetheless meaningful? If we can understand the meaning of these new words, then the meaning must be at least partially antecedent to use. Plus, we frequently use words and expressions quite effectively without always understanding them, as is often the case when learning a foreign language by immersion. For instance, Sarah might learn from experience how and when to say *no hay de qué* in response to a Spanish speaker saying *gracias*, without ever having understood what her response means. That is, if a friend asked Sarah what she said, she might say something like, "I don't really know – it's just something you say when people tell you *gracias*."

The upshot of all this is that theories of truth that sacrifice stance-independent correspondence cannot support realism in a way sufficient to distinguish it from antirealism. Deflationary, internal, or minimalist theories of truth fail to fully accommodate our commonsense attitudes ("platitudes") about truth. Despite their popularity in metaethics today, robust realists should resist these accounts. Moral realism requires a thesis of stance-independence, which in turn entails a claim about moral truth. If the arguments in this section against creeping minimalism have been persuasive, then correspondence emerges as the only remaining tenable model for moral truth. Again, this is not to say that there *is* such moral truth (although robust realists will wish to make this additional claim as well); just that if there is moral truth, that truth must be understood in correspondent language.

2.3 Cognitivism: Giving realists something to talk about

The previous section argued that moral realism is committed to the possibility of moral truth because it is committed to a thesis of the causal and evidential independence of moral truth. We also suggested that the best way to understand this truth was by the traditional model of correspondence. Many philosophers, however, have maintained that the very idea of "moral truth" is incoherent in the first place, and if moral realism is committed to it, then moral realism is incoherent. This objection is raised by those who follow a version of antirealism called *noncognitivism*.

"Cognitivism" is the view that moral judgments essentially involve *beliefs* or belief-like states. "Noncognitivism," by contrast, is the view that moral judgments essentially involve *desires*, or at least *non*-belief-like states.[7] One of the apparent entailments of these definitions is that cognitivism is also committed to the view that moral judgments are truth-apt (i.e. capable of being either true or false) in virtue of possessing propositional content. Unlike other dimensions of discourse such as imperatives, interrogatives, exclamations, etc., propositions are structured in a way that it makes sense to ask of them whether they are true or false. Noncognitivism is, therefore, the view that, whatever else it may do, our moral discourse does not assert genuine propositions that can be evaluated as correspondently true or false in any stance-independent way.[8]

It is important to note that both cognitivism and noncognitivism can each allow for a significant amount of interplay between beliefs and desires. Both definitions specify only what is *essential*, not what is exclusive in moral discourse. After all, any plausible version of noncognitivism will implicate beliefs to some extent. For example, Gibbard's (1990) claim that moral discourse consists in endorsing certain norms presupposes that the agent first recognize something as a norm (where norms are expressed in propositional form) and also be capable of inferring particular actions or situations as instantiations of that norm. Thus, we can see that cognitivism is a necessary (though not sufficient) condition of moral realism, as we defined it above. For, to maintain that moral utterances are sometimes true it must first be the case that moral utterances can be truth-apt, which must in turn require that they can be propositional or belief-like.

Saying that cognitivism allows for desires, emotions, or other non-belief-like states to play important parts in moral discourse (albeit not essential parts), should not be taken as denying that belief-like states and non-belief-like states are nonetheless distinct. Beliefs are essentially propositional in nature, desires are not. The basic difference between the two is best expressed by G. E. M. Anscombe's (1957) famous "direction of fit" account: beliefs try to fit themselves to the world, whereas desires try to fit the world to them. Certainly, recent moral psychology has uncovered tremendous gray areas between beliefs and desires. For one thing, desires are often not random or *ex nihilo*, but are frequently predicated on and shaped by certain beliefs. Thus, desires can be "appropriate" or "inappropriate" to the extent that they are based on true or false beliefs. Indeed, this is a foundational concept in traditional psychoanalysis (Neu 2000), and antecedents can be found in Aristotle's claim that how we perceive and conceptualize a situation fundamentally affects our emotional reaction to it (ff. *Nicomachean Ethics* 1125–26; *De Anima* 403).

In saying that moral realism is committed to cognitivism, we are merely specifying that realism requires moral utterances to be truth-apt, which in turn requires moral utterances to be propositional, that is, essentially belief-like. Not only is this requirement agnostic about the extent to which desires might also be necessary for proper moral judgment, but it is also neutral with respect to the question of *motivation*. Traditionally, contemporary philosophers have sided with Hume's claim that only *desires* can motivate. However, some philosophers have suggested the possibility of ethical beliefs that might themselves supply motivation or justification without any intervention of desire. Mark Platts (1991), for instance, argues that desire alone is often motivationally insufficient: cases of indecisiveness represented by Shakespeare's Hamlet or T. S. Eliot's character J. Alfred Prufrock are very common and familiar, and in such cases, "the desire fails, one might say, to engage my will" (1991: 21). In a similar vein, Jonathan Dancy (2000) argues against what he calls the "desire-based reasons" thesis, namely, the view that all good reasons are based on or grounded in our own desires. Instead, Dancy proposes that belief alone is capable of motivating action. Dancy calls this view "pure cognitivism" and defends it by noting that, "If one is thirsty, one is motivated by the prospect of drinking," not by the thirst itself (2000: 14). J. E. J. Altham (1986) also suggests the possibility of "besires," that is, mental states that are like beliefs on the one hand (in that they are propositional in form), but are also like desires on the other hand (in that they are motivational). The possibility that ethical beliefs could provide justificatory reasons that arise external to a person's preexisting sets of desires has received quite a bit of skepticism among metaethicists immersed in the now-dominant Humean tradition. Many argue that it would render morality "metaphysically queer" (an objection we shall consider in §§5.1 and 5.2) and that it fails to explain the apparent existence of sociopaths who allege to possess moral knowledge, but who evince no motivation to act morally.

So far, we have seen that moral realism presupposes some version of cognitivism, that is, that realism requires moral judgments to be essentially belief-like. The goal in this chapter is primarily to define moral realism rather than defend it, and it goes outside the scope of this book to mount a full attack on noncognitivism in all its various guises. However, if cognitivism is not at least initially plausible, then realism as we have defined it will be *a fortiori* implausible as well. Luckily for the realist, there seem to be several good *prima facie* reasons to put the burden of proof on the noncognitivist.

First, it is important to note that the claim that moral discourse is not truth-apt is a *descriptive* claim. That is, noncognitivists are not claiming that our moral language *should* not be truth-apt, but that as a matter of fact it is not truth-apt. Recall the interpretations of moral utterances offered by noncognitivists like Stevenson (1944) and Ayer (1952): to say "killing innocents is wrong" is just to say "I don't like killing innocents and don't want you to either" or "*Boo!* to killing innocents." These claims are about what moral utterances *mean*, not about the metaphysical status of actions involving the killing of innocents. Suffice it to say that as a descriptive thesis, noncognitivism appears exceptionally counterintuitive. Most speakers of most languages presumably do not mean by "killing innocents is wrong" merely that they do not approve of it, or even that they are simply endorsing a norm, no matter how universal in form. Rather, most speakers think that they mean what they say, namely that killing innocents is *literally* wrong.

Of course, it's always easy for armchair philosophers to say what "ordinary moral language users" actually do or do not mean, and frequently intuitions vary in proportion to the theory defended. For this reason, it is helpful to look to experimental moral psychology, where we find that cognitivism has enjoyed a dominant default status since at least the time of Piaget (1932). Working in the same Neo-Kantian tradition as Piaget, Lawrence Kohlberg's (1971) influential moral stage theory was also expressed cognitivistically by drawing attention to people's moral *judgments*. Much has been made of the "cognitivist legacy of Kohlberg." In fact, Richard Shweder and Jonathan Haidt (1993) claim that the general trend in *all* empirical moral psychology is toward cognitivism. Furthermore, experimental findings concerning the relationship between moral internalization in children and methods of parenting suggest that kids are taught a moral language of truth-aptness. For instance, William Rottschaefer (1999) emphasizes that parents facilitate moral development most efficiently by inculcating norms through an *inductive* process. Whereas strategies of power-assertion (e.g. force, deprivation of privileges) and love-withdrawal (e.g. anger, disapproval) may succeed in capturing a child's *attention*, they fail dramatically when it comes to actually *instructing* the child about what is right. By contrast, inductive methods (e.g. allowing the child to experiment with trial and error, communicating to the child about consequences of actions, etc.) most effectively stimulate empathy in children, which is the best method of inducing guilt, which in turn is the best way of behavior modification. Thus, after hitting her brother, Katie's parents may tell her, "Look, you hurt your brother's feelings" or "How would you feel if someone did that to you?" Through inductive parenting strategies, children learn not just *that* an action is wrong, but *why* it is wrong. Part of the explanation for why it is wrong involves drawing attention to *facts* (e.g. Katie's brother crying) which are appropriate bearers of (correspondent) truth predications.

The "cognitivist legacy" in moral psychology is certainly compelling. But several considerations should caution against overblowing the conclusions of this research. First, even if findings like Kohlberg's and Rottschaefer's support cognitivism, this will not in itself show anything about the truth of moral realism. Unfortunately, although cognitivism is a necessary, but not a sufficient condition for moral realism, many experimental designs tend to conflate the two. For instance, Shweder and Haidt define cognitivism as, among other things, the view that "qualities such as goodness, rightness, justice, or beneficence are real and knowable" (1993: 360). But it could be that inductive parenting amounts to little more than indoctrinating children in a metaethical illusion, as "error theorists" will want to say (see §§4.1, 5.1, and 6.1). Second, it is not clear that many of the findings discussed above "prove" cognitivism in the first place since it is often experimentally underdetermined whether people's moral responses are *judgments* at all. Kohlberg, for instance, *assumed* that people make moral judgments, and he then tried to figure out what those judgments were and schematize them. However, the various ways of accounting for moral reactions to hypothetical scenarios could be explained in a different way. For instance, it is possible that respondents could be merely supplying *post hoc* rationales for their *attitudinal* responses. The ways in which a respondent offers this justification may indeed fall into a division of "stages" as Kohlberg suggests; the division, however, might not be a stage theory of moral judgment *per se*, but rather of how people justify their moral *attitudes*. The attraction to supplying rational justifications for responses which themselves are not rationally formed seems to be a not uncommon tendency in people who generally wish to conceive of themselves as autonomous and responsible decision-makers (Doris 2002: 30–2).

Realists as well as antirealists need to be cautious in what phenomenological and descriptive theses they foist onto "ordinary people." We have seen that there is good evidence that most people appear to implicitly subscribe to some form of cognitivism and that they take themselves to be making genuine truth-apt propositions when they use moral language. But because this evidence is compatible with alternate noncognitivist explanations, it should not be taken as *proving* that cognitivism is true.

Another factor that is suggestive, however, is that the weight of history (especially the history of ethical theory) also seems to be against noncognitivists. With the suspicious exception of noncognitivism itself, moral codes and expressions across cultures arguably share an understanding of morality as something external to a particular speaker's feelings and attitudes. Of course, this is not to say that any of these conceptions are correct; just that as a descriptive thesis, noncognitivism is *prima facie* false for the overwhelming majority of the history of ethics. Indeed, Alasdair MacIntyre (1981) offers a well-known genealogical explanation of the rise of noncognitivism. As MacIntyre sees it, a uniquely modern theory such as noncognitivism can be explained as a remnant of earlier, more stable (cognitivist) worldviews from which modernity has inherited fragmented and perhaps incommensurable parts (recall our discussion of modernist "disenchantment" in §1.1).[9]

Another challenge noncognitivists will need to address is the so-called Frege-Geach Problem (FGP), named in honor of the two philosophers credited with its first articulation (Geach 1965).[10] FGP asks us to consider the following, seemingly ordinary bit of moral discourse: (1) murder is wrong; (2) if murder is wrong, then pressuring someone else to commit murder is also wrong; (3) therefore, pressuring someone else to commit murder is morally wrong. On its surface, this appears to be deductively valid via *modus ponens*. Yet, logical inference patterns such as *modus ponens* can operate only on truth-apt propositions, which noncognitivism rejects. In particular, since noncognitivism reinterprets moral statements as emotional expressions or endorsements, premise (1) would instead mean something like "*Boo!* to murder." But premise (2) cannot be reinterpreted in the same way since it is *not* asserting categorically, but rather making a hypothetical "if" claim. At best, the noncognitivist could say that (2) is stating what someone *would* express or endorse.[11] This would mean that the words "Murder is wrong" as they occur in premise (1) are homonymous to their occurrence in premise (2); which would disallow (1) from affirming the antecedent of (2), and render the conclusion to (3) via *modus ponens* invalid, which flies in the face of the seemingly legitimate discourse with which we started. Since our goal at present is merely to define moral realism in a robust and charitable way, it is not to our purpose to show definitely that FGP is fatal to noncognitivism. But in the absence of a more substantial argument for abandoning the *prima facie* logical structure of everyday moral discourse, we have no reason to rule out moral realism *a priori* just because it is committed to cognitivism.

2.4 Summary

In the previous chapter, we contextualized moral realism as the view that morality is somehow "objective," "real," or "true." In this chapter, we defined these commitments more specifically, so that a "robust" form of realism involves, at a minimum, the view that moral discourse can be truth-apt (cognitivism) and that at least some of this discourse is in fact true, as measured by a correspondence of propositional content to stance-independent properties.

CHAPTER THREE

The metaphysics of realism

The previous chapter specified that a "robust" moral realism must, at a minimum, be committed to the stance-independence of cognitivist moral truths, understood according to a correspondence model. This issue of *defining* the view, however, is quite different from *defending* it, and moral realism is subject to attacks on numerous fronts which the subsequent chapters will examine. In this chapter, we will explore some of the metaphysical challenges facing moral realism, including the question of what realist moral properties actually are, and whether moral realism can be understood against the backdrop of the naturalistic "disenchantment" we discussed in Chapter 1.

3.1 Re-opening the open question argument

Given the position of cultural authority which naturalistic conceptions seem to occupy, perhaps moral realism would fare best if it too could be cashed out in naturalistic ways (if you can't beat them, join them!). If morality were somehow a part of nature, then, as naturalistic beings ourselves, we could presumably tell a plausible story about where morality comes from, how it engages us in practical ways, and why we value it. The "non-naturalist" alternative has been viewed as mysterious, overly romanticist, or "queer"—to use a term from J. L. Mackie (1977) to which we shall return. "Naturalism," by contrast, has typically been associated with an approach to morality that is respectfully scientific and "hard-minded" (to borrow a term from William James). In general, we can think of ethical naturalism as the claim that moral properties are in some way "reducible" to natural properties. Given the variety of ways in which this reduction might be undertaken, it will be useful to investigate the influential arguments for non-naturalistic moral realism, which was very popular in the early twentieth century.

The antireductionist position received its classic expression in G. E. Moore's famous Open Question Argument (OQA), which Moore phrased as follows:

> The hypothesis that disagreement about the meaning of good is disagreement with regard to the correct analysis of a given whole, may be most plainly seen to be incorrect by consideration of the fact that, whatever definition be offered, it may be always asked, with significance, of the complex so defined, whether it is itself good. (1903: 15)

According to Moore, any proposed reduction of morality will always leave open the availability of asking whether the reduction itself is *good*. Thus, if OQA is sound, then the concept "good" is intrinsically distinct (or *sui generis*) from any nonmoral concepts, such that the question "What is a moral concept?" cannot be reduced to merely asking, for example, "What is a concept that causes behavior, represents others in game theoretic ways, involves that which is desired to be desired, etc.?" Moore called these sorts of reductive replacements of moral concepts with nonmoral concepts examples of "naturalism," which he thought violated the logic of OQA—resulting in the so-called naturalistic fallacy. In this way, the success of OQA can be seen as an attempt to maintain a conception of moral agency that is set apart from the contingency, determination, and arbitrariness of nature, and that will ensure that our behavior is "really ours" (Regan 2003: 653; Rosati 2003: 496).

To understand OQA properly, let us recall Moore's distinction between *verbal* definitions which are strictly nominal (i.e. they reflect the usage of a word) and *real* definitions which capture the nature of the entity defined by expressing an "analytic proposition" (i.e. a proposition in which the truth of the predicate is contained in the truth of the subject). OQA deals exclusively with real definitions. Thus, for Moore, the correct analysis of a term should yield an identity between the *analysans* (what is offered as the analysis) and the *analysandum* (what is analyzed). Presumably every word can be verbally defined (i.e. every word can have a specified usage), but not every word can permit of a real definition. Specifically, Moore's view was that simple concepts such as good resist real definition.[1] For Moore, the fact that we can significantly question whether the *analysans* of any offered reductive definition of morality is really the same as the *analysandum* shows that such definitions cannot be real definitions, since real definition involve identities. Since something cannot be questioned as to whether it is itself, we should *not* be able to significantly question whether real definitions of good are really good. Because we *can* so question, such definitions must be wrong. But if such definitions are inapplicable, how *is* good to be defined? Moore's answer is as straightforward as it is frustrating:

> If I am asked 'What is good?' my answer is that good is good, and that is the end of the matter. Or if I am asked 'How is good to be defined?' my answer is that it cannot be defined, and that is all I have to say about it. (1903: 6)

With all this in mind, let us paraphrase the OQA as follows:

P1   If reductionism were true, then some proposition "X = good" is analytically true.
P2   If "X = good" is analytically true, then we cannot significantly ask whether X is good.
P3   But we *can* significantly ask whether X is good.
C1   Therefore, "X = good" is not analytically true.
C2   Therefore, reductionism must be false.

For many, OQA practically represents the very founding of metaethics itself. Whether it started off the field in the right direction, however, has been a subject of enduring controversy. Darwall et al. (1992) limit OQA to a "mere period piece" responsible for what they see as a "rigor mortis" that paralyzed moral philosophy for the next half-century. In Moore's own time, OQA was heralded as definitive and, indeed, inspirational—Bertrand Russell described his first exposure to it "liberating."[2] Throughout the middle of the twentieth century, assessment of OQA varied wildly, and was often what most defined emerging metaethical positions. For example, the traditions of noncognitivism which we discussed in Section 2.3 came to view OQA as formally valid, but unsound. Specifically, they took issue with the enthymeme in P1 that interprets reductionist expressions of "X = good" as *propositions*. This propositional language suggested a cognitivist outlook, which noncognitivists took as constituting a *reductio ad absurdum*: if cognitivist realism leads to morality being *sui generis*, then, since *sui generis* properties were alleged to be absurd, cognitivism must be false. In a similar vein, moral relativists and "error theorists" such as Harman (1975) and Mackie (1977)—to whom we shall return in more detail in later chapters—granted the validity, but not soundness of OQA. Instead of taking issue with Moore's assumption of cognitivism, however, these theorists thought the absurdity of *sui generis* morality should be cause for the rejection of the assumption that propositions such as "X = good" are *true* in the first place.

Let's look more closely at our reformulation of OQA and see how moral realists might react to it. P3 is obviously doing a tremendous amount of work in this argument. It represents a bold empirical claim about "us" and our ability to "significantly ask" something. Moore, however, does not seem to think that this assumption requires much in the way of persuasion or support. He remarks only briefly that, "anyone can convince himself by inspection that the predicate of this proposition—'good' – is positively different from the notion [of any putative reductive definition] . . . which enters into its subject" (1903: 16). So, asking a question "with significance" must mean something like asking a question of a proposition that is not tautologous. Any question of the form "Is S really P?" is significant if "S is P" is not tautologous, and "S is P" is not tautologous if S is distinct from P, that is, if we can, as Moore phrases it, "hold the two things before our mind." Stated this way, the P3 presents an empirical claim about our conceptual abilities. Moore seems to think that it is obvious that, upon introspection, we *do* perceive the distinctness of reductive expressions and good, and that we, therefore, can significantly ask whether the former really are good. Some have denied this, claiming that we simply don't introspect distinctness (Hancock 1960). To define significance as requiring that some expressions be nontautologous, and then to define acceptable definitions as those that *are* tautologous and to require that we significantly question all definitions, begs the question against reductionism. If some reductive theory (e.g. utilitarianism) is true, then "good is the maximization of the greatest happiness for the greatest number" *is* tautologous, and cannot by Moore's standards be significantly questioned. Moore's response to this objection is to simply reaffirm that we *do* significantly question reductive definitions such as hedonism. That is, it's a phenomenological fact that when we think about pleasure we can conceptually separate that thought from good.

Moore's intuition about the conceptual openness of nontautologies as real definitions seems prima facie supported by the history of continual disagreement concerning normative theories. Different theories define morality in different ways, which would suggest that morality as an *analysandum can* be conceptually separated from its *analysans*. However, just because we can introspect distinctness between the *analysans* and the *analysandum* of any reductive analysis, it doesn't follow that the two *really are* distinct. For, consider P2—the conditional that if a reduction of good is true, then we can't significantly question whether the *analysans* is good. The problem here seems to be that the consequent of the conditional is a claim concerning our linguistic or conceptual capacities, but the antecedent is a claim about reality. Assuming that the one claim is dependent on the other seems to involve the assumption that our linguistic or conceptual capacities should have anything to do with our ontology. But couldn't some reductive analysis be true and we simply are unable to recognize it? In other words, just because *we* can think of pleasure and good as distinct does not mean they really *are* distinct.

This point becomes especially salient in the context of *synonyms*. Synonyms are words that refer to the same things, but which may have very different connotations. To use a well-worn example, "bachelor" and "unmarried man" are identical in the sense that they have exactly the same reference and pick out exactly the same items. But "bachelor" may bring to mind certain associations—perhaps with traditional aristocratic caste terminology—that "unmarried man" would not capture. Though our linguistic intuitions will no doubt vary culturally, the point is that it does not seem to threaten the identity that each term permits of different connotation. Thus, it seems that I can think of "bachelor" without thinking of "unmarried man" because, although the two are synonyms, they have different connotations. But OQA would deny this—they could not be synonyms *because* they have different connotations, that is, because I can think of one without thinking of the other.

Philosophers of language since Moore have provided the terminology to state this objection more clearly. We think now that there is a difference between the *intension* (linguistic meaning) of a term and its *extension* (what that term denotes). For instance, we know that water just is H_2O, even though the two terms do not mean the same thing. "Water" means the liquid-stuff of our experience, whereas "H_2O" has a specific chemical meaning. And of course, we can think—and did think for thousands of years prior to the discovery—about water without thinking about H_2O. So, the identity "water equals H_2O" is an identity only at the level of extension. This suggests that meaning is distinct from reference—extension is not determined by intension.

OQA seems to conflate intension and extension. Or rather, it reduces extension to intension, that is, if two things *mean* different things, then they *are* different things. This view denies even the identities of bachelors as unmarried men and water as H_2O. But if these aren't real definitions, then what are? Thus, the problem with Moore is that the conflation of intension and extension seems to lead to a paradox: if true analyses reveal only real definitions, and if real definitions are essentially tautologies, then true analyses will be totally uninformative. In a tautology, the *analysans* and *analysandum* are identical—nothing new is learned.[3] But this means that if an analysis (reductive or otherwise) tells us something about the *analysandum* that we didn't already know from the *analysans*, then the analysis cannot be a real definition. Thus arises the "paradox of analysis"—real definitions must be either trivial or false. Moore's definition of morality as "good, and that is the end of the matter" may not be informative, but it may for that very reason be true. If the conflation of intension with extension leads to such a paradox, if it fails to allow us to talk about synonyms or scientific discoveries, then it should be rejected.

Moore's conflation of intension and extension seems gratuitous to us in light of later twentieth-century philosophy of language. But it might strike us as more plausible if we share Moore's metaphilosophical commitments (his "meta-metaethics," to use the term we introduced in §1.2). Moore was fiercely committed to "commonsense" and, as Brian Hutchinson has characterized him, "the general picture in ethics is one of refinement, not revolt: too much change and we will have switched the subject" (2001: 93). This meta-metaethical view is in line with Moore's indictment of what he called "metaphysical ethics," as being too rarified for nonspecialists to relate to as a sphere of human meaning. The conflation of intension and extension also makes slightly more sense in the context of Moore's aesthete Bloomsbury Group sentiments (Regan 1986). Reductive metaphysics, according to the general Bloomsbury consensus, is misguided from the very start because it overthinks what should instead be spontaneous and immediate. In trying to reduce morality to something else, the assumption must be that morality in its unreduced form is somehow insufficient or unsatisfying. But such an acknowledgment must involve a prior *disappointment* with good—a "cosmic malaise" (Hutchinson 2001: 95)—which Moore emphatically rejected. For him, metaethics (like all philosophy) must be an exercise in beauty as much as in truth.

Moore's non-naturalistic metaethics will only be convincing if we also share his meta-metaethics of re-enchantment. However, although we have seen that re-enchantment is one of the driving forces behind realism, a robust realism cannot settle for a naïve re-enchantment. For one thing, Moore's non-naturalism seems implicitly wedded to a kind of quasipragmatic theory of truth: something is true just insofar as it makes the best sense of our pretheoretic intensions. But such a theory of truth is undesirable for the realist, who wants to maintain some kind of anchor to the world via a correspondence theory (as discussed in §2.2). Thus, OQA fails to prove the irreducibility of moral predicates in the way robust realists would like. The meta-metaethical premise that intension determines extension would force all true definitions to be either trivial or false. This is clearly unacceptable for any but the most deeply committed antitheorists or those who hold a pragmatic conception of truth. However, OQA still deserves to be taken seriously, not only because many antirealists alike wield it in support of their positions, but because it reveals something very important about moral language. Even if we don't agree with Moore about the impossibility of *coextension* between moral and natural properties, OQA seems at least to suggest the impossibility of their *cointension*. Normative talk simply cannot be substituted with non-normative talk and be taken to be talking about the same thing.

3.2 Moral supervenience

OQA was intended as an argument against naturalistic reductionism *tout court*, but we have seen that, unless we share Moore's meta-metaethics (which robust realists should avoid), it is probably only successful against cointensional naturalism. Early formulations of ethical naturalism often failed to heed this lesson, a failure embodied in what Michael Smith (1994: 35) calls "definitional naturalism," that is, the view that naturalism is in the business of *defining* moral predicates as nonmoral predicates in a way which would make their usage interchangeable and synonymous. For instance, R. M. Hare characterized ethical naturalism as, "those theories against which Moore's refutation (or a version of it) is valid." This is not very helpful, for as we have seen OQA is valid as an argument against *cointension*, but invalid as an argument against *coextension*. If Hare meant that naturalism characterizes any view that stipulates cointension, then naturalism is false by definition. And if naturalism characterizes any view that stipulates coextension, then *every* view is naturalistic because OQA is invalid as an argument about extension.

Hare also allows that the validity of some "version" of OQA could define naturalism. One common version of OQA is Hume's oft-cited expression of the "is-ought gap" (1740: 455–70), which claims that one cannot derive normative conclusions from non-normative premises. So, could naturalism be defined as any theory that violates the is-ought gap? Much has been made of this "gap," yet the most charitable interpretation of it (given that Hume himself is traditionally called a naturalist!) is that normative statements cannot be *deductively* proven, except in a trivial way, from non-normative premises.[4] So, could naturalism be defined as "any view that tries to deductively prove normative conclusions from non-normative premises in a non-trivial way?" But this is unfair to naturalism since *no* view can deductively demonstrate normative conclusions from non-normative premises in a nontrivial way. Furthermore, it should be noted that Hare himself thought that the power of the is-ought gap had nothing to do with the constraints of deductive logic, but with the fact that "ought" statements are noncognitivist and prescriptive, whereas non-normative statements are cognitivist and descriptive. But this makes "naturalism" equivalent to "non-cognitivism," and this won't do since many naturalists have been cognitivists.

More plausible recent forms of ethical naturalism have not been "definitional," but instead what Smith calls "metaphysical" (1994: 27). That is, instead of making a claim about moral and nonmoral cointension—which violates the lesson of OQA—ethical naturalism only makes a claim about coextension. Such metaphysical naturalism has proliferated in recent decades. Many of these naturalisms have been explicitly antirealist (e.g. Mackie 1977; Wong 1984).[5] Several recent naturalistic views, however, have attempted to preserve some form of realism. Most notably, the so-called Cornell Realists (prominently including Richard Boyd, Nicholas Sturgeon, and David Brink) have argued that only a cointension of moral and nonmoral predicates would threaten moral realism, and that the remaining possibility of a coextensional reduction is perfectly compatible with realism.[6]

These "new wave" forms of naturalistic moral realism have prompted a refurbishing of OQA in an attempt to problematize even coextensional reductions of the moral to the natural. Most notably, Terence Horgan and Mark Timmons (1991) have undertaken this via their Moral Twin Earth scenario (MTE). MTE presents a thought experiment that is intended to parallel Hilary Putnam's (1973) Twin Earth example, in which the inhabitants of an alternate, but physically identical world used all the same language about water in all the same ways regular humans did, except that, on Twin Earth, "water" was not H_2O, but something else chemically. Putnam argued that this difference in reference will generate compelling intuitions that there is a comparable difference in meaning, such that regular Earthlings and Twin Earthlings are talking past one another when they each pronounce the word "water." In other words, Putnam (1975) thought the thought experiment supported "semantic externalism," the view that, as he phrases it, "meaning just ain't in the head." (Recall our earlier discussion of Putnam's theory of meaning in §2.2.)

Horgan and Timmons ask us to imagine another world (let's call this E2) which is identical to the real Earth (E1) in all natural respects, and on which the inhabitants use the same moral terms such as "good" in translatable and familiar ways as we do. According to naturalistic realists, because moral properties are coextensive with natural properties, and because the natural properties in these two worlds are identical, the moral properties (G for "good"), therefore, should also be identical. This, then, is how the relationship between

the two Earths and their respective meanings of "good" would
look (the downward arrow represents the relation of coextensive
reduction):

$$G1 \quad = \quad G2$$
$$\downarrow \qquad\quad \downarrow$$
$$E1 \quad = \quad E2$$

If E1 is identical to E2, then G1 will also be identical to G2. Such a
relationship is also sometimes called one of "supervenience." For G
to supervene upon E is for G to depend upon E in such a way that
any change in E would result in a corresponding change in G. While
supervenience has been subject to innumerable different formulations
(Kim 1993), moral realists at the very least seem to require some
way of accounting for the instantiation of moral properties in the
world, on pain of realist morality atrophying into a purely formal
or other-worldly thesis with no capacity for practical connection.
Naturalistic realists, however, want this instantiation to involve some
sort of coextensive reduction of moral to natural properties, which is
what Horgan and Timmons claim MTE patently disallows.

MTE proceeds as follows: imagine that "good" for real Earthlings
ends up meaning, say, those actions which produce the greatest
overall pleasure for the greatest number of people. That is, imagine
that Utilitarianism is true on Earth. Now imagine that "good" on
Twin Earth instead turns out to refer to more Kantian considerations.
(And further assume that Utilitarianism and Kantianism are
mutually exclusive.) So, in contrast to the naturalist scheme, here's
the hypothetical scenario Horgan and Timmons suggest:

$$G1 \quad \neq \quad G2$$
$$\downarrow \qquad\quad \downarrow$$
$$E1 \quad = \quad E2$$

Horgan and Timmons contend that this difference between the
meaning of G1 and G2 intuitively implies that inhabitants of E1
and E2 are disagreeing with one another about morality. The ethical
naturalist, by contrast, would apparently be forced to the less

intuitive interpretation that they are not genuinely disagreeing, but rather talking past one another (which is how Putnam diagnosed the situation in the original Twin Earth scenario about "water"). A genuine disagreement presupposes at least enough basic commonality so that the different parties can understand each other; if differences were radically incommensurable, we might not even be able to set them up as differences at all in the first place. The more charitable interpretation of moral dialogue between Earthlings and Twin Earthlings, urge Horgan and Timmons, is to take their prima facie disagreement at face value. This means, however, taking seriously the idea that naturalistic reductions are either (a) not metaphysically necessary across all possible worlds (i.e. G1 apparently supervenes on E1, but not on the naturally identical E2), or else (b) they are not discoverable *a priori* (i.e. the Earthlings or Twin Earthlings, or both, might be wrong about what actually instantiates G1 and G2). To make explicit the affinities between MTE and the older OQA, we can see that Horgan and Timmons are pressing the ethical naturalist on why we cannot significantly ask whether G1 affixes necessarily and to some particular natural state of affairs. The alleged hypothetical coherence of MTE suggests instead that the coextension of "good" with E1 remains an open question.

MTE has accreted almost as much commentary as OQA. As with OQA, some view MTE as definitive against naturalistic reductions. Horgan and Timmons themselves go so far as to say, "all defensive strategies [on behalf of naturalistic realism] are likely to prove futile against Moral Twin Earth" (1992: 171), and R. M. Hare (1995: 342) confesses that MTE is "effective" at defeating ethical naturalism. On the other hand, many naturalistic realists continue to object to both the validity and the semantic soundness of MTE. Stephan Laurence et al. (1999) identify structural disanalogies between MTE and regular (nonmoral) Twin Earth arguments which beg the question against naturalists. Erik Kraemer (1991) argues that the assumption that G1 and G2—Utilitarian and Kantian moral extensions, respectively—are mutually exclusive is not itself obvious, and might bias the way the supervenience onto the two worlds is envisioned. Furthermore, given the outlandish nature of MTE, it is not clear that we have reliable or choate intuitions about moral coextensions in hypothetical alternate worlds in the first place. And if MTE generates intuitions that are inconsistent with ethical naturalism, do we have any independent reasons to avert to the former instead of the later? In a battle of intuitions, it's not intuitively clear who wins, or how.

More importantly, MTE might be guilty of targeting only a caricatured version of naturalistic realism. We have seen previously that OQA might fail at ruling out coextensive reduction, even if it succeeds in disallowing cointensive reduction. Might MTE, which is allegedly analogous to OQA, be subject to the same limitations? As for naturalists in the Cornell Realist tradition, their own positions about the relationship between moral and natural properties are significantly more sophisticated than MTE would seem to give credit. Richard Boyd (1988), for instance, defends the view that moral-natural coextensions are metaphysically necessary across all possible worlds, but explicitly rejects that our knowledge of this coextension is *a priori*. Thus, on Boyd's view, Earthlings and Twin Earthlings who use "good" to refer to Utilitarian versus Kantian categories, respectively, would still be genuinely disagreeing: there would be some fact of the matter that their two natural worlds share, and about which they each might be wrong. Furthermore, Boyd's brand of naturalistic moral realism embraces the possibility that the naturalistic properties E1 and E2 with which good is coextensive might be "homeostatic clusters." Thus, instead of isomorphic rigid designation, Boyd envisions a set of overlapping natural conditions, facts, or states of affairs which might have a vague "family resemblance" to one another, but in a way that is loose enough to permit some wiggle-room in the ways in which G1 and G2 connect to them.

Other critics have leveraged versions of MTE as objections to moral realism in general. Simon Blackburn (1993: 111–29), for instance, asks us to imagine a scenario in which two different Earths are physically different, and in which there is a comparable moral difference too, for example, killing is wrong in one world, but not wrong in the other.

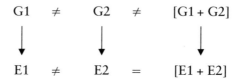

$$G1 \neq G2 \neq [G1 + G2]$$
$$\downarrow \qquad \downarrow \qquad \downarrow$$
$$E1 \neq E2 = [E1 + E2]$$

Because we can imagine each individual world, we should be able to also imagine yet a third world which is a blend of them. But, although we imagine such a world that is mixed in its natural components (E1 + E2), Blackburn thinks it would contradict the essence of moral realism to similarly imagine *morally* alternate worlds (G1 + G2). For, as Blackburn seems to characterize the view, realists envision moral properties as universal, transcending the natural conditions on which they are supposed to supervene or (if the realist is also a naturalist) with which they are supposed to be coextensive. In this way, Blackburn argues that realist morality becomes unmoored from any necessary connection to the real world—a conclusion he criticizes as "mysterious." By contrast, if we take the expression of moral "truths" to involve attitudes which *are* sensitive to changing natural facts, as Blackburn's "quasi-realist" position envisions, then the incoherence of morally alternate worlds evaporates. (Recall our previous discussion of Blackburn's deflationary semantics in §2.2.)

Of course, as supervenience guru Jaegwon Kim (1993) has pointed out, invocations of supervenience are never "metaphysically innocent," and there are a number of ways in which realists might respond to Blackburn's challenge. In addition to reexamining the presuppositions and ecological validity of how such thought experiments are set up to begin with, realists could also jettison a variety of nonessential baggage which Blackburn's version of MTE foists upon them. First, realists might concede that moral properties need not be universal or metaphysically necessary across all possible worlds. Morality might instead be better characterized as "particularistic" (cf. Hooker and Little 2000), in the sense that moral properties are instantiated not in generic action types (as in Blackburn's "killing is wrong"), but in more embodied, situation-specific "thick concepts."[7] Similarly, in the spirit of Boyd's naturalism which we have already explored, realists could distance themselves from the assumption that the natural supervenient base of a moral property must be a single thing; it could instead be a homeostatic cluster of properties with joint family resemblances, which might accommodate the possibility of a morally mixed world.

In summary, moral realists must acknowledge some type of connection between stance-independent moral properties and their actual instantiations in the world. OQA cautions against making this connection so strong as to involve naturalistic cointensional reduction. But naturalism at the level of coextensional property reduction remains a possible venue for realism, but only if such realists can (as most Cornell Realists do) tweak how they envision the necessity or singularity of coextensional reductions.

3.3 The "nature" of ethical naturalism

As we have seen, OQA and MTE are specifically objections against ethical "naturalism"—the former against naturalism tout court, the latter against naturalistic realism. We have seen that OQA may be successful in restricting cointensional reductions, and that MTE can be used to restrict certain coextensional reductions as well, although realists (though no more so than others) will still need to flesh out more fully how they understand supervenience and whether they envision moral instantiations as metaphysically necessary or not. Yet, to fully adjudicate between naturalistic and non-naturalist varieties of realism, we will need a more complete analysis of what it means to call something "natural" in the first place. This section will survey some of the commonest ways of demarcating the natural from the non-natural, which we shall see is difficult to do in non-question-begging ways.

It seems that the common denominator among theories who call themselves "naturalistic" is that there must be a property identity (i.e. a coextension) between moral and nonmoral predicates, *regardless* of whether there is additionally a cointension or whether the view requires any further specific commitments.[8] However, the coextension required by ethical naturalism cannot involve just *any* nonmoral property. There must be a property identity between moral and specifically *natural* properties for the resultant view to be genuinely naturalistic. By contrast, Pigden (1991) has characterized ethical naturalism as involving the reducibility of goodness "to something else." Since it is not specified that the "something else" needs to be this-worldly, there can even be "theological naturalists" on Pigden's view (1991: 422). Indeed, many divine command theorists who think that good is coextensive with God's will have characterized themselves as ethical naturalists (Adams 1979). But if this is ethical naturalism, then what is *not*? If naturalism is committed to anything distinctive, it seems committed to being "not supernaturalism." As Barry Stroud (1996) says, this is what constitutes the "charm" of naturalism in the first place, namely that it frees ethical (and metaethical) inquiry from the constraints of theology and religion.

It is for this reason that many of the leading versions of ethical naturalism beg all the important ontological questions. They affirm a coextension without saying in what way the relevant nonmoral property is appropriately "natural," or even what it means to be "natural" in the first place. Boyd (1988) claims only that there must be a coextension between moral and "non-moral" properties, but we have seen this is compatible with moral properties being identified with supernatural properties. Philip Pettit and Frank Jackson are somewhat more specific, but they still fail to informatively unpack "naturalism": their articulation of "moral functionalism" requires that moral predicates be coextensive with "whatever plays their role in mature folk morality" (1995). But it is not clear why we should call whatever plays the role of moral values in mature folk morality exclusively "natural." Peter Railton (1986) argues that *good* is coextensive with the "objective interests" of an ideal epistemic agent, and that *right* is coextensive with the approval of an impartial spectator. However, it is still unclear precisely why objective interests, ideal agents, and impartial spectators are necessarily "natural"—after all, they are not typically the sorts of entities identified by the natural sciences. (This is not to mention the fact that, even if Railton's view can be said to be "naturalistic," it might nonetheless do so at the sacrifice of robust realism if it requires that good and right are *constituted* by agents' interests or spectators' approval, cf. §2.2.)

An ideal way to demarcate the realm of the natural from the non-natural would be to identify some cluster of necessary and sufficient conditions that are possessed by all and only the properties we want to call natural. But this proves extremely difficult for all candidate conditions. For instance, *existence* or *reality* cannot be the defining characteristic of the natural since this would make naturalism equivalent to realism, and many naturalists have rejected realism, and many realists embraced non-naturalism. Neither can we say that "natural" means "non-normative" since this would make naturalism equivalent to antirealism. Shafer-Landau (2003) considers other proposals of this sort and rejects them all as either not necessary or not sufficient conditions of the natural. For instance, *materiality* (physicality, tangibility) cannot be characteristic of all and only natural properties, because many entities that are vital to the "natural" sciences are not literally physical. Quarks and species are natural (and real!), if anything is, though we certainly cannot touch them; and voids, electrical fields, and black holes are natural (and real!) without being material. *Causal efficacy* also cannot be an intrinsic feature of the natural since many natural properties (e.g. colors, self-identicalness) are not causally efficacious. And "natural" cannot mean anything that is *independent of humans* because humans themselves would then be non-natural.

Many of these candidates for distinguishing the natural can be found in various guises in the history of philosophy. The question of naturalism was especially important during the Enlightenment when philosophers were concerned to ground morality on a basis independent of religion. For instance, Hume called attention to three senses of "natural" (1740: 474–5): when we say that something is "natural," we mean that it either (a) occurs in the world, (b) is universal or innate, or (c) is not created or artificial. Hume's own view seems to be that morality is natural at least in the first two senses, and that *some* aspects of morality (e.g. sympathy and benevolence) are natural in the third sense and some are not (e.g. justice). Hume (1751: 96) says "natural" means either "unusual, miraculous, or artificial." (Interestingly enough, Hume also notes that debates about whether morality is natural in different senses are "merely verbal.") The third sense seems equivalent to being independent of humans, and the first sense equivalent to existence or reality, both of which we have seen to be inadequate to distinguish ethical naturalism. The second sense seems to involve a claim about agreement, which will be considered below. Likewise, in classical Hellenic philosophy, the natural (*physis*) was distinguished from the conventional (*nomos*), but only in a way that made the former equivalent to "real" and the latter equivalent to "not real" (Engberg-Pederson 1995).

Instead of trying to locate necessary and sufficient conditions, Shafer-Landau offers an alternate method of specifying which properties are "natural." He suggests that we "identify the subject matters (and their terms) of the various disciplines related to 'nature'" (2003: 58). This approach jibes with the traditional association of naturalism with *science*—to find out which things are natural, look at which things are studied by science. Of course, it will be important here what one means by "science." After all, Aristotle called ethics a "science," albeit an "imprecise" one (*Nicomachean Ethics* ff. 1094–5). So, what is it about science that distinguishes it from ethics, at least vis-à-vis the question of naturalism? One very common feature thought to be uniquely characteristic of science is *convergence.* Bernard Williams expresses a common version of this opinion:

> In a scientific inquiry there should ideally be convergence on an answer, where the best explanation of the convergence involves the idea that the answer represents how things are; in the area of the ethical, at least at a high level of generality, there is no such coherent hope. (1985: 136)

Of course, there is an influential tradition that denies that even science converges. Those sympathetic to Thomas Kuhn's (1962) outlook will see the history of science not as a progression toward some unified end, but rather as a succession of incommensurable paradigms.[9] But even without engaging this tricky debate, there could be other reasons to resist drawing a science/ethics distinction on the basis of convergence. But this reason cannot, of course, be convergence itself, for to say definitively that ethics *cannot ever* converge but that science can is to beg the question against the moral realist.[10]

It could instead be maintained that as a matter of fact ethics has not converged *so far*. But even if this were true, it should not motivate the conclusion that ethics cannot or will not eventually converge.[11] After all, during the so-called dark ages of the early Medieval period, science failed to progress for centuries. Perhaps we are in an "*ethical dark age.*" And ethical dark ages should not derail the potential of ethical convergence any more than scientific dark ages have derailed scientific convergence. Besides, even discounting the Kuhnian hypothesis mentioned above, we should not overblow the degree of present scientific convergence. The enduring failure of physics to be made satisfactorily consistent with the biological and social sciences—not to mention our current inability to identify a plausible "grand unified theory" for physics itself—shows that scientific convergence is, at present, largely a matter of faith. This is not to say that science will not eventually surmount these difficulties. But it should caution against the hypocrisy of denying the similar potential for ethical convergence. If we believe that the laws of quantum mechanics and the laws that govern the macroquantum world will eventually converge, then why can we not believe that entrenched ethical conflicts—for example, between consequentialist and nonconsequentialist outlooks, or between different values—could similarly converge?

If science cannot be differentiated from ethics of the basis of convergence, can it be distinguished on the basis of anything else? Shafer-Landau (2003) identifies four ways in which he thinks science (which he associates with naturalism) differs from ethics:

1   Science is *quantifiable*, ethics is not.
2   Science involves *physical necessity*, ethics involves metaphysical necessity.
3   Science concerns *prediction and causal efficacy*, ethics does not.
4   Science is *theoretical*, ethics is practical.

However, it seems we can think of paradigm examples of both science and ethics which threaten to collapse each item on this list; and *a fortiori*, any clear boundary between naturalism and non-naturalism.

Consider the first claim, that only science is quantifiable. First, we do frequently speak of actions and people being *better* or *worse* than others, for example, we think that supererogatory actions are not only good, but *better* than obligatory actions. Most people probably don't think in terms of someone or some action being wholly good or wholly bad, but instead as holding some variable position on a moral spectrum. This alone might suggest some type of ranking or scaling implicit to moral attributions. Of course, the ability to be ranked is not the same as being literally quantifiable— being literally quantifiable seems to require units of measurement. But even if ethics is not (literally) quantifiable, is science itself? First, we should resist the urge to associate quantification with the ability to be expressed mathematically. More importantly, if quantification involves units of measurement, then many scientific disciplines are *not* quantifiable. What are the units of psychology or sociology? "Units" such as beliefs, feelings, "states," people, etc. all seemed to be shared to some extent by ethics. And if being quantifiable means being nomological or law-like, then the biological and human sciences seem to resist quantification.[12] If it turns out that only physics is literally and robustly quantifiable, then "quantification" is too narrow a way to distinguish science and ethics.

Maybe instead science and ethics can be distinguished by the degrees of necessity to which they appeal. Could science alone be physically necessary and ethics metaphysically necessary? First, as we saw earlier, some naturalistic realists might be willing to sacrifice the necessity of reductive coextensions in the face of MTE. While metaphysical necessity might be attractive vis-à-vis re-enchantment, there is nothing in the bare-bones formulation of robust realism, as we unpacked it in Chapter 1, which requires that moral truths obtain equally across all possible worlds. Second, "physical" cannot mean "scientific" or "natural" without begging the question. It also cannot mean "material" or "tangible" because both science and ethics involve immaterial and intangible entities. Third, there are many metaphysically necessary principles (e.g. self-identity) that are not uniquely moral, many of which inform scientific reasoning.

Perhaps science and ethics differ in that only the former is concerned with or admits of predication and causal efficacy. However, on the one hand, "natural" properties like color or self-identity are not causally efficacious. And certain areas of even the "hardest" sciences resist prediction—meteorological and quantum phenomena, for instance, appear persistently chaotic. On the other hand, to say that ethics is not at all causally efficacious is to beg the question against a prevalent conception of morality as being inherently action guiding (see §§5.1 and 5.2). Furthermore, it seems that moral judgments *can* predict behavior with a relatively high degree of accuracy. We do so all the time with people we know. If I observe that Stefan habitually cheats on difficult exams, I know not to sit too close to him on the next one. If I know that Eric has been trustworthy in the past, I will feel confident confiding in him. This is to say that I can predict Stefan's cheating, and that I can predict Eric's discretion, based on antecedent moral judgments. If Stefan took a failing grade rather than cheat, or if Eric blabbed my confession to everyone he knew, I would be *surprised*. Ethical judgments have just as much predictive power as scientific judgments. Indeed, Hume observed that ethics may in some cases have *more* predictive power: a prisoner who wants to escape will try to break down the cell walls rather than plead with his jailer, reasoning that the jailer's "inflexible nature" is even more predictable than the hardness of the stone door! As Hume writes, "No union can be more constant and certain, than that of some actions with some motives and characters" (1740: 406).

Finally, could science and ethics be distinguished on the basis of the former being theoretical and the latter being practical? Maybe, but what do "theoretical" and "practical" mean? The terms cannot mark a difference in stance-independence (i.e. "practical" means "concerned with humans" and "theoretical" means "concerned with reality") because this begs the question against realism. And the two certainly cannot be mutually exclusive or else "ethical theory" and "practical science" would each be oxymoronic. "Practical" also sometimes means "action-guiding" or "motivating." But it is not clear that scientific judgments do not guide action—they clearly guide *scientific* action![13] In fact, it seems difficult to articulate what is theoretical and what is practical in a way that is not ultimately just a restatement of one of the three conditions of quantification, necessity, and prediction or causal efficacy considered above. But if these features fail to differentiate science from ethics, trying to additionally distinguish them by calling one theoretical and the other practical will be vacuous.[14]

Perhaps the natural could be adequately distinguished in some way we have not yet considered. But, as Hume said, "'Tis impossible to refute a system, which has never yet been explain'd" (1740: 464). The upshot of this discussion is not that ethical naturalism is false, but that it is unclear exactly how it differs from ethical non-naturalism. Of course, we could simply stipulate a demarcation between the two, but this would be arbitrary. Moral realism, as we have defined it, is compatible with a number of possible coextensions with other properties, and the question of the necessity, singularity, and supervenience of these coextensions is much more significant than in-fighting about an ultimately irrelevant nomenclature of "naturalism."

3.4 Where in the world are moral properties?

Although we have defined moral realism and considered its possible relationship with nonmoral instantiations, we have skirted the thorny question of *ontology*. What sorts of entities are envisioned as existing according to moral realism, and in what ways are they thought to exist? We have spoken loosely of moral "facts," "properties," and "values," but realists owe a more detailed metaphysical picture. What particular type of thing is "morality" for it to exist allegedly in such a way that we make cognitivist judgments about it? To what aspect of the world would true moral judgments correspond—what sort of "truthmakers" can moral realists countenance?

Moral realists have unfortunately been rather reticent on the issue of ontology, rarely addressing the question of what it is that moral judgments are true in virtue of or what aspect of the world it is to which true moral judgments correspond. But if realists have been wary of confronting ontological issues, their opponents have been quick to supply ontological pictures on their behalf. One of the most damaging, but pervasive ontological accounts foisted upon realists has been a primary quality model of *objects*. For example, J. L. Mackie (1977: 17) famously characterized realism as the view that moral values are somehow part of the "furniture of the world." Antirealists are not to blame for this distortion: objects are a familiar and relatively easily articulated entity, and realists have simply not provided many explicit alternatives. Silence on behalf of realism, however, should not imply consent.

The object model has subtly infiltrated realist ontology in the form of the notion of "objectivity." Indeed, numerous influential twentieth-century metaethicists (both realists and antirealists) have used "realism" and "objectivism" synonymously, for example, Mackie (1977), Rachels (1978), Wong (1984), and Platts (1991). For reasons we shall see, however, the two notions pull apart in important ways. For one thing, objectivism is often characterized by what Williams (1985) has called an "absolute conception of reality" (cf. McNaughton 1988: 83–5; Smart 1963; Stroud 2000). According to Williams, something admits of an absolute conception if and only if it is "non-perspectival."[15] It is exceedingly unclear, however, how a conception of reality could be in principle nonperspectival, for there seems to be an obvious absurdity in the idea of a nonperspectival conception of reality when our very act of conceiving constitutes a perspective. How can agents characterize reality by absolute conception if agents are prevented from using their concepts in the first place? Or as Peter Railton has put it, "a standpoint without any subjectivity is a standpoint with no point of view – which is to say, no standpoint at all" (1998: 63).

Thomas Nagel's (1986) critique of similar attempts to construct an impartial "view from nowhere" also illuminates some of the problems which face objectivism. As Nagel observes, there is a tension in any attempt to reconcile the sense that a particular experience is uniquely one's own with the impulse to abstract from anything peculiar to an individual perspective. Though we feel pulled in the direction of objectivity, we find it impossible to leave behind our subjectivity fully, since our subjectivity is itself a part of the very world which the objective perspective seeks to identify. In this way, exclusively catering our ontology to such a perspective results in what Nagel calls "objective blindness." David Wiggins (1976) makes a similar point, arguing that one of the incoherencies of reductive views such as noncognitivism is that they collapse what he calls the "inner view" we subjectively take toward our first-personal experiences into the objectifying "outer view" according to which we view things from the third-person perspective. As Wiggins says, "The outside view must pay some heed to the differences that the inner view perceives" (1976: 100).

It is in just this way that we can distinguish moral realism from moral objectivism. *Realism*, recalling our discussions in the previous chapter, is the view that moral properties exist in a way that is stance-independent, whereas *objectivism* is the view that moral properties exist in a way that makes no reference to any features of agents whatsoever. This sort of objectivism threatens to divorce morality from human sensibility completely, which would certainly not serve the meta-metaethical goal of "re-enchantment" with which we started this inquiry. Moreover, objectivism doesn't add anything ontologically vital to morality that robust realism doesn't already countenance. This would suggest that realism fares best when objectivism is denied: morality may be essentially about us, but it is no less real for this fact. Furthermore, jettisoning objectivism would keep realist values in good ontological company with other familiar entities. Most people are presumably realists about books, for instance, and believe that books exist independently of anyone's beliefs about them, even though it would be impossible to meaningfully articulate the concept "book" without reference to anthropocentric intensions. Similarly, moral claims such as "capital punishment is morally wrong" cannot be meaningfully expressed without reference to concepts such as death, rights, justice, desert, suffering, or deterrence—none of which make sense independently of features of our biology, psychology, and social-political frameworks. Imagine trying to explain the content of the sentence "capital punishment is morally wrong" to someone unfamiliar with the definition of "capital punishment." How else are we to define "capital punishment" without bringing anthropocentric concepts such as death, law, or government into the discussion?

Another reason to distinguish realism from objectivism is that the latter connotes an ontology of *objects*, which is a mode of existence obviously inappropriate to values even as construed by the realist. Morality is not spatiotemporally bounded, that is, we do not say that goodness exists "over there." Although particular actions, events, and characters that instantiate moral properties might be spatiotemporally bounded, the properties themselves are *sine loco et anno*. Despite the obvious absurdity of envisioning moral properties as literal, spatiotemporal objects, this is unfortunately the *de facto* characterization which often tacitly dominates many discussions of the metaphysics of moral realism. Mackie, it will be remembered, described the objectivist properties which he indicted as erroneous as "structural elements" of the world (1977: 23). Furthermore, he utilized Hume's discussion of the mind's "propensity to spread itself on external objects" as representative of what he saw as the objectivist's error. Commenting from the realist side, Brink has also stated that moral realists are "usually" characterized as analogous to scientific realists about disciplines such as physics and chemistry, which in turn are taken to involve the study of "real objects" (1989: 6). The point here is not that such writers themselves are intending to envision moral properties as spatiotemporal, but that the default language of "furniture," "structural elements," "objects," and entities similar to those studied by physics has engendered an implicit association of moral realism with a *primary quality* ontology.

If realist moral properties do not exist as primary qualities, do they not then exist simpliciter? Even antirealists, however, should be wary of a rarefied ontology of exclusively spatiotemporal objects. After all, we do commonly recognize the reality of entities that are not spatiotemporally bounded, for example, subatomic particles, gravitational forces, and electromagnetic fields. Only a "rough desert-dweller" (Lewis 1989) would conceive of an ontology strictly limited to spatiotemporally bounded objects. But if the ontology of morality is not modeled on primary qualities, what alternative models can realists look to?[16] On the one hand, realists might fall back to the *sui generis* view of moral properties popular among non-naturalists. As we have seen in Sections 3.1–3.3, though, even if we are attracted to a *sui generis* ontology (which, after all, seems more like a refusal to articulate any positive ontological model at all), we shall still have to face the challenges inherent in OQA, MTE, and the ambiguous demarcation from the sphere of the "natural."

In the remainder of this section, by contrast, we shall consider an alternate ontological model for realism. Instead of refusing to articulate an ontological model (i.e. non-naturalism) and instead of being saddled with an implausible primary quality model (i.e. objectivism), perhaps realist properties could be modeled on *secondary qualities*. If primary qualities are objects in the sense of entities permitted by a nonperspectival absolute conception, secondary qualities, by contrast, will allow for some sort of relational or dispositional connection between reality and sensibility. John McDowell (1985), for instance, has suggested that moral properties might have the same ontological status as color.[17] The color red, for example, might be understood as the disposition of an object to produce in an observer "red" perceptions in appropriate epistemic situations. Although the perception is stance-dependent, the *power* that produces the perception is not: it is ontologically grounded in external states of affairs, for example, reflectance properties of physical surfaces. By analogy, moral properties could similarly exist as powers to produce corresponding moral reactions in appropriately situated or constituted agents. If successful, this sort of secondary quality ontology would preserve the realism of moral properties by locating them in states of affairs that are stance-independent, while avoiding the quietism of non-naturalism or the implausibility of objectivism.

The "dispositional realist" will need to insist that colors would still exist even in a world of no actual color perceivers, and that moral properties would still exist even in a world of no actual moral agents. In such worlds, there would obviously be no color or moral perceptions since there would be no color or moral perceivers. But the powers to produce the corresponding color or moral perceptions in appropriately situated agents would still obtain even if there were no such agents. The colors and properties would exist, as it were, un-actualized (cf. Cohen 2009). As Robert Schwartz as put it, "experience results from contributions of both the environment and the perceiver, and these contributions are inextricably joined" (2006: 250).

Dispositional realism, however, faces several potential challenges, which can be grouped into two camps. First, many dispute the dispositionalist analysis of secondary qualities in general. This kind of objection usually stems from either alternate interpretations of the canon of philosophical texts related to secondary qualities,[18] or else from contemporary accounts gleaned from color science that seem to suggest some form of color antirealism.[19] Second, whatever the fate of color, morality might be viewed as fundamentally disanalogous in a variety of ways. For one thing, color and morality might respond differently to what Crispin Wright (1992) has called an "order of determination test" for whether or not a concept is "constructive" or "extension-determining," that is, whether it is our concept that determines which items fit that concept, or whether it is instead the items themselves which determine the concepts we have about them. Wright maintains that secondary qualities pass this test, but that moral properties fail it. Thus, for Wright, secondary qualities are not stance-independently real, but moral values are: moral judgments *track* moral properties whereas color judgments *constitute* color properties.

Wright thinks that one of the reasons why our concepts of secondary qualities are antirealist is because we are able to articulate *a priori* informative conditions for when we are epistemically justified in making color judgments. The fact that these conditions serve as the best explanations of color judgments suggests, claims Wright, that there is nothing more to color judgments than the satisfaction of these conditions and therefore that our color concepts determine their extensions rather than the other way around. Suffice it to say that this criterion for the order of determination test seems already to presuppose an antirealist interpretation of secondary qualities which the dispositional realist will not accept. If secondary qualities are instead interpreted as stance-independent powers, then it is the extensions of color concepts (i.e. the powers themselves) which determine the correct application of those concepts after all. Furthermore, it is ironic that, even if Wright's test is legitimate, moral properties emerge as *more real* than secondary qualities: realists might lose the battle for dispositionalism, but thereby win the war for stance-independence!

Let's consider some other objections to dispositional moral realism. First, it might be thought that whereas color terms are predicated of objects, moral properties are instead predicated of events, actions, and characters. The objection here is that the color-morality analogy commits some kind of category mistake by conflating objects with actions and events. However, it may be possible to rephrase events and actions in terms of strings of objects and the properties thereof, such that to predicate something of an action is no different than to predicate something of multiple individual objects. Moreover, we know that our manifest image of physical objects as macroscopic solids bearing colors is not supported by our scientific image of them as composed of microscopic entities. We predicate color of manifest objects, but if manifest objects are themselves relations between smaller scientific objects, then color is in fact predicated on relations. If this is right, then there is no disanalogy with values being predicated of events. To put the matter differently, there is no disanalogy between color and morality if we think of the surface-reflectance properties of objects upon which colors supervene, as well as the actions and intentions upon which moral properties supervene, as all simply different sorts of states of affairs.

A second alleged disanalogy between color and morality is that morality is intrinsically motivating, whereas color is motivationally inefficacious and "just sits there" (Blackburn 1993). However, it is not clear that moral realism, even dispositional moral realism, needs to require that moral beliefs are intrinsically motivating. Indeed, as we shall explore in Section 5.1, it seems possible for an individual to possess certain types of moral beliefs, and yet be unmoved to act. Plus, it is also misleading to say that color "just sits there" in a completely causally inert way. After all, the colors of things determine how we sort those things in ways that are more than merely aesthetic. There is evidence that color judgments played vital evolutionary roles as well—for example, certain colors indicating that something is poisonous ("aposematism")—such that an object's color would motivate us to avoid it (King 2005; Sharpe 1999; cf. Darwin 1859: 72). Again, the point here is merely to preserve the color-morality analogy: if color is not motivationally efficacious, then neither does morality need to be, and if color is ultimately motivationally efficacious, then morality can be too.

As a third potential disanalogy, recall Blackburn's version of MTE, which we examined in Section 3.2. We can conceive of a Twin Earth in which people see everything as blue which we (on regular Earth) see as red; but, goes the argument, the moral realist would not want to say that we could similarly change to think of as bad everything we currently think of as good. Blackburn (1993) claims that we would judge the inversions on Moral Twin Earth as horribly mistaken. However, wouldn't we also judge inverted color perceptions on Twin Earth as horribly mistaken, albeit not *morally* horrible? Indeed, accounting for an inversion of moral perception as constituting a "mistake" seems to presuppose a standard of moral value that is independent of what we currently think about or could ever come to think about it, and this sounds extremely similar to what the realist wants to say all along. Indeed, the scenario of morphed color perceptions seems supported by the possibility of such phenomena as inverted or absent *qualia*: why could these phenomena not be possible in an analogous way in the case of moral values? For example, we think that most nonhuman animals have different mental faculties than we do, and we also think that most animals are not aware of moral values as we are (or certainly not to the same extent), which is why we think it's inappropriate to morally judge them. Likewise, certain psychological pathologies may cause those afflicted to think of morality in a way very different than we do, or maybe not to think of it at all. Thus, the problem with the sociopath, for example, is that she suffers from a kind of absent *moral* qualia (cf. §5.1).

Furthermore, if we *did* radically change vis-à-vis our color or moral perceptual capacities, the dispositionalist could account for this by arguing that we are simply no longer occupying the requisite epistemic situation. But the powers to produce color and moral experiences needn't be affected concomitantly. Morality is no more illusory just because animals and sociopaths are insensible to it, any more than gamma rays are illusory just because humans are epistemically unequipped to directly perceive them.[20]

A fourth putative disanalogy between color and morality could be that we disagree much more about moral matters than we seem to about color. As we shall see in Sections 4.2 and 4.3, however, the extent or significance of moral disagreement might be greatly overblown. Furthermore, this alleged disanalogy might itself overblow the extent of color agreement. For example, while it is well known that there is much cross-cultural agreement about certain basic or paradigm colors (Berlin and Kay 1969), there is much less agreement about shades and uncommon colors. This is not merely a function of not being familiar with the *names* of these colors. Rather, it seems that there can be actual epistemic difference between color perceptions. For example, a trained artist may actually *see* more colors than someone who is untrained: she may be able to distinguish two shades of blue in a way that an untrained person cannot, even if the latter is familiar with the names for each color. Color is like *taste* in this way: an expert wine taster will be able to identify more tastes in a wine, or differences between two similar wines, than a nonexpert, even if the latter's wine vocabulary is very good. The nonexpert simply cannot taste a difference; but we would not conclude from the nonexpert's ignorance that there is actually no difference, especially when it is revealed that the winemakers really included the very things which the expert tasted. Thus, in both moral and perceptual cases, we agree on basic or paradigm cases: blue versus red, sweet versus dry wine, torturing babies versus giving to charity. And we similarly disagree on finer discernments: beige versus terracotta, a 1989 Sauternes versus a 1990 Sauternes, whether we should we tell a lie to produce a greater good or not.

Consider one final alleged disanalogy between color and morality. According to dispositional moral realism, moral properties would have to be articulated by reference to at least *potential* moral agents, just as the color purple would require potential color observers. Again, in neither case is the existence of the color or moral property *qua* disposition impugned by the lack of *actual* existence of such perceivers. However, while we seem to be able to articulate the conditions for potential color perception, the conditions for potential moral perception seem quite different. The difference, so the present objection goes, is that moral properties are essentially prescriptive in a way that colors are not. As McDowell (1985: 175) himself notes, "The disanalogy, now, is that a virtue (say) is conceived to be not merely such as to elicit the appropriate 'attitude' (as a colour is merely such as to cause the appropriate experiences), but rather such as to *merit* it." McDowell offers a comparison to the quality of "fearfulness" or dangerousness. According to McDowell, fearfulness (as opposed to fear itself) shares common ontological characteristics with his picture of realist moral properties: both exist as external states of affairs that obtain independently of anyone's belief in them, even though the content of each necessarily requires mentioning features of agents. As above, we must distinguish the claim that something is expressed by reference to features of agents from the claim that it exists only in virtue of agents' beliefs, agreements or endorsements. Thus, something is really fearful regardless of whether there are any actual feelings of fear, even though it would be impossible to talk coherently about fearfulness without mentioning anthropocentric aspects which make the fearful thing dangerous to us. McDowell's point here is that, whereas color *causes* us to have certain reactions, fearfulness and moral properties more properly *merit* certain reactions.

McDowell himself is not explicit about what "meriting" means. But to distinguish it from mere "eliciting" we might say that meriting a response implies that the response is not necessarily guaranteed. Thus, to merit a response means that we ought to have the response even if we do not in fact have it. In this way, fearfulness merits fear in the sense that we should be afraid of dangerous things even if we are not. This seems the only tenable way to significantly contrast meriting from mere eliciting. Yet, if this is the main difference between meriting and eliciting, there is no longer a disanalogy between morality and color. Moral realists, after all, could abandon the view that moral beliefs "elicit" their own intrinsic motivation or justification for action (cf. §§5.1 and 5.2). Furthermore, colors themselves do not always perfectly "elicit" actual color experiences, for example, in color-blind people or in perceivers equipped with different sensitivities to the electromagnetic spectrum. We could say that colors elicit color experience in humans *ceteris paribus*, but this is equally true of moral properties: they too elicit motivation to act all things being equal. Of course, it could be objected that even if colors do not always elicit, they still do not merit, and that is enough to secure a disanalogy with morality. However, is it really so odd to conceive of colors as themselves meriting responses *in some way*? Indeed, the fact that colors are real might itself merit our perception of them, such that the color-blind person "should," in some sense, perceive colors *because the colors are really there*. Obviously this "should" is not associated with moral responsibility since we do not blame the colorblind for being insensitive to colors. But such a "should" is nonetheless normative in a nonmoral way since we do, after all, describe the color-blind person as suffering from a deficiency. How else are we to make this assessment unless we are appealing to a standard of what the color-blind individual's color perceptions should normally be like?

There would still be a disanalogy between morality and colors, though, if the sort of *ceteris paribus* conditions for reliable perception were radically different in the cases of color versus value experience. When we examine scenarios in which we recognize that color perception is not reliable, however, we find that the analogies to moral perception are quite plausible. For example, color perception is not veridical if the perceiver is not wearing corrective eyewear when needed; by analogy, so too is moral perception defeated in cases where the perceiver lacks the requisite epistemic apparatus. Exactly what this apparatus will be in the moral case will depend on what theory of moral knowledge we think is accurate. Theories that associate moral knowledge with the possession of certain cognitive capacities or emotions will reject any moral perceptions in which the perceiver lacks these capacities or emotions. For example, say we are persuaded by Damasio's (1995) findings about how pathologies of the prefrontal cortex enable psychopathic behavior, or by Blair's (1995) work identifying a "violence inhibition mechanism" in humans, the possession of which is necessary for the ability to draw the moral-conventional distinction. If such theories are on the right track, then putative moral response would be defeated in cases where the agent lacked things such as a healthy prefrontal lobe or a violence inhibition mechanism. This is analogous to rejecting the veridicality of color judgments of a person with bad eyes. The point here is not to say what specific theory of moral epistemology is correct (we'll explore the epistemology of moral realism in Chapter 6), but simply to observe that whatever theory of moral knowledge we opt for will provide the epistemic conditions for when moral perception is veridical and when it is not, and in an analogous way to color perception.

Consider another situation in which we judge color perception unreliable: viewing an object in an unnatural environment. For example, an orange object will not properly appear orange if viewed in red light. Moral experience again seems analogous to this phenomenon: moral perception may also be defeated in environments, say, of extreme moral depravity or extreme beneficence. This is because the background "moral atmosphere" partly shapes our moral judgments. A "victimless offense" might be permissible in our world, but judged a horrifying transgression in some ideal moral heaven. A simple act of sharing a piece of food may be viewed as morally trivial in the real world, but might become quite heroic in the Hobbesian world of *The Hunger Games*. Similarly, we often express heightened moral praise for a right action performed by someone from whom we typically do not expect much; just as we can often be harsher in judging the moral failure of someone whom we hold to very high standards. It seems plausible to think that evaluations in such environments can distort the actual moral status of actions and characters. It is not that the weak-willed person who finally acts rightly is really more praiseworthy than the strong-willed person who slips up just once: it is just that the actions seem more or less pronounced relative to our background understanding of each character. Just as an orange object will not look orange in a red-lit room, neither might a praiseworthy action appear as such in a moral heaven, nor a blameworthy action seem blameworthy in a moral wasteland. Jonathan Haidt (1993) has similarly found that educational and socioeconomic conditions greatly dampen or amplify the severity of moral evaluation. So too does distance mediate the reliability and strength of both moral and color judgments. Color becomes difficult to identify at great spatial distances, just as moral obligations to people that are not immediate or proximate can feel disconnected. But the realist will insist that the far-away object is still colored, and that the obligation to remote people is still there, even if we are not fully sensible of them.

3.5 Summary

Moral realism still needs to respond to a host of other objections, which it shall face in the subsequent chapters; but we have at least explored how it might articulate a satisfactory and "re-enchanting" metaphysics. Specifically, we have seen how different formulations of robust moral realism can be "naturalist" or "non-naturalist" depending on how they envision moral properties being instantiated in the world. In lieu of the Open Question Argument, realists should, at a minimum, resist extreme forms of naturalism which reduce the intensional meanings of moral language to nonmoral language. Realists should, however, allow for some sort of coextensional reduction, identity, or supervenience, although whether or not this can coherently and stably be called "naturalism" (as Cornell Realists envision) was problematized.

Furthermore, different realisms will emerge depending on how realists respond to the following questions about coextension or supervenience:

- Are these coextensions metaphysically *necessary* or contingent across all possible worlds?

- Are these coextensions known *a priori* or not?

- Are the things with which moral properties are coextensive merely functional or are they ontologically robust?

- If realism opts for ontology instead of mere functionalism in the previous question, is the envisioned ontology singular or does it permit cluster properties, and are moral properties understood as objects or dispositions?

Finally, as a guiding thread through these debates, and also because I argued that it is the most independently plausible version, we considered a specific formulation of moral realism which grants contingent moral coextensions with stance-independent (even if not "objective") dispositions, modeled on a secondary quality analogy.

CHAPTER FOUR

The anthropology of realism

Even if moral realists can articulate a satisfactory metaphysics, how can we account for the fact that so many people seem to disagree so profoundly about moral matters? In particular, if realist moral properties can be thought of as dispositions, as we suggested in Section 3.4, shouldn't people who are similarly situated vis-à-vis the same dispositions be similarly disposed? Such considerations about the apparent diversity of moral beliefs and practices have furnished a powerful objection to the feasibility of moral realism, and a defense of a form of antirealism commonly called *moral relativism*.

4.1 Cultural differences and relativism

"Moral relativism" has wide currency even outside academic metaethics. This popularity, unfortunately, has rendered the term something of a conceptual black box, housing an untold superfluity of different views and commitments. As relativist Gilbert Harman has noted, moral relativism is often viewed as "confused, incoherent, and even immoral, at the very least obviously wrong" (1975: 3). It will help to distinguish three levels of moral relativism:

1 Descriptive relativism

2 Normative relativism

3 Metaethical relativism

Descriptive relativism frequently assumes many aliases.[1] But what is central is the idea that, as a matter of empirical fact, different parties disagree in their moral beliefs and practices. By contrast, *normative* relativism adds to the descriptive thesis an evaluative claim that such differences *ought* to be morally respected. *Metaethical* relativism is a view about the meaning or truth-status of moral claims, namely that they only refer to (or are only true relative to) particular sociocultural practices or institutions. In other words, for the metaethical relativist there are no such things as realist moral properties that correspond to features of a stance-independent world. Since, as we have seen in Sections 2.1 and 2.2, this is a necessary feature of moral realism, metaethical relativism is for this reason mutually exclusive with moral realism.

Metaethical relativism is not itself monolithic. For example, David Wong (1984) defends a metaethical relativism based largely on the causal-historical theory of reference, according to which something's meaning is established by some initial "dubbing ceremony." Since different dubbing ceremonies can stipulate different meanings, the transmission of reference can, thus, yield multiple extensions of moral predicates. Alternative metaethical relativisms, however, might be defended on the basis of alternate considerations. For instance, Torbjörn Tännsjö (1990) defends what he calls "ontological metaethical relativism," according to which morality is relative to "moral universes" (i.e. a socially constructed system of commonsense moral standards and rules). Tännsjö says his type of metaethical relativism differs from Wong's by being grounded in metaphysical considerations about truthmakers rather than semantic considerations about meaning and reference. Yet, both Wong's and Tännsjö's accounts deny the existence of the sort of stance-independent properties we have seen are necessary for robust realism.

Note also that normative relativism presupposes descriptive relativism. That is, if there are actually no moral differences, then *a fortiori* we will not have any differences to respect. Conversely, descriptive relativism does *not* presuppose normative relativism: we can believe that people and cultures have different moral beliefs without thinking that we should respect or tolerate these differences. This attitude is sometimes taken to its extreme in the form of so-called cultural imperialism, that is, the view that, although one culture descriptively differs from another, only one of the cultures is "right" and is, therefore, entitled to judge and intervene with the other. In addition, normative and metaethical relativism do not presuppose one another. Even if metaethical relativism were false and there *are* stance-independent moral properties, we might still be justified in subscribing to something like normative relativism for purely prudential reasons. The existence or knowledge of realist values does not entail any particular actions with respect to those with whom we disagree: you can believe in the existence of realist properties without thinking that you know what those properties are, and even if you *do* know which properties are the realist ones, you might still justifiably refrain from judging or intervening in others' lives. In fact, your moral knowledge might actually *include* the knowledge that interference would be morally arrogant. (More on this later when we discuss the metaethics of toleration in §7.2.) Indeed, it seems plausible to interpret the "political correctness" movement for many people as a subscription primarily to normative relativism: I may think that what you are doing is wrong, but may also think that it is not my place to intervene. Conversely, someone can believe in metaethical relativism without thereby believing in normative relativism. Consider, for instance, Richard Rorty's (1989) "ethnocentrism," which recognizes that metaethical relativism is true and that there is no "supercultural observation platform," but which nonetheless defends the legitimacy of favoring one's own culture for pragmatic reasons of solidarity.

Vis-à-vis moral realism, the most important relationship is that between metaethical and descriptive relativism. Moral realism is compatible with all moral relativisms except metaethical relativism, and metaethical relativism is often defended by appeal to the truth of descriptive relativism. The *locus classicus* of the inference from descriptive relativism to metaethical relativism is J. L. Mackie's (1977) Argument from Relativity (AFR). Mackie supports descriptive relativism by citing, "the well-known variation in moral codes from one society to another and from one period to another, and also the differences in moral beliefs between different groups and classes within a complex community" (1977: 36).

This premise is then used to infer metaethical relativism in the following way: "Radical differences between first order moral judgements make it difficult to treat those judgements as apprehensions of objective truth" (1977: 36). Mackie grants that many people may think, talk, and act *as if* moral realism were true, but because of this "well-known variation in moral codes," such commitments are fundamentally *errors*. For this reason, Mackie's defense of metaethical relativism is often referred to as "moral error theory," or more recently, "moral fictionalism" (Joyce 2001; Kalderon 2005).

AFR has endured as perhaps the most common and accessible defense of metaethical relativism, and it has popped up in various alternative forms. For example, James Rachels (1978) considers what he calls the Cultural Differences Argument, which does not differ notably from Mackie's version. Indeed, Rachels says that this style of argument for metaethical relativism has been common in twentieth-century ethics since at least as early as William Graham Sumner's (1906) statement that, "a tradition is its own warrant" and that "in the folkways, whatever is, is right."

What is the logic of the AFR? Obviously, the inference from descriptive to metaethical relativism is not *deductively* valid. For one thing, AFR rather egregiously derives a normative conclusion from a purely descriptive premise. And in general we do not typically think that *ad populam* considerations alone determine truth in any area, let alone in ethics. However, a more charitable interpretation of AFR is that it is not intended as deductive at all, but as *abductive*: it is an argument about metaethical relativism being inferred as the "best explanation" of the truth of descriptive relativism. The *abductive* interpretation of AFR fares much better than its deductive cousin. After all, other realms in which we posit realist entities (e.g. physical, scientific, perceptual claims, etc.) do not seem to suffer from the same degree of disagreement. Isn't the best explanation of the "well-known variation" in moral and cultural codes that there simply are no realist moral values, but instead that some form of metaethical relativism is true? Furthermore, whenever there is disagreement in these other realms, we have certain established standards of hypothesis, experimentation, evidence, and replication which we believe can in principle resolve the disagreement, but we have no such universally agreed upon standards with respect to ethical disagreements. This may not deductively "prove" metaethical relativism, but it seems at least to locate the burden of proof on moral realism to explain how realist moral truths could be consistent with such apparent intractable disagreement and confusion about them.

Thus, even the abductive interpretation of AFR must assume that morality is largely unique in the disagreement to which it gives rise. If a significant number of other areas to which we want to extend stance-independence turn out to be similarly conflicted, however, then it is no longer clear that the best explanation of disagreement in the moral sphere is metaethical relativism. Mackie asserts that moral disagreement is "well-known," yet he cites no studies or examples in support of this belief. Of course, no one needs *studies* to show that people and cultures disagree, right?[2] But, again, the mere fact of disagreement about an issue does not in itself entail that there is no truth of the matter concerning that issue: one party might not have as much of the relevant information, or be in as good an epistemic position, as the other party.[3] This sort of disagreement does not threaten moral realism, which is a thesis about the stance-independent existence of moral properties, not about the variety of ways these properties can be interpreted or instantiated. Thus, Mackie needs to show that moral disagreement is *fundamental*, in the sense that the disagreement must concern basic values, principles, or justifications.

One thing to note is that, regardless of whether we disagree about specific values and conflicts, people seem to agree at a minimum about the *status* of morality. As we saw in Section 2.3, there is persuasive reason to think that a minimal form of cognitivism accurately describes our moral language. But since cognitivism is a necessary but insufficient condition for realism, do we have any further reason for thinking that moral realism is true? One illuminating finding that might be taken as evidence of people's commitment to realism is the fact that most people draw very similar distinctions between what is moral and what is merely conventional (Nucci 2001).[4] Indeed, so entrenched is the moral/conventional distinction, that the rare lack of it is often used as a symptom of psychopathy (Blair 1995). On the metaethical relativist hypothesis, though, no such distinction could obtain—the moral sphere would collapse into the conventional sphere. Again, the fact that people do not think in relativist terms does not mean relativism is false; it is, after all, called an *error* theory because it maintains that people are simply mistaken in their conception of morality. However, if one of the main reasons for adopting an error theory is that it can best explain fundamental disagreement, then the fact that people do not disagree about the status of moral values serves to return the burden of proof to the relativist.

We should not, however, overblow these findings about the moral/conventional distinction. Indeed, two sets of research have suggested that the moral/conventional distinction is not as stable or universal as realists might like. First, Jonathan Haidt (1993) found that poor and uneducated classes in different societies draw the moral/conventional distinction in fundamentally *different* ways than do upper class citizens of the same society. Whereas "victimless yet offensive actions" are judged merely conventionally wrong or "disgusting" by educated members of both societies, they are judged *morally* wrong by poor or less educated individuals in each society. Haidt explains this result by noting that more educated individuals based their judgment on a criterion of *harm* while less educated individuals based theirs on their own emotional response. This suggests that less education or lower socioeconomic status is associated with greater affectivity, which in turn is associated with a conflation of moral and conventional offenses.

As interesting as these findings are, they do not obviously threaten the claim that people are intuitively moral realists. First, though poor and less educated individuals may draw the moral/conventional line differently, they still draw *some* form of the distinction. Second, in the case of the poor and uneducated respondents, the conflation of the distinction vis-à-vis some specific example collapsed the conventional into the *moral*, not the other way around, as is the case with sociopaths. If anything, poor and uneducated respondents demonstrate intuitions of *hyper*-moral realism! Third, and most importantly, in order for disagreement about the status of morality (in this case, about the moral/conventional distinction) to be relevant to AFR, it needs to be *fundamental*, which involves among other things the disagreeing parties occupying similar epistemic positions. If you simply have more information than I do on a certain issue (e.g. by being better educated in that respect), then our disagreement is not fundamental and the best explanation of it is that I am mistaken. Similarly, it is not outlandish to claim that the lack of certain basic material conditions can and does hamper moral response (cf. §3.4).[5]

It has also been observed that the moral/conventional distinction frequently collapses among university undergraduates. This is a much more serious obstacle for the view that people agree about the status of morality. This is because, though we may be able to discount poor or uneducated disagreement as relevantly fundamental, it is much harder to do so with university students since they are arguably in a *better* epistemic position than most people because they have received more education. However, examining the experimental work done on undergraduates' moral commitments reveals several serious methodological flaws.

Philosophy instructors may be familiar with the fact that students are often hesitant about making universal or objective moral claims or judgments.[6] Harman (1985) in fact uses this as a starting point for his own defense of metaethical relativism. However, rarely is this phenomenon tested experimentally. And when it has been, it has proven exceedingly difficult to isolate all the important metaethical issues. Sarkissian (2011), for instance, concludes that "folk metaethics" in college undergraduates leans toward metaethical relativism on the basis of a documented increase in hesitancy to pass moral judgment as the morality of a hypothetical culture becomes less familiar. Yet, the questions and scenarios posed to respondents conflate important semantic, epistemological, and normative considerations. It is often unclear (presumably even to the students themselves) whether refusals to pass judgment are instead motivated by awkward experimental design (e.g. moral scenarios so unfamiliar that the respondents do not have any immediate intuitions), politeness (e.g. it's rude to come right out and say that someone is immoral), cageyness (e.g. the students smell a trap and don't wish to be called out by their professor to defend something they can't), or a commitment to *normative* relativism (cf. §7.2).

In a similar study, Nichols (2004) claims to "discover" metaethical relativism in populations of undergraduate students, but claims also to find that this phenomenology does not lead to nihilism or undermined moral motivation. Nichols asks students to respond to a fictionalized disagreement between two interlocutors concerning the moral permissibility of "hitting people just because you feel like it." One interlocutor (John) claims that it is morally permissible to hit someone because "everyone he knows" thinks it's permissible and the other interlocutor (Fred) claims that the hitting is impermissible, citing that "everyone he knows" agrees.

Respondents are then asked to select a statement that they think best explains the disagreement between John and Fred: they may conclude that either (a) John is right and Fred is wrong, (b) that Fred is right and John is wrong, or (c) that neither is right or wrong since "there is no fact of the matter." They were additionally asked to provide their own short justification of why they answered as they did. Seventeen out of forty students selected the third response, namely that there is no truth of the matter. Nichols concludes that "a sizable group of undergraduates are nonobjectivists about some canonical moral transgressions" (2004: 9). Thus, even if people are realists as children, their commitment is defeasible in college. Realists sometimes claim as support for their position the fact that denial of moral objectivity would lead to negative practical consequences, for example, nihilism, lack of moral motivation or action, or insensitivity to suffering. However, Nichols goes on to argue that the very same undergraduates who deny moral objectivity nonetheless are still capable of drawing the moral/conventional distinction.

Even disregarding a rather small sample size, however, we can note several serious methodological problems with Nichols's experiment. First, Nichols labels as "nonobjectivists" students who respond to the hitting example by denying any truth of a matter. But what does Nichols mean by "objectivism?" Apparently, "objectivism" includes the view not only that moral claims are truth-apt and at least occasionally actually true, but that they must refer to moral values that are intrinsic (i.e. nondispositional), categorically motivating, and general in form. But, as we saw in Sections 3.2–3.4 and as we shall also see in Section 5.1, none of the latter commitments are necessary to the realist position. Defining "objectivism" in such an overblown way makes a strawman out of moral realism. If we keep moral realism distinct from other metaethical positions, it is not clear that the third response (i.e. that there is no truth of the matter) uniquely reveals relativism. Indeed, *all three responses* explicitly included as a reason an appeal to what people think. If the third response is relativist because it recognizes that moral values are based on culture, then the other two responses are just as relativist since they say that hitting is right or wrong because everyone thinks so. A robust realist would say that the truth-value of hitting is independent of what everyone says (cf. §2.2), but this anticonstructivist option was not provided to respondents.

Moreover, even if undergraduates are truly metaethical relativists about "canonical moral transgressions," examples such as "hitting" might be too trivial or vague to be representative of students' moral outlook. Future studies would do well to substitute examples of killing, genocide, and rape since it might be that students are realists when it comes to these more serious things.

4.2 Interpreting disagreement

Consider more wide-ranging examples of alleged cross-cultural moral diversity, for example, Herodotus's well-known observation that, while Greeks customarily cremated their deceased fathers, Callatians instead ate them, and each group was morally shocked (*shocked*!) by the "barbaric" practice of the other. In another commonly cited example of anthropological moral difference, consider the traditional Inuit practice of abandoning elders to die alone in the cold. Ruth Benedict (1934) famously delineated several more well-documented examples of anthropological variation judged to be "abnormal" by different cultural standards, for example, institutionalized values of treachery and betrayal (among the Dobuan), ritualized headhunting (among the Kwakiutl, the Ilongot, etc.), and radically divergent valuations of medical conditions such as epilepsy (in traditional Hmong culture). Often, such moral variation is just as intracultural as it is intercultural. Just look at the fiercely divisive attitudes evident in many industrialized Western societies regarding issues like same-sex marriage and abortion.

But again, as we saw earlier, variation does not equal disagreement, let alone fundamental disagreement. For example, although words in different languages (e.g. English "red" and Spanish *roja*) vary, they denote the same thing in the world. A simple transcendental argument against fundamental disagreement between languages is supplied by our ability to translate. There must be a good deal in common between "red" and *roja* for us to be able to translate one to the other. The assumption of a certain amount of agreement is necessary for any hermeneutic project to even get off the ground—a presupposition famously analyzed by Donald Davidson (1974) as the Principle of Charity (cf. Wong 1984: 105–20). Indeed, if there is *no* common ground between two viewpoints, then representatives cannot genuinely be said to disagree at all, but are instead merely talking past one another. To be sure, something is always lost in translation, for example, nuance, connotation, the length and sound of a word, and all the other "poetic functions" of a language. Furthermore, many languages seem to have words that are not easily translatable into English. For example, comparative philosophers are familiar with the frustrating fact that the Greek *eudaimonia* or the Chinese *lǐ* (禮) do not exactly match the English "happiness" or "ritual," respectively. Some have concluded from this that translation is impossible, but surely this is unjustified. Even if something important is lost in translation, what is lost might not be fundamental. Indeed, languages cannot be completely incommensurable for the simple reason that multilingual speakers can express and understand the same concepts using different words. Complicated foreign words (and also native words, for that matter, as the difficulty of philosophical conceptual analysis reminds us!) may take a very long time to fully understand, but they are still in principle translatable.

The possibility of translation between languages suggests that linguistic variation is not fundamental. One way this has been explained in linguistics is by what Noam Chomsky (1965) has described as a "deep structure" across different languages, revealed in a "universal grammar" by our ability to acquire competency in any natural language. Of course, the notion of a universal grammar is contentious among linguists; the point, though, is simply that moral realists could appeal to an analogous strategy with regard to moral variation, since moral commonality across cultures seems to theoretically admit of the same *prima facie* support that undergirds linguistic translation. The very fact that we can acquire dual citizenships and hybrid cultural identities suggests that there must be a large cross-cultural common denominator. But we will need more than theoretical considerations to deflect AFR. What does empirical anthropology tell us about the possibility of a deep structure similarity underlying apparent cultural differences? Is moral disagreement between cultures about values and practices truly *fundamental* as AFR requires?

To address this question, we first need to understand that the very nature and assumptions of "cultural anthropology" have changed drastically over the years. Prior to the early twentieth century, most anthropology presupposed a great deal of cross-cultural similarity, although this assumption frequently went hand in hand with a condemnation of alternative practices as "primitive." E. B. Tylor (1871) expressed the dominant Western attitude with his theory of "cultural evolutionism," which envisioned non-Western civilizations as simply less evolved. Over time, anthropology inverted its judgment of non-Western cultures. Though still dubbed "primitive," this could sometimes be a term of praise rather than abuse for foreign societies. During periods in which Western social criticism turned inward, "primitive" cultures suddenly became standards of innocence, simplicity, and freedom from oppressive religious, industrial, and economic forces. The Noble Savage became an archetype for moral courage, harmony with nature, and personal (often sexual) liberty.

Even praiseful stereotypes, however, are dangerous and distortive. It was not until the turn of the twentieth century that anthropologists recognized the insufficiency of Noble Savagism and began to replace it with a methodology that attempted to neither condemn nor praise. After generations of anthropological conclusions made from the comfort of a study (and fed only on a diet of biased and sparse sketches by traders, naturalists, and explorers), anthropology finally began utilizing first-hand accounts of different cultural practices. When Bronisław Malinowski (1922) studied the peoples of Papua New Guinea and the Trobriand Islands, thereby effectively founding ethnography, readers were confronted with the undeniable fact that native subjects were *not* primitive, noble, or savage. But they certainly appeared quite different. People such as Franz Boas (1911) articulated various renditions of relativism in response to the variation being revealed by this burgeoning field of ethnography which they were helping to define. Their common methodology came to be generally called "cultural relativism" and represents the *descriptive* relativism we discussed above.

Mackie's articulation of AFR was not unoriginal, and it should not be rejected just because the ideology that underlies it can be historicized. However, the trajectory of anthropology during the middle of the twentieth century does help explain how Mackie could assume that cultural variation was "well-known": he was addressing an audience already incubated in the relativism of Boasian ethnography. But in fact, the Boasian approach has come under serious philosophical criticism in subsequent decades. First of all, even if cultural relativism is methodologically or descriptively acceptable, the inference to a deeper metaethical relativism certainly goes beyond the actual experimentation and observation of ethnography. There are also serious problems about attaining the sort of epistemological objectivity required by methodological relativism, which dictates that no value judgments are to be passed. Bias, however, is a notoriously difficult thing to recognize (especially in oneself), let alone eliminate. And certain types of valuation might even be an ineliminable feature of descriptive judgment if we take certain criticisms concerning the fact/value distinction seriously. For instance, it might be that it is impossible to be "value free" as an ethnographer if standards of observation and intervention, as well as the very act of conceptualizing and framing a culture or practice, count as values, let alone if "being value free" itself counts as a value (cf. Appiah 2006: 23–31).

Furthermore, ethnographers are familiar with the necessity of acquiring ethnographic knowledge from inside a practice, that is, experiencing a practice first-hand as a native herself would. But this also threatens to invite bias. Thus, anthropologists striving for complete objectivity (as Boasian relativism would seem to prescribe) either they remain aloof, in which case risk their own cultural biases and also fail to attain genuine insider knowledge; or else they become intimate enough with a practice to acquire inside knowledge, but thereby develop new biases. This dilemma is probably not inescapable in actual ethnographic practice, as ethnographers negotiate middle grounds between objectivity and submersion; but it has nonetheless worried ethnographers who have been reared in the Boasian tradition of suspending *all* evaluative judgment (cf. Geertz 1983).[7]

Additional worries concerning Boasian relativism have been more theoretical. For example, to evaluate the view that there is no cross-cultural standard of moral truth, we will need to know what we mean by a "culture." However, "cultures" stubbornly resist admitting of necessary and sufficient conditions. For one thing, cultures are almost never self-contained or what Michele Moody-Adams (1997) calls "windowless monads," but instead experience constant contact, interaction, and negotiation with other cultures. Cultural solipsism is naïve, historically inaccurate, and dangerous, for it threatens to stifle the organic nature of living cultures and can give rise to blind conservative impulses to "preserve" an often mythological version of a "pure culture" (Rosaldo 1989). Conversely, what we call "cultures" are in fact rarely internally integrated units. The pervasiveness of subcultures and countercultures, mixed ethnicities, dual citizenships, immigration and emigration make problematic any attempt to characterize a culture monolithically. Consider what it means to talk about "American culture." What is the common denominator that all and only Americans share? If the only answer to this question is "those who live in America," then we have conflated culture with nationality and must give over anthropology to the historians and geographers.

We have already noted the *exoticism* of anthropological approaches that judge other cultural practices. Whether condemning them via imperialism or praising them via Noble Savagism, both outlooks distort the degree of difference between "us" and "them." But AFR, which infers metaethical relativism from Boasian descriptive relativism, commits the same exoticism. Whereas imperialism and Noble Savagism render foreign practices too commensurable to our own in order for them to be judged as superior or inferior, Boasian relativism renders them unnecessarily incommensurable, which is just as much of a self-serving distortion (Nussbaum 1997: 113–47).

As we have seen, the success of AFR requires widespread moral disagreement at a "deep structural" level, which may contain justifications that we recognize as legitimate, even if we wouldn't otherwise understand the practice to which the justifications are applied. And even *unfamiliar* justifications may be understood and condoned after seeing them in the context of the rest of a web of beliefs. For instance, imagine a foreign culture in which human sacrifice was practiced in a very bloody, public way. On the one hand, cultural imperialists might immediately understand it by the standards under which such an action would be judged in their culture, and morally condemn the practice. On the other hand, Boasian relativists might immediately immunize the practice from any moral assessment *tout court*. A more sophisticated anthropologist, however, might seek to understand the practice based on the justifications and webs of beliefs given by the practitioners themselves in support of the practice. If this culture justified human sacrifice as punishment for criminal offenses, would we be able to condemn it without condemning our own practices of capital punishment? If the sacrificial "victims" volunteered for the practice, would our moral assessment change?

Justifications may also be relative to certain material conditions and background assumptions. For instance, we might understand the sacrifice if the culture in question was suffering from a severe food shortage and the only way to sustain the community was to turn to cannibalism. We might even morally admire the practice for its sensitivity to its tragic circumstances as evidenced by the fact that sacrifice is ritualized and solemnized (cf. §7.1). If the justification of a practice is embedded in a web of other beliefs, we may come to understand and respect the justification (and perhaps by extension the practice) even if we don't share the other beliefs. A culture might believe that this life is pain, but that the afterlife will be heavenly, or that the gods demand sacrifice and will punish those who disobey, or that sacrifice metaphysically ensures the continuance and stability of history; for such a culture, human sacrifice might represent an admirable way of efficiently and morally coordinating society.

We may not agree with the background assumptions which contextualize the justification of the practice, but if this disagreement is not a moral one, then it is irrelevant to AFR. That is, if we disagree with human sacrifice because we disagree with a premise concerning the will of the gods or the nature of the afterlife, then our disagreement is metaphysical or factual, but not moral. We may think that different metaphysical or scientific beliefs are wrong, but "wrong" in this context must mean "factually false," not "immoral." An erroneous scientific belief may give rise to a practice which we see as morally wrong, but since the error grounding it was factual and not moral, we cannot pass moral judgment on the practice. This does not mean a practice should be allowed to continue with no intervention. It is just that the intervention should take a factual tone, not a moral one.

This may be a tough pill for moral realists to swallow. After all, many historic examples of injustice were justified on the basis of presumed "scientific evidence." Practices of racist and sexist discrimination frequently appealed to the "fact" that minority groups were biologically inferior, incapable, or even dangerous (Gould 1981). Must we forego moral judgment of such atrocities because they were justified by what were taken to be facts? If practices are justified on the basis of errors of fact, then the committed moral realist should answer *yes*. Slave holders or bigots who actually believed that racial minorities or women were innately inferior may be morally exculpated if their prejudice was the result of inherited factual errors. Of course, this exoneration does not imply that such practices should be immune to *any* criticism. After all, they are based on factual *errors*, and errors should be fixed. Indeed, arguably the most effective programs to alleviating prejudice have taken the strategy of addressing the factual premises of that prejudice. For example, in *The Subjection of Women* (1869), John Stuart Mill points to all the ways in which women have equaled or could equal men, and how they are not given the same opportunities to achieve their potential. He rarely just moralizes, for that would have restricted his audience in such a way that he would be merely "preaching to the choir." Similarly, in his *Letter from a Birmingham Jail* (1963), Martin Luther King Jr. addresses the perception that African Americans were biologically, spiritually, and intellectually inferior. Like Mill, King did not just preach what *should* be the case, but pointed out what *was* the case. In these ways, moral reform has often proceeded most effectively as factual reform.[8]

Of course, figuring out whether a certain justification is grounded in factual as opposed to moral error is not easy. An obvious complication is that much of the pseudoscience mobilized to justify racism and sexism was an *effect* as much as a cause of prejudice, trumped-up to rhetorically reinforce and defend antecedent biases or practices (cf. Said 1978). We will need good social scientists and historians to determine precisely what causal role factual assumptions played in each particular case of prejudice. The epistemic difficulty of determining the relationships between moral and factual errors seems especially intractable at the level of individual belief. More than likely, at least some antebellum Americans endorsed slavery because they had never actually met a slave and had only received biased information about them; others may have endorsed it simply out of economic motivations, sadistic motivations, or just plain did not like Black people. The point is that the first group might be morally exculpated, though still in factual error; the second group, by contrast, is guilty of moral error. Since such a distinction needs to be made at an individual level, differentiating who is deserving of moral versus merely factual blame could prove epistemically impossible. But this may not necessarily be a bad thing, and robust moral realism is perfectly compatible with a humble agnosticism regarding whether we actually know what those values are. For the realist, there is a fact of the matter concerning whether a practice is morally acceptable even if we cannot ever determine it. Factual errors need to be remedied, but we should not become too morally self-righteous in doing so, since we ourselves might be in factual error about a great many things (cf. §§7.1–7.3).

Consider another practice such as female genital cutting (FGC).[9] Is FGC morally permissible, impermissible, or unable to be evaluated because there are no cross-cultural moral truths? The answer a realist should give is that it could be either morally permissible or morally impermissible *depending on the justifications* given for the specific practice. After all, there are numerous different incarnations of FGC around the world, for example, the pricking or ritual washing of the prepuce, the whole or partial excision of the clitoris, the additional removal of the *labia minora*, or infibulation (i.e. the complete sewing shut of the vulva). Different versions of FGC in different regions can have quite different justifications, many of which are not dissimilar to ones we give for our own practices.[10] For instance, as a statement of group identity and solidarity (e.g. religious, ethnic, gendered, or as shared opposition to globalism), such a justification is not unrecognizable to us. Indeed, we might even admire certain forms of the practice as supplying a ritualized and celebrated expression of coming-of-age that is often lacking in contemporary Western societies. Alternately, aesthetic appeals are also sometimes given as justifications of FGC. But how foreign does this render the practice when measured alongside pervasive Western practices such as breast implantation, penile enlargement, or the shaving of pubic hair?

Moral evaluations of a practice need to be informed about the actual nuance and diversity of the practice, and also about the justifications and beliefs supporting the practice—something to which we shall return in the context of considering how a moral realist might regard global debates concerning "human rights" (§7.3). As Ellen Gruenbaum reminds us,

> Simplistic condemnations are not only ineffectual but can also stimulate strong defensive reactions . . . a sound analysis requires looking at female circumcision from many angles, listening to what women who do it have said about it, and trying to understand the reasons for resistance to change. (2000: 25–6)

If we can recognize the justifications given for a particular practice as morally valid, then a sufficient deep structure similarity seems to exist which serves to undermine AFR. This is not to say that

FGC *is* morally permissible—that will depend on what kind of a deep structure similarity obtains, if any. In cases where less invasive forms of FGC are justified by, for example, religious or gender identity or by a desire not to have any more children, a deep structure similarity *does* exist between the practice and our own outlook, such that we have should neither condemn the practice nor infer metaethical relativism on the basis of it. If a practice of FGC is explained as an effort to maintain physical cleanliness, then the practice ought not to be morally condemned, though it might still be factually criticized by pointing out some of the many health risks.

If a practice is justified by something unrecognizable to us morally and not on the basis of factual errors, however, then realists ought to morally criticize it. For example, the best ethnographic efforts to understand the traditional Igorot (Philippines) practice of headhunting have revealed that the justification given by practitioners involves a psychological expression of a "rage" experienced in reaction to grief. Surely cultural outsiders can understand what it is for grief to transmute into uncontrollable rage. Indeed, Western civilization is canonically founded on the very idea (as embodied by Achilles in Homer's *Iliad)*. And Renato Rosaldo (1989), one of the leading ethnographers of the Igorot, has argued that a personal experience with a comparable emotion is a necessary methodological prerequisite for accurate ethnographic understanding.

However, though we can *understand* it, we do not morally *condone* it. It is morally unacceptable for a grieving widower in our society to become a vigilante because his wife died. So too for the Igorot. There are no additional beliefs or justifications that have been identified by ethnographers or supplied by Igorot huntsmen that could exculpate the practice. For instance, there is not a shortage of resources such that population control might be warranted, nor do victims agree to be victims. This would, therefore, appear to be a practice which realists cannot exculpate by appeal to a possible deep structure moral similarity, nor by a mistake about facts, nor by a tragic material environment. It is this scenario that best distinguishes the realist from the metaethical relativist: the realist can say that the practice is morally impermissible—as indeed have many Igorot moral commentators themselves, such that the practice has been culturally abandoned since the 1970s.

The passing of this judgment will need to be (even, or maybe especially for the realist) tempered by considerations of epistemic humility as well as pragmatic efficiency. That is, the realist needs to realize that her moral judgment could be misguided; maybe there could be an adequate justification or reason for headhunting for some individuals or in some contexts. And the realist also needs to be sensitive to the pragmatic repercussions of her judgment. Condemning a single practice of a culture should not extend to condemning every individual of that culture, nor the culture as a whole. American slavery may have been morally unjustified, but this does not mean that every individual American thereby contracted moral blame, or that "the United States is immoral." Furthermore, the condemnation of a practice need not, and often times *should* not, lead to intervention. For example, in the case of the Igorot, British colonizers brutally exterminated many Igorot tribes putatively to "stop headhunting." But this ostensibly constituted a worse moral evil than the headhunting itself.

4.3 Metaethical pluralism

So far, we have considered anthropological objections to moral realism which attempt to infer metaethical relativism on the basis of alleged cross-cultural disagreement. In rebuttal, we explored hermeneutic limitations on such disagreement and also examined some instances of possible *agreement*. One of the difficulties facing this rebuttal, however, is the fact that ethical theories do not themselves always agree on the standards or definitions of what qualifies as properly "moral" in the first place. Disagreement at this theoretical level makes it difficult to assess the extent to which we truly agree or disagree at the anthropological level. The history of moral philosophy has revealed several instances of apparently intractable disagreement at the level of general theory. For example, are intentions more or less praiseworthy than effects? Is it better to maximize happiness or to do our duty come what may? If it comes down to a choice, which value trumps—benevolence or justice? Partiality or impartiality? Duties to others or duties to ourselves?

Most of the history of normative ethics has assumed that such questions are in principle answerable. The universalist aspirations of the great Enlightenment theories were to articulate some general algorithmic principles capable of resolving tricky moral tensions like those noted above. Thus, Kantians tell us to value individual dignity over cold, calculating sacrifices in the name of the greater good. Utilitarians, by contrast, tell us to stop being naïve and shortsighted, and to lie to the axe murderer who is chasing our friend. The problem with each of these theories, independent of any internal inconsistencies or ambiguities they may have, is that none of them seem quite correct. Or, more accurately, *all* of them seem partially correct. After all, no plausible theory prescribes anything too phenomenologically unfamiliar: we understand the attraction of each position, but are unable to reconcile often diametrically opposed values. This is not merely an inadequacy of *theory*—we can imagine a person torn between a duty to herself and a duty to another who is completely ignorant of (or agnostic about) particular normative frameworks. Plausible normative theories have withstood the test of time precisely because they reflect things we pretheoretically value (cf. §1.2). And it seems that we pretheoretically value different and potentially mutually exclusive things.

Rather than seek some totalizing super-theory that tries to resolve such tensions unambiguously, the best explanation of persistent disagreement at the theoretic level could be that there is an irreducible *plurality* of goods. Furthermore, this pluralism is perfectly compatible with moral realism. The possibility of "pluralistic realism" has been a neglected option in metaethics, which typically presents *absolutism* (the view that there is a single moral value) and *metaethical relativism* (the view that there is no realist moral value) as the only two shows in town with respect to moral ontology. Pluralistic realism, though, holds that the dichotomy between absolutism and metaethical relativism is a false one. Realism and metaethical relativism are theses about the *existence* (or nonexistence) of transcultural moral values; absolutism and pluralism are theses about the *number* of moral values. Articulated in this way, the question often put to realists as to whether there is "a single moral value" is misleading, conflating two distinct questions into one. Is there moral value? The pluralistic realist answers *Yes*. Is this value singular? The pluralistic realist answers *No*.

One initial worry about pluralistic realism is that it is indistinguishable from the (metaethical) relativist alternative, and so should not be properly called "realism" at all. For, how can we say that morality is *real* if there can be multiple conflicting values?

Expressed this way, the objection seems to question the feasibility of separating absolutism from realism in the first place. This objection would have us view pluralistic realism as logically inconsistent. Pluralism maintains that there could be two right things to do in a single situation. This is not merely due to different agents evaluating the situation from different perspectives or in light of different abilities or positions, that is, "particularism" (Hooker and Little 2000). Instead, pluralism of the deep nonreductive ontological type we are exploring holds that a situation could involve multiple conflicting obligations for a *single* individual. And if moral realism is true, then the justification for the conflicting obligations must be due to the stance-independent existence of a truthmaker. That is, the conflict cannot be explained by relativizing value without sacrificing moral realism, and it cannot be explained by citing some single, more basic moral value without sacrificing pluralism. So, pluralistic realism would appear to leave us in an impossible position: I am obligated by value A to Φ, but I am told by value B to Ψ, then if A and B are inconsistent, then Φ and Ψ may be inconsistent.

However, we should not conflate logical inconsistency with practical inconsistency. Consider the example of someone confronted with any of the sort of hypothetical moral dilemmas so beloved by philosophers, in which one mutually exclusive and forced option involves saving a loved one, while the other mutually exclusive and forced option involves saving an innocent person. Pluralistic realism maintains that in this case there may be two moral obligations: "save your loved ones" and "protect innocents." Fulfilling both of these obligations is impossible within the confines of the scenario. But this impossibility is characterized by *practical*, not logical inconsistency. There is no formal contradiction between the propositions "I should save my loved ones" and "I should protect innocents," since we can easily think of cases in which the two are conjoined, for example, where my loved ones are innocents, where I am able to save both parties, etc. If the conflicting moral obligations were expressed instead as "I should save my loved ones" and "I should not save my loved ones," then there *would* be a logical inconsistency. But pluralistic realism need not (nor would any plausible ethical theory) maintain that we have duties *against* helping loved ones. We may have countervailing considerations that outweigh saving loved ones, but this hardly constitutes a duty not to save them. Thus, pluralistic realism recognizes the existence of multiple, fundamental, and realist moral values which may generate practically incompatible moral obligations.

We shall consider some of the possible implications and applications of pluralistic-realist dilemmas later in Section 7.1. However, we might wonder at present whether we should properly call a view "realist" if it affirms an infinite number of fundamental moral values. Would allowing for more than one ultimate moral value open the floodgates, inundating the realist's ontology in an objectionable way? To prevent this, a pluralistic realist will need to articulate nonarbitrary *constraints* on the sort of fundamental values they have in mind.

To be clear, the objection here is not that a huge number of conflicting moral values could not all be real or would be logically inconsistent; the objection is rather that a huge number of values would make pluralistic realism *practically indistinguishable* from metaethical relativism. This would either render metaethical inquiry concerning the foundations of morality irrelevant to normative practices, or else would force realists back to absolutism. Fortunately, the pluralistic realist does not need to decide precisely *which* properties are actually real. In fact, a benefit of the position is that the pluralistic realist may assume a humble agnosticism about particular moral truths. Pluralistic realism is a thesis about the status of moral properties, not necessarily about their content; the pluralistic realist claims only that there *are* (belief-independent) moral properties, not that she knows what they are.

As for the worry that the plurality of moral values could slippery-slope into affirming so many values as to effectively affirm none, it has so far been unrealized. We simply do not think that "anything goes" just because we may discover certain intractable moral disagreements. Indeed, once again, empirical research gives us at least some reassurance that the plurality of moral values is constrained to a small, finite handful even at the level of normative theory. For example, Richard Shweder and Jonathan Haidt (1993) have noted that experimental moral psychology is moving increasing toward an affirmation of pluralism. Recall that Carol Gilligan's (1982) critique of Lawrence Kohlberg (1971) was not that his theory of the progression of moral judgment was *wrong*, but that it was *incomplete*, namely, Kohlberg's initial experiments were conducted exclusively with males. When Gilligan conducted similar experiments on females, she observed that women tend more often to evaluate moral dilemmas from perspectives of partiality. Instead of the highly abstracted, generalized, and principle-based responses which Kohlberg identified in his highest-stage male respondents (who tended to focus on a kind of Kantian impartial justice), Gilligan observed that female respondents expressed more empathetic role-taking, personal associations and feelings, and considerations about particular positions and capacities of the agents involved.[11]

Similarly, cross-cultural analyses have revealed that moral disagreements tend to collate around a very small number of fundamental values, perspectives, or what Thomas Kasulis (2002) has called moral "orientations." Precisely *which* moral values are the fundamental ones, and on what basis commitment to them is distributed, of course, remains somewhat controversial. Whereas Gilligan identified pluralism with respect to values of *partiality* and *impartiality*, which she thought were distributed according to gender, others have observed pluralism about alternative value sets distributed according to alternative factors such as nationality.[12] An absolutist explanation of this variation might be that one value was more primary than the other, or that one group is mistaken about fundamental moral reality. And a relativistic explanation might simply deny any ability to legitimately compare competing values, arguing that *no* values are stance-independently true. Pluralistic realism helpfully furnishes a third option: several of these values might *all* be robustly realist.

Though a particular group or individual may not give as much moral salience to a competing fundamental value, such a value is nonetheless recognized as an acceptable moral alternative. One cultural orientation may place less moral importance on social role expectations, but this doesn't mean that alternative emphases are morally incomprehensible. For the pluralistic realist, the reason *why* we understand most fundamental values (at least those most frequently identified by cross-cultural moral psychologists) as morally acceptable alternatives is because we recognize a constrained plurality of values as robustly real.[13]

Obviously, we should be wary of oversimplifying groups or even individuals as being wholly committed to only one fundamental value. Even if Kohlberg and Gilligan's research shows general trends and stereotypes, it is obviously false to conclude that *all* men value justice and *all* women value caring. Too much rigidity with respect to generalizations about value commitments can only lead to pernicious essentialism. Presumably every culture, and even every individual, shares some degree of commitment to each value. This is why we are able to recognize competing fundamental values as morally familiar. Different cultures or individuals might decide to emphasize or "foreground" (Kasulis 2002: 133) a particular value for a variety of reasons—perhaps environmental or historical considerations come into play—but this need not threaten the reality of that value or imply the ontological exclusion of alternative values. The pluralistic realist does not need to defend a view of precisely which moral values are the fundamental ones, or precisely how particular groups or individuals wind up emphasizing one over another (if they do). What is important is that empirical moral psychology and cross-cultural anthropology have given us no reason to think that the number of fundamental moral commitments is so unconstrained as to trivialize the concept of moral value. Whether one grouping is more accurate than another is less important than the fact that there appears to be *some* constraints on the plurality of moral values that cultures and individuals consistently judge morally acceptable.

Based on the considerations discussed so far in this chapter, though, we can at this point offer a tentative and partial enumeration of the values that are strong candidates for the sort of fundamental (and potentially conflicting) values which the pluralistic moral realist might recognize:

1 **Utility**: the production of the greater good, etc.

2 **Fidelity**: promise-keeping, voluntarily assumed responsibilities, etc.

3 **Society**: expectations generated by social roles and positions, etc.

4 **Self-improvement**: cultivation of personal projects, self-defense, etc.

5 **Caring**: differential concern for loved ones, etc.

6 **Liberty**: freedom of choice, belief, expression, opportunity, etc.

7 **Noninjury**: the protection of innocent life, etc.

8 **Equality**: no moral distinctions made on morally irrelevant grounds, etc.

This list is tentative and incomplete at best. It is an attempt, however, to represent the basic values which are: (a) cross-culturally morally recognizable to us, (b) appear recurrently in ethnographic reports of justifications given for diverse practices, and (c) figure prominently in enduring and plausible normative theories. For instance, the value of producing the best overall state of affairs has been a hallmark of consequentialist accounts; the value of fidelity and promise-keeping is emphasized in deontological theories; Confucianism has endured as a powerful justification for the value of social-role expectations; virtue ethics (particularly in its contemporary resurgence) has stressed the ineliminable importance of personal projects and duties to oneself; and the existence of special nonderivative duties to loved ones is at the heart of the "ethics of care" movement. A more complete defense of pluralistic realism will ultimately need to provide greater clarification of the above values through systematic conceptual analyses, whereupon it could be revealed that some values ultimately reduce to one another, or to some more all-encompassing super value.[14] The main point, however, is simply that it is compatible with robust moral realism that there might be incommensurable and potentially conflicting features of the moral landscape.

Before concluding this chapter, let's consider how pluralistic realists might respond to other possible objections. An obvious initial worry is that such a view is unparsimonious. Even a small number of fundamental moral values are baroque compared to the elegant singularity alleged by absolutism. Wouldn't it be more parsimonious either to preserve moral realism by jettisoning pluralism or to preserve pluralism by abandoning realism? The pluralistic realist might respond to this objection in a number of ways. For instance, one thing to note is that parsimony is only *one* principle of abductive warrant. Other considerations affect whether a hypothesis is the "best explanation." In particular, pragmatic concerns will presumably have some bearing on the acceptability of a view that should not be totally overshadowed by considerations of simplicity. A different way to put this might be to contrast different types of "simplicity." Canonical expressions of the familiar principle of Ockham's Razor involve *ontological* simplicity, where the concern is for the most economical and efficient number of entities in an ontology. But this is not the only way in which something can be simple. For instance, recalling our discussion in Section 1.2 of the "meta-metaethics" driving some of the *a priori* attraction to realism, we might also think in terms of *phenomenological* simplicity, according to which a hypothesis is privileged which makes the best sense of our experience. Thus, even if pluralistic realism fails standards of ontological simplicity by multiplying entities, it might nonetheless constitute the simplest explanation of our experience of certain competing goals and of the reality of moral value.[15] Phenomenological and pragmatic standards of simplicity will affect whether a proposed view is, in William James's language, a genuinely "live option." A theory that tells me that everything my senses and reason reveal to me is ultimately illusory will not strike me as a very rational possibility, no matter if its ontological simplicity has been demonstrated.

Furthermore, even if standards of simplicity are uncontroversial, the pluralistic realist may object to their exclusive rights to dictate rational acceptability. That is, even if pluralistic realism is ontologically unparsimonious, so what? *Why* is the (ontologically) simplest explanation necessarily the most true? To be sure, we have an entrenched impulse to unification, but this might only represent something idiosyncratic and contingent about human rationality. The world, perhaps especially the moral landscape, might be messy and defiant of our desire to simplify it, such that it could be anthropocentric hubris to think that reality must answer to *our* conceptual needs. Of course, if morality turns out to be the *only* domain of human experience with such a degree of ontological complexity, antirealists may find this suspiciously unique and self-serving. As we have seen in Section 4.1, this concern about morality's suspicious uniqueness is part of the motivation undergirding relativist arguments such as AFR. And in Sections 5.1 and 6.1, we shall also address objections that realism requires metaphysical and epistemological postulations that are unparsimonious or "queer." For our present purposes, however, we might observe that the pluralistic component needn't make moral realism any more queer or unique than other nonmoral domains. As we saw in Section 3.3, despite a widespread anthropocentric impulse to theoretic simplification, many aspects of the sciences persistently elude unification: it remains a challenge to articulate a robust conception of a "law" that accurately accommodates the diversity of empirical generalizations across the different natural sciences; theoretical physicists continue to struggle to specify a "Grand Unified Theory" capable of reducing the quantum and macroscopic phenomena (see Kellert et al. 2006 for applications of these debates to the question of ontological pluralism); and even the very notion of "science" itself defies universality (see Lloyd 2009: 153–71 for a survey of divergent cross-cultural and historical understandings of "science"). We might have faith that *eventually* such scientific unifications will be identified; but would it really be so disastrous if physical reality resisted our attempts at unity? After all, theoretic unity is not necessary to *predict* physical phenomena. So, exactly what role does the impulse to unification play? A pluralist about physics would have no problem accepting multiple fundamental entities if such pluralism was revealed by science. Indeed, it might be thought bad science to insist *a priori* that reality must be a certain way. We should instead listen to how reality actually characterizes itself, and if this is done in pluralistic terms, then so be it.

One final objection which we shall consider is that pluralistic realism, which countenances potentially inconsistent moral obligations, renders morality psychologically impractical. In Section 7.1, we shall consider the psychology of so-called moral dilemmas, and what a moral realist (pluralistic or otherwise) might say about them. But the central worry at present is that, by affirming an irreducible plurality of fundamental and "real" values, pluralistic realism gives us no guidance concerning *which* values we should follow. Thus, pluralistic realism might be thought to result in some kind of moral *nihilism* or what Nicholas Rescher (1993) has characterized as "indifferentism."

Of course, indifferentism is a possible psychological response to pluralistic realism, not a logically necessary entailment. Even if fundamental values, being on equivalent ontological footing, can provide no intrinsic reasons for preference, it does not follow that no *extrinsic* reasons are available. For instance, the pluralistic realist may recognize that impartial justice and social role expectations are both equally real and fundamental values, but still allow for the fact that particular environmental, cultural, or personal factors could tip allegiance to one specific value commitment. If it really is the case that Americans on the whole privilege impartial justice and Indians on the whole privilege social role expectations (Miller and Bersoff 1992), then this contingent cultural fact could constitute a legitimate, albeit circumstantial, reason for an American to prefer justice if a situation of practical inconsistency arises. Consider fundamental conflicts between values of partial love and impartial justice: for the pluralistic realist, both values may be real and unsystematizable, even though a legal judge might have a professional reason to prefer impartial justice, while a different person might prefer partial love on the grounds that it was more dominant in her upbringing. Rescher calls this response to pluralism "contextualism" or "perspectival rationalism," and characterizes it as follows:

> There is no good reason why a recognition that others, circumstanced as they are, are rationally entitled *in their circumstances* to hold a position at variance with ours should be construed to mean that we, *circumstanced as we are*, need feel any rational obligation to abandon our position. (1993: 119–20)

This sort of preference is not arbitrary: it is justified (extrinsically) by considerations of circumstance.[16] Furthermore, the fact that we rarely freely choose our circumstances may constitute a certain type of "moral luck" (Williams 1981)—not with respect to questions of responsibility or character-trait attribution, but with respect to fundamental value commitments. The reason why someone values impartiality most might be because she was born in a society that emphasizes it, or raised by parents who stressed it, or biologically constituted to prefer it, not necessarily because it is the only realist fundamental value or because there are no ultimately realist values. However, although environmental, cultural, or personal factors may justify a group or individual's commitment to a specific value, this is still compatible with a recognition that commitment to an alternative fundamental value may nonetheless be equally justified in different circumstances.

4.4 Summary

In this chapter, we see how moral realism can be more than an abstract metaphysical or semantic thesis, but can begin to address real-world anthropological issues of cultural differences and moral disagreement. Specifically, we unpacked one of the most prevalent objections against moral realism—namely that a form of relativism is the best explanation of observed moral variation. After analyzing different formulations of "relativism," as well as some of the historical, methodological, and normative motivations in favor of it, we looked at the evidence for moral disagreement. In addition to critiquing recent experimental findings that allege relativism, we also pointed to hermeneutical reasons that should caution against overblowing the extent of moral diversity. Most importantly, we examined specific ways in which apparent surface moral differences can reduce to "deep structural" similarity. Many moral realists may wish to stop here, but we went further to explore the possibility that even robust realism could still permit a deep-structural, intractable ontological pluralism of fundamental values and justifications. Objections to this particular breed of moral realism were rebutted and we even offered a tentative list of the sort of basic values which pluralistic realists might recognize, in ways that help pragmatically adjudicate real-life moral conflicts.

CHAPTER FIVE

The psychology of realism

Recall that one of the main challenges for moral realism is to explain how moral values can be both robustly real, but still sensitive to features of embodied human agency. We have seen in Section 3.4 that the stance-independence of moral value is consistent with nonetheless allowing the expression of values to reference features of agents. In this chapter, we will consider a separate, but related problem for moral realism. As we have already seen, one of the main explanatory concerns motivating *ethical naturalism* is the difficulty of articulating how moral values can engage our wills—for it is a common thought in metaethics that moral values, unlike other entities, come prepackaged with their own intrinsic to-be-pursued quality. For example, it is often thought that whereas the belief that there is a table in front of me does not in and of itself cause me to want to act in any certain way, the belief that it is morally right to help the person who has fallen down in front of me does or should typically entail a desire on my part to help them. In other words, it has been thought that part of what it *means* to call something morally right or good is to view the value in question as inherently worthy of corresponding action. If moral values exist in the way that realists claim, can we explain how they are able to engage our will in this unique manner?

Ethical naturalism seeks to account for the interaction between moral values and our wills by reducing value to something "natural" that can affect us. For instance, if morality boils down to something like pleasure, adaptive fitness, social coordination, or human flourishing, then the reason why we should be inherently attracted to morality is that we are already attracted to these other things: if it is an axiom of human nature that we all pursue evolutionarily stable survival strategies, then, if moral goodness is nothing above and beyond these strategies, we have thereby explained why we should pursue moral goodness. Although Section 3.3 presented a variety of ways in which the nomenclature of "naturalism" might be ambiguous and unhelpful, the challenge to explain how morality engages our will nonetheless requires an answer from the realist.

In Section 5.1, we will address this worry by explaining how realist moral values can relate to our motivational structures, regardless of whether such values are properly "naturalistic" or not. After considering dominant accounts of moral motivation, it will be proposed that realist moral values need *not* necessarily provide their own inherent motivation and that, furthermore, this lack of intrinsic motivation is a well-established item of moral phenomenology. In Section 5.2, however, we will consider the distinct question of whether or not moral judgments provide their own justifying reasons for action, independent of whether someone is actually motivated on that basis. Section 5.3 concludes by considering another important dimension of the psychology of realism—namely, how realist moral values engage our emotional capacities and responses. In this regard, special attention will be devoted to recent views about the role that "retributive emotions" such as guilt and regret might play in the realist debate.

5.1 Moral motivation and the possibility of sociopaths

Moral realism posits the belief-independent existence of certain properties to which true moral propositions correspond. One of the biggest worries facing such a view—which we have explored in Section 3.4—is the danger of placing morality so far outside human sensibility in an effort to preserve its objectivity, that its practicality is thereby sacrificed. This danger is especially glaring when we consider moral motivation. Much of the time, the linkage between a moral judgment and the subsequent motivation to act on that judgment run smoothly, and does not seem to require any special analysis or explanation. For instance, when Sarah forms the judgment that she should give money to a charity, we are not surprised when she then proceeds to give money to a charity. But often people in Sarah's position who make exactly the same judgment seem to not follow through with concomitant action. Not only do such phenomena require explanations in their own right, but realists also need to ask whether these explanations jibe with their other semantic and metaphysical commitments.

Consider the following description of Tim's deliberative process: (1) Tim identifies strongly with the value of compassion and helping those in need. (2) As he is walking across the street, Tim sees another person, Jerome, drop his groceries and look around in obvious distress. (3) Tim forms a judgment that it would be morally right, in keeping with his values of compassion, for him to try to help Jerome. (4) But Tim instead walks right past him. In Section 6.4, we will analyze what a moral realist might be able to say about the linkage between (2) and (3), that is, about how Tim's perception of Jerome's distress leads to the corresponding judgment to help him, and what it might mean to say that Tim "sees" Jerome's distress in the first place. But for this chapter, our focus will be on what happens between steps (3) and (4) in Tim's deliberation. What accounts for Tim's failure to act on his moral judgment, and can moral realism accommodate this failure?

For one thing, Tim's failure to act might be due to insufficient motivation—perhaps the "rightness" of his judgment simply wasn't enough to move him to help. The view that moral judgments supply their own intrinsic impulses to act is called *motivational internalism*. Thus, according to motivational internalism, the very act of making a moral judgment (e.g. that it would be right to help someone in distress) will, all by itself, supply some degree of prepackaged motivation to act accordingly. Motivational internalism can further be distinguished in terms of the *strength* of the motivation inherent in moral judgments (cf. Brink 1989: 61). *Strong* motivational internalism maintains that moral judgments provide overriding motivation that will always lead to corresponding action in the absence of physical impediments (McDowell 1978; Nagel 1970). *Weak* motivational internalism maintains only that moral judgments provide *some* degree of motivation, but this may be defeasible in light of other motivations or considerations (Blackburn 1984; Johnston 1989; Pettit and Smith 1993).[1] By contrast, *motivational externalism* maintains that moral judgments can still motivate us, but only when they are fortified by other nonmoral antecedent desires. Which of these theories makes the best sense of Tim's failure to help Jerome despite judging that it was morally right to do so, and what implications does the answer to this question have for a theory such as moral realism?

First, it should be noted that realists have good *prima facie* reasons to be attracted to motivational externalism. This is because motivational externalism supports *cognitivism* in a way that internalism seems unable to, and cognitivism (as we have seen in §2.2) is a necessary condition for any robust realist view. At least on the traditional Humean picture, only desires or desire-like states can move us to action. If this picture is correct, though, motivational internalists would need to interpret moral judgments as essentially expressions of desires, desire-like states, or some kind of belief-desire compound in order to account for how moral judgments can alone move us to action. It is for this reason that motivational internalism has long been associated with noncognitivism (cf. Blackburn 1984).

For similar reasons, motivational internalism has also been used as a premise for moral error theories (the anthropological dimensions of which we discussed in §4.1). J. L. Mackie, for instance, argued that if realism is committed to the inherent motivational power of moral judgments, realism would be suspiciously unique or "queer." In Mackie's view, no other category of judgments contains its own intrinsic motivational power in the absence of some hypothetical desire on the part of the judger to act on the judgment. I can earnestly judge, for example, that I should go to the gym tonight, and yet fail to do so for completely nonmysterious and unsurprising psychological reasons. To require moral judgments to magically motivate people would, in Mackie's mind, seem to put morality on a completely different plane from other realms of judgment—which would be unparsimonious and suspiciously question-begging. In Mackie's words,

> An objective [realist] good would be sought by anyone who was acquainted with it, not because of any contingent fact that this person, or every person, is so constituted that he desires this end, but just because the end has to-be-pursuedness somehow built into it. (1977: 40)

Thus, if Mackie is right and motivational internalism would be suspiciously queer, then perhaps the easiest maneuver for a moral realist is just to abandon commitment to motivational internalism from the get-go. Motivational externalism provides a much simpler and straightforward way to reconcile cognitivism and motivation. If moral judgments are essentially belief-like, then they can be attained in a cognitivist manner and do not need to move us to action at all. In other words, those already attracted to realism should also be attracted to motivational externalism.

But are there any reasons to favor motivational externalism for its own sake, independent of any commitment to moral realism? On the one hand, the history of ethics furnishes many assumptions of motivational internalism. For instance, with respect to *strong* motivational internalism, Plato famously believed that if someone *knows* what is morally right, she will automatically seek to *do* what is right (cf. *Protagoras* 352a–358d; *Republic* 439a–441c). This is known as the "Socratic view of evil"—or, for those like Mackie who find it implausible, the "Socratic paradox."[2] A similar romantic faith in the intrinsic motivational power of morality can be found in the writers of the eighteenth-century "Intellectual School." For instance, Richard Price (1757) achieved notoriety for his claim that, "When we are conscious that an action is fit to be done, or that it ought to be done, it is not conceivable that we can remain uninfluenced, or want a motive to action". The opposing "Sentimental School," with its focus on a so-called moral sense, was much less friendly to this sort of internalism. Although many Sentimental writers maintained that people *are* frequently motivated to act morally, they stressed that this is not due to any internal quality of moral values, but requires the participation of some aspect of our human nature. Thus, Lord Shaftesbury (1699) famously stressed that the motive to be good is embedded in our nature, not in moral values themselves.[3]

And yet, there are just as many familiar cases of failures to act on what we judge to be morally right or obligatory. Scenarios such as Stanley Milgram's (1974) experiments concerning people's obedience to authority appear to showcase the fact that subjects will inflict pain on others even though they express knowledge that what they're doing is morally wrong. And the unnerving case of Kitty Genovese, in which onlookers watched as a woman was repeatedly stabbed to death without acting to call the police (Gansberg 1964), should also instill some skepticism regarding any overriding motivational power internal to moral beliefs. Most of us are also familiar with much less exotic examples of motivational failures involving temptation or "weakness of the will." Often it is not the idealized and forgiving experience of Socratic ignorance which we are aware of in our moments of moral failure, but rather something closer to Augustine's confession that we often deliberately seek "what we *know* to be not pure" (1961: 47, my italics).

If these phenomenologically familiar cases are at all legitimate, they would seem to debunk any strong version of motivational internalism. Clearly, people's moral judgments do not always provide overriding or indefeasible motives to act morally. However, we are also familiar with scenarios in which moral judgments appear to lack *any* motivational power at all. Such possibilities are often showcased with unnerving explicitness in fiction. Think, for example, of Shakespeare's Iago, whose externalism seems evident in his unapologetic assertion, "Evil, be thou my good." In the *Book of Jeremiah* (2.20), motivational externalism seems to be present when the Israelites are chastised for their deliberate wickedness, saying "I will not serve" directly to God—words famously quoted by Milton's Lucifer as explaining his fall from grace. More recently, this type of moral rebellion and nonchalance has been expressed in literature by characters such as Hannibal (in Thomas Harris's *Silence of the Lambs*) or Pat Bateman (in Bret Easton Ellis's *American Psycho*). What is unnerving about these individuals is that they seem to possess knowledge that what they are doing is wrong (or at least that it is *considered* wrong), but do not seem to *care*. Hannibal and Bateman are even presented as being of above-average intelligence, and are extremely adept at knowing how the rest of society uses moral language, which of course helps them to "blend in."

Most writers describe these scenarios as cases of "amoralism." If we take cases of amoralism seriously, then we must allow for the disturbing possibility that moral judgments do not always entail motivation to act morally. In other words, an individual may possess true moral beliefs—indeed, she may even know that they are true—but be unconcerned about them or unmoved to act on the basis of them. Such an individual may coherently say "I *know* that upholding agreements is morally obligatory, but I just don't particularly *feel* like upholding agreements." The amoralist who says this is not merely claiming that: (a) she is *unable* to uphold her end of the agreement, (b) she does not know what her duty is, or (c) she does not want to because of competing moral considerations that outweigh the duty to uphold the agreement. Rather, she is saying that even though she knows her duty, and is able to perform her duty, and finds no competing moral duties, she still simply does not feel like doing her duty.

It is an interesting empirical question as to what is the most frequent culprit for failures to act morally—not knowing our duty, trying to do our duty but failing, or simply not caring about our duty. One of the difficulties facing any investigation of this question, of course, is that people are often unwilling or unable to admit when they have failed to fulfill a moral duty. Given that most assessments of moral responsibility occur after the opportunity for moral action has already passed, psychological strategies of denial and avoidance make it difficult to determine the real cause of a moral failure. For example, when we are confronted with a television injunction to send aid to starving children across the globe, why do so few of us refuse to do so? It might be that the phenomenon of children starving all the way around the planet is interpreted as being too large of a problem for any single individual to help: the obligation might, therefore, be defused by considerations that "ought-implies-can," that is, that because we cannot fix the problem, we are not morally obligated to fix the problem.[4] Or it might be that we recognize a legitimate moral obligation to give aid, but do not do so because we think that the obligation is outweighed by other moral considerations, for example, saving our money to pay debts, send our own children to school, etc. If we take the purported cases of strong motivational externalism seriously, however, we must admit that some people could simply be motivationally unaffected by the images of starving children.

One way that motivational internalists have attempted to account for the apparent existence of amoralists is by denying that such individuals really possess genuine moral knowledge or make genuine moral judgments in the first place. Of course, amoralists certainly *appear* to make moral judgments. After all, they seem to use moral language and terms in the same way that other moral agents do. Indeed, in many cases, they are actually able to use moral language *better* than ordinary moral speakers: Hannibal Lector and Pat Bateman are highly educated, articulate, socially polished, and very charismatic. The motivational internalist, therefore, needs to explain, in a nonstipulative or question-begging way, how the amoralist does not actually make legitimate moral judgments despite the fact that she nonetheless appears to do so. One of the most influential explanations of this is the view that, although the amoralist utters moral terms, she does not fully understand the words coming out of her mouth. As R. M. Hare (1952) argued, she uses moral predicates only in an "inverted commas" sense. On this theory, someone like Hannibal is able to talk about murder being wrong, but only by using the term "wrong," as it were, tongue-in-cheek. What Hannibal really means is that murder is *considered* wrong—he is literally paying lip service to its wrongness. If he really meant that murder was wrong *simpliciter*, says the internalist, he would *ipso facto* feel some motivation not to do it.

David Brink (1989) argues that this internalist strategy fails to take the cases of amoralism seriously, conveniently attempting to explain them away as due to a kind of false consciousness: the amoralist thinks that she makes moral judgments, but in fact is mistaken. The burden of proof, of course, is on the internalist here. Reducing the amoralist's purported moral judgments to a merely inverted-comma usage of moral predicates distorts what the amoralist actually says. After all, moral judgments seem more akin to pain judgments: if you say that you are in pain, then (provided you are not lying) *ipso facto* you are in pain, if you claim to be making a moral judgment, then (provided you are not lying or confused) *ipso facto* you are making a moral judgment. Obviously, your moral judgment could be mistaken, but it is much less clear that you could be mistaken that you are making a moral judgment in the first place. At any rate, internalists and externalists can argue forever about what counts as a genuine moral judgment. But, as Michael Smith (1994: 70) points out, both positions will be stipulative and question-begging. What we need are independent reasons to evaluate whether the amoralist actually makes genuine moral judgments.

Smith himself offers an argument for motivational internalism in line with the inverted-commas strategy by drawing a parallel between moral language and color language. According to Smith, we would deny that a person would possess legitimate color concepts if she did not also have the attendant perceptual experiences of colors, no matter how adept she is at using color vocabulary. Similarly, says Smith, we should be suspicious that amoralists possess legitimate moral concepts (i.e. make genuine moral judgments) because they do not have the same motivational experience that ordinary agents do, no matter how well they are able to use moral terms. In neither case do we think that mere use of a term determines possession of the corresponding concept.

Smith's argument serves to illuminate some of the reason why motivational internalists might be attracted to the inverted-commas theory. Smith's intuitions regarding the use of color terms, however, seem somewhat idiosyncratic: why would we not allow that the person who uses color terms with perfect accuracy and reliability thereby possesses the corresponding concepts? Could we not merely say that such a person possesses the concepts and just lacks the personal experience of colors—in the same way that I might possess the concept of "Mt. Shasta" without having had the personal experience of seeing or climbing it, or might possess a certain abstract mathematical concept without necessarily being able to nonmathematically envision the corresponding entity? Such a person could learn to discriminate between colors by learning which objects are associated with certain colors. In addition, Smith's analogy with color judgments is at best a possibility-proof of motivational internalism. The burden is still on the internalist to explain why and how the amoralist's judgment motivationally misfires in the way it does.

Smith attempts to satisfy this burden by noting that it is analytically built-in to the definition of a "good person" that she is motivated by her beliefs. Of course, the motivational externalist can recognize this, but insist that the motivation is contingent on the "goodness" of the person, and not inherent in the moral judgments themselves. Smith argues, however, that to interpret the good person's motivation in this way is to interpret her motivation in a *de dicto* way that would disconnect the good person from any direct or nonderivative concern for what she thinks is right. For example, consider the moral judgment that one's friend is in the hospital and that one should visit her: according to Smith, a *de dicto* interpretation of one's motivation would involve desiring to visit one's friend *because* it is the right thing to do. But this would involve giving our moral obligations what Bernard Williams famously derided as "one thought too many." In other words, requiring agents to be motivated by highly reflective and self-conscious concerns for being good distorts actual moral decision-making. Indeed, our friend might even be insulted if we explained our desire to visit her solely as a result of wanting to do the right thing. Instead, says Smith, the good person's motivation should be interpreted *de re*. That is, the good person is not motivated to visit her friend because it is the right thing to do, but simply because she cares about her friend.

Smith's analysis of our moral phenomenology seems accurate: most people would be insulted by an impersonalized explanation of our moral concern for them, and most morally good agents are not typically aware of abstracted and overly reflective *de dicto* considerations. Indeed, these kinds of motivations can actually slow down moral response, which in some cases needs to be more immediate and instinctual. On the other hand, we also believe that moral behavior cannot be arbitrary or random for it to be praiseworthy. That is, on the *de re* reading of motivation, the good person's concern for her friend runs the risk of being based only on contingent whims and personal inclinations if it is not justified by the *de dicto* desire to act morally. Indeed, if the *de re* interpretation of motivation were satisfactory, the moral value or worth of our friend need not ever enter into our decision-making: the fact that we desire to help our friend would alone suffice to explain our motivation. This would make it very difficult to distinguish the actions of morally good people from other people since morally bad individuals can still have the desire to visit a friend.[5] A purely *de re* interpretation of motivation would abandon the importance of grounding our actions in specifically *moral* considerations.

This is not to say that our moral responses should have no *de re* considerations at all. Williams's worry about having "one thought too many" is absolutely right: the person who visits her friend solely out of abstract considerations of duty lacks something morally important just as much as the person who acts solely out of inclination. Rather, proper moral response should incorporate *both* *de re* and *de dicto* considerations. Marcia Baron (1995: 117–45) offers a helpful way of reconciling *de re* and *de dicto* considerations. In response to Michael Stocker's (1976) worry that modern ethical theories like Kantianism are "schizophrenic" because they too sharply distinguish inclination and duty, Baron argues that *de dicto* considerations are not inherently "repugnant" or "alienating" (Stocker's words).[6] As Baron points out, the only thing that seems wrong about acting out of purely *de dicto* considerations of duty is when the actor presents herself falsely as acting out of *de re* considerations. In other words, what strikes us as morally repugnant or alienating is when someone whom we thought was visiting us as a friend is discovered to only be motivated by abstract duty—if someone were explicitly and straightforwardly visiting us out of *de dicto* considerations, we would not feel alienated because we would not feel misled (Baron 1995: 119–20). Furthermore, even if we would still find the straightforwardly *de dicto* visitor morally distasteful, *de dicto* considerations do not necessarily need to be explicitly in the forefront of one's mind when performing one's duty. That is, we may need *de dicto* considerations to justify a moral response as moral, but we need not be consciously aware of (let alone offer) these sorts of considerations during actual moral actions. In this way, Baron points out that *de dicto* considerations may be more appropriate as "secondary motives" which provide limiting conditions on what may be done, while the actual motivation to do what should be done arises from personal inclination and *de re* considerations (1995: 129).

In summary, strong motivational externalism is not only plausible by its own lights, but it also might sync best with moral realism. Common examples of moral failure discredit idealistically strong forms of motivational internalism. Taking the possibility of genuine amoralism seriously also makes weak motivational internalism implausible. Attempts to reduce apparent amoralist judgments to inverted-comma usages fail to take amoralism seriously, as well as force us to interpret the good person's motivation in a morally suspicious way. What this shows is that moral judgments do not necessarily provide their own inherent motivational power, such that an individual may possess legitimate moral knowledge and still fail to be motivated to act accordingly.

5.2 Justification and reasons for action

Let's return to our example of Tim's failure to act on the basis of his judgment that he should help Jerome. In the previous section, we examined the motivational linkage (or the lack thereof) between Tim's judgment and action. Yet, many philosophers who allow for both the weak-willed person and the amoralist have nonetheless wished to maintain that such agents still have *reasons* for acting morally, even though those reasons do not apparently generate corresponding motivations. This section will explore the suggestion that moral judgments can generate their own reasons independent from motivational force, and we shall see what stance the moral realist might take on this debate.

Debates about reasons are often much more abstract in metaethics than debates about motivation. After all, we seem to have a pretty clear grasp of what it takes to motivate us (viz. *desire*, at least on the standard Humean picture), but it is less clear what it means to say that we have "reason" to do something above and beyond whether we are motivated to do that thing or not. In general, there seem to be two different ways we speak of "reasons" with respect to moral judgments. On the one hand, we often use "reasons" in an essentially *explanatory* sense. When you are asked why you helped someone who has fallen down, your response "I did it because it was the right thing to do" is sometimes intended as an explanation of why you helped the person. On the other hand, we might intend our response as a *justification* of our action, that is, that we were entitled or allowed to act as we did. Explanatory reasons try to make sense of our action by expressing it as stemming from an appropriate consideration of means-to-ends reasoning. Given the goal of wanting to do the right thing, my judgment that I should help the person who has fallen down makes good sense as an appropriate means. Justifying reasons can be envisioned as concerning the ends themselves. In this way, someone may have an explanatory reason for action without necessarily having a justifying reason for action. For example, imagine that I am asked why I punched you in the face. If I answer "because I felt like it," this might *explain* my action, but it would not *justify* my action (cf. Brink 1989: 40). However, if I answer "because I thought you were attacking me" or "because I was trying to push you out of the way of danger," then I have offered a plausible justificatory reason for punching you.

Just as we can distinguish motivational versions of internalism versus externalism, so too can we speak of *reasons-internalism* versus *reasons-externalism*. Here, though, the terminology is orthogonal to how it is used in the motivational sense. Reasons-internalism is the view that the only reasons which have any bearing on my deliberation and behavior are those which arise inside my own subjective motivational set (e.g. Williams 1981). So, whereas "internalism" in the motivational sense refers to something that is allegedly internal to a moral judgment, "internalism" in the reasons sense refers to something that is internal to an agent herself. By contrast, reasons-externalism is the view that there can exist reasons for actions that are outside my or anyone's subjective motivational complex (e.g. Korsgaard 1996; Nagel 1970). Thus, reasons-externalism recognizes what we might call "objective reasons"—reasons that make sense of or morally justify why we acted on our judgment in the way that we did. Furthermore, based on the distinction we have considered between the explanatory versus the justificatory senses of "reasons," we can define *explanatory reasons-externalism* as the view that moral judgments reference explanations of our behavior that obtain objectively or in a way external to our subjective motivational set. *Justificatory reasons-externalism* is the view that moral judgments reference objective or externally grounded justifications for acting in accordance with those judgments. This section will focus primarily on justificatory reasons-externalism (JRE). Seen in this light, the main thrust of reasons-externalism is the attempt to answer the perennial question "Why be moral?"

Again, reference to our old friend Tim may be helpful: Tim judges that he should help Jerome, but then does not help Jerome.

- **Strong motivational internalism**: Tim's judgment was sufficient all by itself to have motivated him to help; since he didn't, either there must have been some physical inhibition or else Tim's judgment was not truly a "judgment" at all. Perhaps he only deliberated in an inverted-commas sense.

- **Weak motivational internalism**: Tim's judgment contributed some motivational oomph, but obviously not enough to override countervailing motivational considerations. Perhaps Tim was too weak-willed.

- **Motivational externalism**: Tim's judgment supplied zero motivation—he had to independently care about morality for his judgment to move him, and obviously did not. Perhaps Tim is a sociopath!

- **Justificatory reasons-internalism**: Had Tim helped Jerome, his actions would have been morally justified, but only because he made the specific judgment that he did. Tim's helping would, thus, be "hypothetically imperative" and justifying of his actions just in case he cares internally about morality and helping people. Morality has to make its own case to Tim for it to govern Tim's deliberation and behavior.

- **Justificatory reasons-externalism** (JRE): Tim's helping Jerome is morally justified regardless of whether Tim himself felt moved to do so. The moral justification is thus external to Tim's subjectivity, such that the action could be "categorically imperative" even if Tim personally doesn't care about helping.

To which of these accounts should the moral realist be committed? We have suggested that motivational externalism (even perhaps the strong version) might render realism more psychologically realistic, given the apparent existence of amoralists as well as the unattractiveness of purely *de re* or purely *de dicto* moral considerations. And it would seem that moral realism has strong ties to justificatory reasons-externalism (JRE) since this alone recognizes the existence of moral considerations and standards independent of an individual's beliefs. But what precisely does JRE entail?

JRE is sometimes expressed as the view that having a good reason for action inherently entails the *capacity* to be motivated. Yet, whether someone is actually motivated by a moral judgment she makes is a separate question from whether or not that moral judgment provides someone with good justifying reasons for action. It may be that someone has a good reason that would justify her action, but that she is nonetheless psychologically, epistemically, or emotionally unable to feel motivated. Motivation is internal to our subjectivities, but the realist needs to maintain that morality itself is not. Consider, for example, Damien who is deeply sadistic. The moral realist will want to say that it is the wrongness of inflicting pain on others for fun which makes Damien's sadism unjustified, even if Damien himself is psychologically incapable of being motivated by moral appeals, and even if he makes the judgment that it would be wrong.

This highlights two important features of justificatory reasons. First, having a justifying reason for action is not the same as *recognizing* that one has a justifying reason for action. The fact that we are unaware that something is good for us does not mean that that thing is not in fact good for us. For example, we have good reason not to drink salt water even if we are critically dehydrated and stranded on a boat in the middle of the ocean—regardless of whether or not we are aware of this fact—because salt will only dehydrate us more. Second, even if an agent does recognize something as a good justifying reason, she may not necessarily be *capable* of feeling any corresponding motivation. For example, Shafer-Landau (2003) draws our attention to a severely depressed and reclusive person who may be aware that it would be *better* for her if she socialized more frequently, but who, because of her condition, nonetheless does not *want* to socialize, that is, not only might she not be motivated, she might even be *unable* to be motivated.

With these caveats in mind, we can refine the position of JRE as the view that true moral judgments provide their own inherent justifying reasons for action, regardless of whether an agent recognizes them and regardless of whether an agent is capable of being motivated by them (and certainly regardless of whether she is actually motivated by them). Expressed in this way, JRE seems highly intuitive: we are familiar with cases in which people have good (justifying) reasons to act in certain ways even if they are blind to them and unable to be motivated by them. This suggests that the burden of proof rests on the reasons-internalist. But before siding wholly with JRE, let's explore what arguments might support the reasons-internalist view.

First, it might be thought that, although moral demands might be "obligatory" in the sense that they apply to agents regardless of personal interests and desires, this does not imply that they are also obligatory in any categorical sense (Foot 1972). If moral demands are only binding in a hypothetical sense, then they would not differ essentially from the demands of etiquette or games. After all, the "rules" that govern a game of chess, a fencing match, or choosing which fork to use during the salad course of a fancy dinner apply to agents irrespective of whether they know the rules or not; that is, the games still hold players accountable for ignorant violations. But we do not thereby think that the rules of chess, fencing, or dining etiquette obtain external to the game itself. And we can change the rules of chess or a fencing match simply by stipulating new ones. Even though we can say that an individual who was ignorant of the rules of dinning etiquette still committed a *faux pas* in using the wrong utensil, we do not think that there are reasons why one particular dining convention is *intrinsically* better than another. According to this objection, JRE must show how moral demands are different from the demands of etiquette or games; and the proponent of JRE cannot merely cite the fact that moral demands obtain regardless of individual interests or desires because this feature is shared by the demands of etiquette and games.

Of course, one of the fundamental ways in which morality and etiquette differ seems to be with respect to the *scope* of their demands—what Russ Shafer-Landau (2003) calls "jurisdiction." The demands of etiquette and games have a very local and limited jurisdiction: they obligate us in a way that is relative to certain specific roles we occupy only at particular times, places, and situations. For example, one of the demands placed upon a competitor in a fencing match is that she cannot cross one leg in front of the other while advancing. Once she ceases the fencing match, however, this demand vanishes, that is, it would be very strange for someone to tell her that she is doing something "wrong" if she walks normally while, say, heading to the restaurant down the street. Moral demands differ from demands of etiquette and games by having a more universal scope. On this view, the demands of morality, unlike those of games, obtain everywhere and always; they are unconditional and do not depend on any specific roles or positions of agents.[7] Thus, the obligations of fencing are optional (someone may choose when and whether or not to fence), but the obligations of morality are not.

A defender of JRE, however, should be hesitant to accept Shafer-Landau's explanation of this as due to a difference in "jurisdiction."[8] For one thing, the moral realist sees moral demands as differing from the demands of etiquette not only in terms of their scope, but importantly in terms of their *source*. Moral demands, for the realist, are causally independent of our conceptions, interests, and desires, whereas the demands of etiquette are not—they are invented by us, which is precisely what the realist wishes to avoid saying about morality. Distinguishing morality from etiquette in this way also allows us to be agnostic about whether there is a difference in jurisdiction between the two. Thus, even if we were to identify some demand of etiquette so basic as to be universal (e.g. a Confucian account of social propriety that grounds moral development and relationships), we could still distinguish morality from etiquette so long as we accept moral realism. Of course, this means that JRE is only as plausible as moral realism, and cannot therefore be used noncircularly as a premise for realism. But JRE does help strengthen moral realism by showing how moral judgments can link up with our agency: even though moral judgments do not always provide inherent motivation, they *do* refer to reasons that would justify corresponding behavior in a way that the demands of etiquette do not since the latter are not belief-independent in the way that realists envision the former as being.

Note that this objection is intended only to counter attempts to reduce moral obligations to the status of optional demands of games such as fencing. Of course, to call the latter "demands of *etiquette*" might beg certain questions about the relationship between morality and social rules of conduct. In fact, I think there might be good reason to view many "demands of etiquette" as instantiations of certain moral values. Thus, the "obligations" to cover one's mouth when yawning or to take off one's hat when indoors may not be shared by other cultures, but the underlying values these practices represent (e.g. not showing boredom when another person is talking, not being vulgar in a way that might make an onlooker uncomfortable, showing humility, etc.) seem best understood as legitimately *moral* values. On this reading, many of the demands of etiquette would receive the same nonarbitrary status as the moral demands which they instantiate. Perhaps even the demands of games and sports can ultimately be understood as incarnations of a more general (and *moral*) value of, say, respect for fairness, etc.

JRE, however, has been subject to a separate critique of its very coherence. This objection can be seen as a more challenging version of Mackie's worry about metaphysical queerness discussed above. The original version of the queerness argument has already been deflected in Section 5.1 by simply noting that moral realism is not committed to motivational internalism. But we can refurbish Mackie's basic position as an objection to JRE as well: if moral judgments refer to intrinsically justifying reasons for action independent of whether we care about such action, then they would be utterly unlike any other kinds of judgments with which we are familiar. According to this objection, it would be just too much of a coincidence for moral values to exist independently of our beliefs about them, but still exist in precisely the sort of way that inherently supplies creatures like us with reasons for action. Proponents of this argument conclude that such suspicious uniqueness or "queerness" should be sufficient to engender skepticism about reasons externalism.

There are several problems with this argument. First, since it is really an appeal to the best explanation of an alleged uniqueness, rather than a deductive proof, it is at best only suggestive of reasons-internalism. JRE is still consistent, logically possible, and might be attractive for other reasons. For instance, it might be thought that JRE is the best way to preserve the many intuitions which we seem to have in its favor, as discussed above. Second, why should we agree with Mackie that just because something would be unique or queer, it should, therefore, be purged from an acceptable ontology? After all, we might think that morality is special enough that it makes sense to evaluate it by unique standards.

Mackie's argument is ultimately unpersuasive, however, because it falsely assumes that morality is the only realm which supplies inherently justifying reasons. There seem to be several other noteworthy realms that appear to be more like realist morality than irrealist games or etiquette. Mackie himself anticipates this objection, but denies that the identification of any such "companions in guilt" would alleviate the suspicions facing JRE. External justifications would be so inexplicable that, even if other nonmoral entities supplied similar external reasons, these too should be purged from our ontology. The reasons-externalist cannot allow for too many companions in guilt, however, without undercutting the putative queerness of reasons externalism. What would be allegedly queer about morality is that it would be inexplicably reasons-giving; and what would be inexplicable about external reasons is that nothing else besides morality would provide them. Yet, if a sufficiently large amount of additional entities or realms other than morality turn out to also supply their own external justifications, then the abductive evidence against JRE begins to shift. This would be especially undermining for Mackie's argument if the other nonmoral realms that were revealed as supplying justifying reasons for action turned out to be very important to us, that is, ones that we would be hesitant to purge from our ontology.

A little consideration reveals a number of companions in guilt which are important in precisely this way. *Pleasure*, for example, seems to also reference external reasons: the judgment that something is or would be pleasurable provides an inherent and *prima facie* (though perhaps defeasible) reason that would justify corresponding action. Similarly, *aesthetic* predicates seem to generate their own reasons for action, external to an individual's subjective motivational set. It would be weird to say that something was "beautiful," without attributing some sort of *prima facie* value to that thing, for example, without generating a reason that would justify acting to preserve beautiful things. Most importantly, it seems that *alethic* predicates also provide their own justifications. To say that a proposition is "true" seems to involve an endorsement of that proposition, that is, to assent to its truth by believing it. It is for this reason that it seems incoherent or perverse to ask of a proposition which is admitted to be true, *why* it should, therefore, be believed. If judgments concerning pleasure, aesthetic predicates, and even truth predicates can supply their own justifications for acting or believing, then what is so queer or unique about moral judgments supplying their own justifying reasons as well? Moral judgments seem to be in quite good company with other important aspects of our discourse that we should be extremely hesitant to discard.

In summary, we have seen that JRE and moral realism seem well suited to support each other. JRE gives realism a way of differentiating social constructions from genuine moral demands, and realism gives an account of what JRE might mean by "external reasons." Conjoining realism with JRE, however, implies that we might not always be able to rationally persuade individuals who do not recognize reasons that they nonetheless have reasons. Amoralists such as Hannibal, or regular old Tim (who fails to help the fallen Jerome), still have external reasons that make their actions unjustified, even if they do not or cannot recognize such reasons or ever feel motivated by them.[9]

5.3 Realism and the retributive emotions

If moral realism recognizes external reasons which would justify behavior, then realism should also recognize the appropriateness of the emotions which are activated in response to these external reasons. For instance, even if Tim's judgment that it would be morally right to help someone fails to motivate Tim (as the motivational externalist acknowledges), Tim's failure was still morally unjustified (as the reasons-externalist insists)—and doesn't it also make sense to say further that Tim should, therefore, *feel bad* about his unjustified failure? After all, moral realism is not solely an abstract metaphysical thesis about the existence of values: it must also address the ways in which values engage us as embodied moral agents, and one of the ways this happens is through our *emotional* experience with morality. Moral values ground moral obligations, and it is the success or failure to adhere to these obligations which in turn give rise to our "reactive attitudes" of praise and blame. In this section, we will analyze how realists might try to make sense of the emotional dimensions of our moral successes and failures.

First, let us understand reactive attitudes as emotional responses to perceptions of moral right or wrongdoing. While some reactive attitudes are not obviously evaluative in nature (e.g. anger, fear, etc.), many others seem thickly moral. Righteous indignation, guilt, and forgiveness, for example, are constituted not merely by affective feelings, but also by a cognitive dimension that references some moral standard. I could feel afraid for all sorts of reasons, but I only properly feel guilty when I believe that I have done something wrong. In this way, the moral content of an action will often be deeply entangled with our psychological response to it. Discussions of the reactive attitudes are prevalent in the philosophical literature concerning free will—do we have deliberative control over our attitudes, and are attitudes mollified if someone could not help but commit the action to which we are reacting?—but less attention has been given to their metaethical significance. On the surface, it might appear that taking reactive attitudes seriously would commit one to some version of metaethical noncognitivism (as discussed in §2.3): if we cannot disentangle our moral assessments from our emotional reactions, perhaps that is because our moral assessments *just are* emotional reactions (or expressions or endorsements of norms, etc.). This is yet another instance of the familiar worry, which has been the focus of much of this chapter, that moral realism divorces morality too much from actual human sensibility and experience. Yet, before we are forced to choose between moral realism versus our emotional phenomenology, let us first look more closely at the moral psychology of these reactive attitudes.

We have already distinguished the reactive attitudes that are intrinsically evaluative from those which are not: fear and anger may accompany moral assessments, but they need not, whereas righteous indignation and guilt necessarily presuppose some evaluative stance. Let us call the latter category of reactive attitudes—the ones which are intrinsically moral—"retributive emotions."[10] We may further differentiate retributive emotions into those which are other-regarding and those which are self-regarding. Take guilt, for instance. Like other retributive emotions such as vengeance or indignation, moral guilt involves a negative or unpleasant affective response (typically experienced as sorrow, rather than anger) that is predicated on certain judgments about having done wrong.[11] Unlike those other retributive emotions, however, guilt is specifically self-regarding: one may feel vengeful or indignant at another, but one can only feel guilty with oneself. Furthermore, guilt is normative in the way all retributive emotions are: someone who has done something morally wrong *should* feel guilty and, reciprocally, someone should only appropriately feel guilty for having done something morally wrong.[12] Indeed, it is this normativity that seems to connect self-regarding moral emotions such as guilt with other-regarding moral emotions such as vengeance and indignation: when I cause a moral violation, not only should I feel guilty, but you also would be justified in feeling vengeance or indignation toward me as a result of my violation. Thus, in a certain sense, the reflexivity or inwardness of guilt "completes" the outwardness of the other-regarding moral emotions. Indignation at someone who feels no guilt is frustratingly incomplete; just as the retraction of another's indignation can serve to ameliorate one's own guilt (i.e. forgiveness).

Patricia Greenspan (1995) has offered one possible way of seeing normative emotions such as guilt as possessing deep relevance for a view like moral realism. Drawing on developmental moral psychology, Greenspan argues that moral emotions can help cash out what realists might have in mind when they envision the sort of "external reasons" we explored in Section 5.2. On the one hand, external justificatory reasons need to be more intimately connected with our embodied psychologies than mere abstract moralizing or abstruse metaphysical concept-chopping; but, on the other hand, external justificatory reasons cannot become reduced *solely* to our sensibilities without thereby sacrificing the metaphysical independence required by a properly realist view. The normativity inherent in moral emotions such as guilt, however, helps provide the missing link between the independent ontology of realist properties and the dependent motivational elements of human moral-psychological development. (This is a psychological/phenomenological analogue to the attempt to bridge realist morality and human subjectivity via 'dispositional properties, which we explored in §3.4.)

To articulate this possible emotional version of moral realism, Greenspan looks to a suggestion by Mackie (1977: 108). In his argument against what he saw as the psychological queerness of realist normativity, Mackie invokes a distinction between the classical Greek concepts of *aidos* (moral shame) and *dike* (justice), which he describes as "Protagorean," in reference to Protagoras' famous aphorism that "Man is the measure of all things." As Mackie sees it, the concept of *dike* refers to the *de jure* sanctions of norms and social-legal codes, and the concept of *aidos* plays the role of motivating and inculcating those norms and codes. Yet, realists could requisition this same view of the motivational and developmental role of moral emotions such as *aidos*, but harness it to a realist property (perhaps a dispositional one, as we suggested in §3.4) instead of a socially arbitrary norm. Thus, *dike* and *aidos* might be seen as the independent (objectivist) and dependent (subjectivist) sides of the same realist coin: the latter cashes out the normativity of the former from "within" the experience of realist morality, as it were.[13]

Emotions such as guilt, regret, shame, indignation, and forgiveness represent the lived experience of our everyday moral lives. Moral realism needs to accommodate the centrality of this phenomenology in order to avert charges of psychological queerness or irrelevance. The suggestion we have considered in this section is that moral emotions and moral realism might complement one another: realism anchors the cognitive content of the emotions, and the emotions supply the normativity we experience in the form of external justificatory reasons. Obviously, much more could be said regarding the conceptual relationship and anthropology of these emotional encounters with morality. But for our purposes, it is enough to be reminded that moral realism needn't be insensitive to our everyday psychology.

5.4 Summary

This chapter addressed psychological issues connected to the moral realist position. At the theoretical level, we considered the objection that realism might locate morality too far outside human sensibility to account for the practical and action-guiding quality it is thought to possess. In response, by examining not only commonplace experience and intuitions, but also experimental evidence from moral psychology, we conceded the possibility that morality does *not* always motivate us. We also considered the even more radical possibility that morality—even for a realist—might fail to provide reasons that would be rationally accessible to all people, although we saw that realists must at a minimum insist that such reasons would justify concomitant action. Finally, at the more practical level, we considered a dimension of the psychological debate typically neglected in discussions of realism, namely, the role that moral emotions play in our conception of moral reality. In particular, we considered arguments that the phenomenological dynamics of certain "retributive emotions" such as guilt, blame, and regret might help cash out an otherwise esoteric doctrine such as realism; and, vice versa, that realism provides a theoretic grounding for such experiences.

CHAPTER SIX

The epistemology of realism

The previous chapters have been concerned with defining moral realism and demarcating the assorted semantic, metaphysical, cultural, and psychological debates with which it intersects. Although we have seen a wide variety of available interpretations and combinations of positions which might all be glossed as "realist," we have also explored the possibility of a specific realism that is cognitivist, pluralist, and naturalist. In this chapter, we will consider another dimension of the realism debate—namely, how realist moral properties are or could be accessible to us epistemologically. That is, if moral properties are truly as belief-independent as the realist claims, how can it still be possible for us to form beliefs about them at all? The worry is that in order to preserve the "reality" of moral values, realists have thrust them too far outside our epistemic ken.

We have seen in Chapter 5 that realism needs to respond to what J. L. Mackie (1977) called a metaphysical "queerness" about how independently existing values could possibly move us to action. Mackie famously raised an analogous worry that realism is also queer because it seems completely quiet about how people could come to know these values. The motivational charge of queerness was rebutted in the previous chapter by arguing that moral knowledge may contain prepackaged reasons that would justify corresponding action, even if actual motivation itself is sometimes lacking. But how is this moral knowledge acquired in the first place? The frequent reticence of realists concerning issues of epistemology has given license to a bevy of caricatures. For example, in the absence of any explicit alternatives, Mackie himself assumed that realists must be committed to some version of mysticism, according to which moral values are known by gongoozling some otherworldly Form of the Good. In Mackie's own words,

> None of our ordinary accounts of sensory perception or introspection or the framing and confirming of hypotheses or inference or logical construction or conceptual analysis, or any combination of these, will provide a satisfactory answer [to the question of how realists account for the acquisition of moral knowledge]; 'a special sort of intuition' is a lame answer, but it is the one to which the clear-headed objectivist is compelled to resort. (1977: 39)

Of course, Mackie is raising the objection of epistemological queerness against a type of moral realism which he assumes must involve categorical motivation (which is part of what he also finds metaphysically queer about it). Yet, we have seen in Section 5.1 that this sort of strong motivational internalism might be a strawman for a more nuanced form of externalist realism. Moreover, Mackie's language of "objectivism" might tempt a critic to associate realism with the view that moral values are objects totally independent from human sensibility, rather than the sensibility-dependent dispositionalist realism we explored in Section 3.4. Nonetheless, Mackie's dismissal of overconfident and hand-waving epistemologies is an important reminder that the realist owes a more worked-out position.

On the other hand, it might be objected that quietism about epistemology is perfectly acceptable. After all, realism is a metaphysical thesis about what is real and therefore it might be thought to be insulated from mundane concerns about whether we puny humans are or are not able to know that reality. This is a seductive possibility for realists since it promises to absolve them of the need to offer an attendant epistemology. Furthermore, it may be motivated by a legitimate and honorable commitment to moral humility or fallibilism. Indeed, one common response (perhaps not as common as the condemnatory alternative, unfortunately) to being presented with different moral practices or being pressed to articulate rational justifications for moral opinions is to embrace a "Who am I to know?" attitude. Undergraduate students in introductory ethics courses, for example, having learned to appreciate both the complexities of human nature as well as the difficulty of standing their ground by defending a fully worked-out ethical position, may often default to a quietist epistemology—whether out of genuine moral respect, faux humility, or simply because it is perceived to be the simplest way out of an uncomfortable Socratic confrontation.

Despite these potential attractions, realists should not hide behind epistemological quietism or humility. A metaphysical view about what is real that lacks an attendant account of how we get knowledge about such reality should be a philosophical last resort, since it would fly in the face of the broadly held conviction that ethics (even metaethics) is ultimately a practical discipline that provides some degree of guidance about what we should do, how we should live, and what we should value. An ethical theory that neglects these central concerns might not even be considered legitimately "ethical" any longer.

With this in mind, let us clearly state the epistemological problem facing moral realism by first recalling the traditional philosophic definition of knowledge as "justified true belief." Chapters 2 and 3 examined how "truth" and "belief" might be understood by the moral realist. The present chapter, therefore, can be seen as trying to account for the "justified" part of the definition of moral knowledge in a way consistent with other semantic, metaphysical, anthropological, and psychological commitments of realism. This challenge can be divided into two separate, but ultimately related prongs:

- First, what is the *relationship*, if any, between moral beliefs themselves and the realist's insistence regarding truth-making properties which are independent of those beliefs? Do putative realist properties play any legitimate explanatory role, or are they so *ad hoc* as to be objectionably queer?

- Second, what is the epistemological *process* by which moral knowledge is acquired? Is this process reliable and does it jibe with other legitimate modes of knowledge acquisition, or must the realist default to an unhelpful mysticism or quietism?

Section 6.1 examines the first prong in light of the famous debate between Gilbert Harman and Nicholas Sturgeon regarding the role that realist properties might play in explaining "moral observations." After articulating and defending an ineliminable explanatory role for realist properties, Section 6.2 will analyze the possible conditions under which such observations could be reliably justified. After presenting a variety of influential moral epistemologies, it will be argued that a type of *foundationalism* best complements moral realism. Foundationalism has historically been at the heart of ethical intuitionism. However, since the romantic vagueness frequently tolerated by early intuitionists became the impetus for Mackie's queerness objection in the first place, Section 6.3 will examine recent attempts by realists to refurbish the view with greater precision and plausibility, and Section 6.4 will outline a new theory of moral perception capable of satisfying both Mackie's charge of queerness and Harman's worry about explanatory power.

6.1 Explanatory power and moral observation

Given the difficulties facing realist attempts to explicate a theory of moral knowledge, it is appropriate first to ask what epistemological difference, if any, realism would actually make if it were true. Regardless of how moral beliefs might be reliably formed, if realism turns out to be completely irrelevant to how we normally talk about and justify those beliefs, then realism would be revealed as suspiciously *ad hoc*. This, at least, is the antirealist strategy proposed by Gilbert Harman (1977). Harman asks us to imagine witnessing a group of kids gleefully burning a defenseless cat. According to Harman, this would likely cause us to form the belief that such wanton cruelty is morally wrong and that the kids are morally depraved. With this, the realist presumably agrees.

Harman's point, however, is that when it comes time to *explain* our negative evaluation, we can give a comprehensive account by citing various sociological, emotional, behavioral, and perceptual causal factors. We don't need to appeal to there being any additional factor called a "realist moral property" in order to explain our attitude. Harman's position is that an explanation of why we condemn animal cruelty that merely involves saying "Because it is wrong!" is really more of a *rephrasing* of the condemnation itself, rather than a legitimate "explanation" of it *per se*. A genuine explanation ought to shed some light on the factors that went into the condemnation, and Harman thinks this role is played instead by appeals to psychological or perceptual facts, for example, "I wasn't raised that way," or "Look at that poor suffering cat," or "That burning cat smells horrible." These facts already suffice to explain why we have the moral belief that we do; what else does the belief in correspondence to belief-independent properties add? Thus, argues Harman, we should cut out the middle-man and limit our epistemic commitments solely to belief in naturalistic explanations. In this way, Harman locates the epistemic burden of proof on the realist:

> Is your reaction [to observing the kids burning the cat] due to the actual wrongness of what you see or is it simply a reflection of your moral 'sense,' a 'sense' that you have acquired perhaps as a result of your moral upbringing? (1977: 4)

This alleged explanatory impotence of moral realism, Harman believes, furthermore constitutes a disanalogy with other forms of nonmoral explanatory inference. For example, when a seasoned astronomer looks through a telescope and observes the distortion of light around a certain point in distant space, she may quickly infer the existence of a Black Hole. This, of course, is an inductive leap since by definition she is not literally or directly "seeing" a Black Hole. And yet, her inference may be justified on the grounds that postulating the existence of a Black Hole sheds light (so to speak) on why she observed the distortions she did. In a more everyday vein, we make similar inductive leaps every time we think we see someone in pain: we don't after all literally or directly "see" their internal mental states, but an immediate attribution of such a mental state helps explain why they exhibited the grimacing or screaming they did. Harman's point is not to dispute the legitimacy of these sorts of inferences—in this way, he avoids the sort of extreme naturalism (what McDowell calls "bald" naturalism) which we analyzed in Section 3.3—but rather to limit ourselves solely to postulations which actually aid our explanatory goals. Inference to the best explanation is always an inductive leap, but why add insult to injury by overcomplicating things with unnecessary moral postulations that do not tell us anything which we didn't already know from our initial perceptual and psychological postulations? To put it simply, the astronomer explains her observation by making *one* postulation ("There must be a Black Hole"), whereas the moral realist would explain her condemnation of cat-burning with *two* postulations ("There is cat-burning, which violates my moral convictions" and "There are realist properties to which my moral convictions correspond").

Nicholas Sturgeon (1985), however, has argued that second-order metaethical properties *can* play legitimate explanatory roles, for the simple reason that they are cited in people's justification of why they find the torturing of animals morally wrong. Thus, for Sturgeon, what will count as the "best explanation" of a phenomenon—namely, the phenomenon of morally condemning the torturing of an animal—must be understood in the broader context of our overall explanatory goals, one of which will be to make sense of why we think that torturing animals is objectively wrong in the first place. Ironically, part of Sturgeon's response might have been suggested by a snarky comment Mackie himself makes about the prospects for realist epistemology. Immediately after deploying the queerness objection, Mackie (1977: 39) proposes that realists might, at best, seek out "companions in guilt," namely, other putative entities or bodies of discourse which are committed to similarly queer epistemologies. Mackie says he is skeptical that other areas would turn out to be even remotely as queer as realist morality; but even if they should, they'd be subject *a fortiori* to the same objectionable queerness as realism.

However, Mackie's "queerness" (like Harman's charges of explanatory impotence), if they are to mean anything at all, require not merely a contrast class of nonqueer things, but a contrast class that is overwhelmingly larger than the putatively queer entities. Mackie's and Harman's epistemological problem with realism, after all, concerns its alleged *uniqueness*; but if a critical mass of other entities and modes of discourse involve the same epistemic commitments, realism is no longer unique, so *ipso facto* no longer queer.[1] Sturgeon makes this point by noting that Harman's view holds realism to an impossible standard, setting the bar for explanation so high that too many other areas of inquiry would fail along with moral realism. As Sturgeon says, Harman's epistemic objection to realism is actually,

> just the application of a familiar *general* skeptical strategy, one which, if it works for ethics, will work equally well for unobservable theoretical entities, or for other minds, or for an external world (and so, again, can hardly be what constitutes the distinctive [read: queer] problem with *ethics*.) (1985: 230)

The specific companions in guilt which Sturgeon mobilizes are drawn from scientific principles, for example, Newton's universal law of gravitation or the principle of natural selection. While Harman does acknowledge the well-known view within the philosophy of science that observation underdetermines theoretical explanation (cf. Duhem 1914), such that there are never any "pure" observations which are entirely devoid of theoretical overlay or filtering, Sturgeon charges that he fails to acknowledge that ethical observations and scientific observations alike are embedded within a web of other beliefs that establish the conditions for empirical testability. The astronomer's postulation of the existence of a Black Hole in order to explain why she observes light distortions makes sense within the context of a host of other beliefs she has about how the laws of physics, her telescope, and her eyes work. The realist's postulation of the existence of moral depravity in the characters of the cat-burning hoodlums similarly makes sense within the context of her beliefs that there is some connection between action and character; for what *else* is causing those kids to do what they are doing?[2] Just as the astronomer's beliefs in the principles of optics are "tested" against her postulation of the Black Hole, so too are our beliefs in moral principles (e.g. that needless animal cruelty is wrong) are "tested" against the postulation of realist values.

For instance, part of what explains our observation that burning cats for fun is morally depraved is the additional belief that it *really is* morally depraved. Harman would account for the former only by describing our upbringing, attitudes, etc.; but Sturgeon's point is that part of what explains *why* we have the upbringing and attitudes we do in the first place is the additional belief that these are true. As Sturgeon puts it, "Isn't it plausible that Hitler's moral depravity – the fact of his really having been morally depraved – forms part of a reasonable explanation of why we believe he was morally depraved?" (1985: 234).

At root, Sturgeon's response to Harman's strategy is part of a concern regarding reductionism in general. (Recall our discussions of this issue in the context of ethical naturalism and Cornell Realism, of which Sturgeon is a proponent, in §3.2.) Harman would deny explanatory power to the belief in realist moral properties because he thinks that such a belief can be reduced to or explained away as nothing above or beyond psychosocial factors. But through what process is this reduction or explaining away to be done, and in what language? If the very domain that one seeks to reduce into a naturalistic metalanguage makes references to entities which would not have any correlate in the metalanguage, then the reduction cannot hope to be total or without semantic remainder (i.e. the reduction would not satisfy the requirement of "completeness" in the logical sense). Sturgeon considers the reductive aspirations of physicalism as an example, and notes that,

> although physicalism certainly entails that biological and psychological properties (and ethical properties too, if there are any) are physical, nothing follows about whether we have any but biological or psychological or ethical terminology for representing these particular physical properties (1985: 240).

Thus, in order to reduce or explain away belief in realist moral properties, Harman must first allow their *prima facie* existence; but once realist values are provisionally admitted as playing explanatory roles, Harman cannot make a convenient *volta-face* and cease talking about them. Morality must be talked about in the language of morality (even if it can ultimately be reduced at a more metaphysical level to something nonmoral). Barry Stroud has made a similar point, albeit in the context of color realism rather than moral realism. Stroud goes so far as to call such reductive goals—or what he calls "unmasking explanations"—conceptually "impossible." If the unmasker does not provisionally believe in the reality of the entities which are to be unmasked (a.k.a. reduced, explained away, etc.), then there is nothing to be unmasked in the first place.

> An explanation, even an unmasking explanation, needs an *explanandum.* By restricting ourselves exclusively to the language

of the physical sciences [or in Harman's case, the language of psycho-social influences], the *explananda* we wish to account for would not even be part of the only world we accept . . . So in trying to restrict our thinking from the beginning to the body of physical [non-moral] truths alone, we would lose the very *explananda* involving human beings' perceptions and beliefs [e.g. realist beliefs that cat-burning is wrong] that the goings-on in that purely physical world are supposed to be enough to explain. This means that an unmasking explanation that has anything to explain away must countenance something more than purely physical facts as part of the world. (Stroud 2000: 78)

If Sturgeon and Stroud are correct, then there is no *prima facie* or unique problem facing moral realism vis-à-vis explanation. Plenty of other epistemic problems might face the moral realist—such as how to account for the acquisition and justification of moral knowledge, which will be the subject of the next sections—but at least realism can defend itself by starting the debate on equal footing.

6.2 The conditions of epistemic justification

Even if realism can be defended on grounds of explanatory power, realists still need to provide an account of the processes by which knowledge of realist properties is obtained and justified. This section will survey the terrain of what a successful theory of epistemic justification will look like, and the subsequent sections will leverage these observations against historical and contemporary theories of how moral knowledge is acquired.

In general, to say that a belief is justified is to say that it is epistemically acceptable for the believer to hold that belief. Clearly, much more needs to be said about this. For one thing, following Walter Sinnott-Armstrong (1996), we might want to distinguish between *negative* justification and *positive* justification. A belief is negatively justified if there are no external reasons for the belief being false. In other words, to say that a belief is negatively justified is to say that it is innocent until proven guilty, that is, that a person is free to believe anything in the absence of reasons to the contrary.

Thus, for example, although a theist may not have evidence *for* her belief in God, her belief could still be negatively justified because she also has no evidence *against* it.

Negative justification allows us the freedom to believe many matters of faith with justification. But it is perhaps too epistemologically egalitarian. Indeed, it appears to elevate all items of faith to the status of knowledge. In addition, the history of positivism reminds us how difficult it really is to verify or falsify many beliefs conclusively. Belief in God may be unfalsifiable or unverifiable, but so is belief in skepticism about the external world, or the belief that I am a superhero, but that I have temporarily lost my powers and memories (which, after all, seems to happen to superheroes with suspicious frequency). Without a more restrictive criterion of justification, we run the risk of granting justification to too many insane beliefs.

Epistemic justification requires something more constraining than mere negative justification. Specifically, a true belief counts as knowledge only if the believer actually has good reasons or evidence *for* her belief. Sinnott-Armstrong calls this "positive justification" and associates it with the requirement that the belief must be based on "adequate positive support." Sinnott-Armstrong notes two ways in which a belief may have adequate positive support. First, it might be based on another belief that has its own adequate positive support. Thus, I might believe something not because I have direct evidence in favor of it, but because it is an entailment of something else that I believe on the basis of good evidence. Furthermore, a belief that is only believed on the basis of another belief is not, for that reason, believed strictly on the basis of its *own* truth. In other words, beliefs that are justified in this way might be purely instrumental, for example, someone believing in God merely to avoid going to hell, or believing in genetic racial inferiorities in order to justify racial prejudices *ad hoc*.

The kind of justification which moral knowledge requires needs to be both positive and evidential. That is, a moral belief will be justified (and thus a candidate for knowledge) if the believer has good reasons or evidence for the truth of that belief itself, above and beyond any benefits that might accrue to her for so believing. Of course, this still leaves unanswered precisely what counts as "evidence" or "good reasons" for a moral belief. (This question will be addressed in the next sections where we will consider the possibilities of "self-evident" moral beliefs and a reliabilist model of moral perception.) But for now, we can note a few more features of the positive-evidential account of moral justification.

First, it is important to remember that, although evidence provides justification for moral beliefs, it does not *make* them true because, for the realist, the truth of moral beliefs is evidence-independent. Second, positive-evidential justification does not require that the truth of justified moral beliefs be logically necessary. Sinnott-Armstrong has defended a strange kind of moral skepticism by arguing that genuine moral knowledge requires specifically "philosophical" justification, rather than merely "everyday" justification. This distinction stems from the recognition that justification is often relative to contrast classes. For example, the belief that "skyscrapers are big" may be justified relative to an anthropocentric scale, but unjustified relative to an astronomical scale.[3] Everyday justification involves weighing a belief against the familiar and ordinarily encountered contrast classes; philosophical justification involves weighing a belief against every logically possible contrast class. Sinnott-Armstrong is right to distinguish levels of justification by reference to contrast classes, but it seems implausible that moral knowledge (or any kind of knowledge, for that matter) requires exclusively philosophical justification. Philosophical justification is an attractive ideal for beliefs because it promises utter certainty. But requiring that a belief be justified relative to every single logically possible contrast class is too demanding—it would deny justification to all but beliefs about logically necessary propositions. Moral realism need not be committed to moral values being necessary in this way, or even to them being insensitive to particularistic representations: realist values can still generate obligations and true moral propositions which are nonetheless relative to particular contexts and situations.

One final feature needs to be noted about the requirement that moral justification consist of positive-evidential justification. When we talk about justifying our beliefs, we often make distinctions between being able to justify them to ourselves and being able to justify them to others. One person might find a belief personally sensible and yet be unable to justify it to another person because of limitations of linguistic representation or differences in experience. For example, I might be justified in my belief about the grandeur of a view from a tall mountain, but be unable to justify that belief to someone who has not experienced anything similar or because the view cannot be "put into words." For this reason, we can distinguish *personal* justification from *public* justification. Many philosophers (e.g. Robert Audi) have assumed that justification requires intersubjective consensus, reportability, and the capacity to persuade others.[4] I see no reason for this. One person simply might be privy to unique experiences that justify her belief, but which cannot be replicated or shared in an effort to justify the belief to others.

In summary, we have seen that epistemic justification must be formed on the basis of good positive evidence for the truth of the proposition that is believed, and not just because there is no evidence against the possible truth of that proposition or because such belief would produce desirable consequences. Such evidence need not be of a public or reportable nature, and it certainly need not deal exclusively in only necessary math-like truths. With these caveats about justified true belief in mind, let us turn to a brief exploration of some of the leading contemporary theories of epistemic justification. Again, the guiding thread throughout this discussion will be that *foundationalism* emerges as the theory most conducive to realism vis-à-vis the requirements that epistemic justification be of a positive-evidential nature.

The advantages of foundationalism can be seen by briefly surveying some of its alternatives. One influential contemporary theory of epistemic justification is *coherentism*. Coherentism is the view that a moral belief is justified if it is part of a network of other beliefs, all of which are "jointly consistent, comprehensive, and connected by logical, probabilistic, and explanatory relations" (Sayre-McCord 1985).[5] According to coherentism, justification is necessarily circular. In this way, the justificatory structure of coherentism has been famously compared to a *raft* (Sosa 1991): beliefs have no deeper justifying foundations, but instead float together by means of mutually supporting one another. The problem for realists, however, is that there is no provision within coherentism that any of the beliefs in the justificatory network actually be *true* (at least in the sense of correspondence to external facts which we examined in §2.1). An entire set of false beliefs could still be logically consistent with one another. Indeed, coherentism seems unable to address the possibility of epistemic *bias* by providing a disincentive for ever entertaining new beliefs (even true ones) that do not match one's current beliefs. Furthermore, whether a belief is consistent with a set of other beliefs is largely a matter of whether or not that belief is *not* logically *in*compatible with the set. But in this way coherentism seems to fall back on a negative form of justification—where a belief is epistemically acceptable insofar as there are no reasons or evidence against it—which we have seen is unsatisfactory.

Another influential theory of moral justification has been offered by *contractarianism*.[6] Contractarianism can be expressed as the view that moral justification is gleaned through some process of rational agreement. But again, from a realist perspective, it is not clear that contractarianism fares any better than coherentism as an adequate theory of epistemic justification. For one thing, the contractarian tradition has been historically associated with antirealism and constructivism (cf. §2.2), where statements about moral values become true *because* of rational agreement or consensus. But more importantly, contractarianism seems too grounded in our own self-interest to adequately accompany a theory like moral realism. After all, it may not be strictly "irrational" to agree to a rule or law according to which people with green eyes are killed so long as you do not personally have green eyes. The realist might want to maintain that this kind of distinction is arbitrary and immoral, and yet there could still be certain nonmoral or instrumental reasons to make such a distinction. Contractarianism would apparently be unable to condemn the killing of green-eyed individuals if this practice were the result of a process of rational agreement on the part of the majority or those in power; the killing would be *ipso facto* justified *because* it was agreed upon.

Coherentism and contractarianism both fail to support moral realism as well as the requirement that moral-epistemic justification be positive and evidential. Moral *contextualism* has been a third influential theory of epistemic justification—yet, this option has largely represented various compromises and combinations of coherentism and contractarianism. For example, understood as the view that justification is partly dependent on certain facts about oneself or one's environment, contextualism is uncontroversial and compatible with any number of other theories of justification. Mark Timmons (1996) calls this sort of view "circumstantial contextualism" and attributes it to Alvin Goldman, Joshua Cohen, and Ernest Sosa. Timmons also distinguishes "normative context-ualism" (according to which justification is dependent on some "relevant set of epistemic practices and norms") and "structural contextualism" (according to which justification is dependent on other beliefs, terminating in "contextually basic beliefs" that are not in need of justification). Normative contextualism is incompatible with moral realism—it views moral truths as *constituted* by epistemic practices or norms. And, at least as Timmons has defined it, structural contextualism is not substantively different from foundationalism, which we shall examine in the next section.

None of this is to say, however, that either coherentism or contractarianism is necessarily false or even incompatible with the truth of moral realism. After all, as we have seen, moral realism is only a thesis about the existence of moral properties, not about whether or not we are able to justify beliefs about those values. It might be that realist moral properties exist, but that our epistemic capacities are limited in such a way that we cannot know when or if our moral beliefs are justified. Indeed, it may be that coherentist or contractarian justification is simply the best our moral beliefs can hope for. This might make it possible to be a moral realist *metaphysically*, while being a coherentist or contractarian *epistemologically*. On the other hand, since both coherentism and contractarianism are unable to rule out the possibility of justified moral beliefs that could nonetheless be false, it would be nice if realists could defend an account that requires epistemic justification to somehow link up with the truth of the propositions on which those beliefs are based. One traditional way of securing this linkage between justification and the correspondent truth of propositions has been by appeal to *foundationalism*.

Foundationalism may be expressed as the view that beliefs can receive justification by being grounded by other beliefs that are "foundational" or "basic," meaning that they themselves do not require external justification. As Ernest Sosa (1991) has famously expressed it, foundationalist justification is structured like a *pyramid*, where beliefs at the "top" are only as sturdy as their foundations. The motivation to identify foundational beliefs has typically been to avoid the apparent threat of an infinite regress of justification. For example, if I am asked why I believe that I should put on a coat before I go outside, I may appeal to my antecedent belief that it is raining outside. And if I am asked why I believe it is raining outside, I may appeal to my belief that I hear the sound of rain. It is easy to see how this line of questioning could threaten to go on *ad infinitum* until I either beg the question or arrive at some rock-bottom indubitable fact that resists this sort of questioning.

Foundationalism, however, it has foundered on controversy concerning precisely which beliefs (if any) are the foundational ones. Very often candidates for basic beliefs are suspiciously self-serving. Plus, what one person claims is "indubitable" is often open to doubt by another person. In moral epistemology, such basic or "self-evident" beliefs have historically been referred to as "ethical intuitions," to which we turn in the next section.

6.3 Ethical intuitionism

Coupled with the influence of post-Kantian idealism, analytic metaethics in the nineteenth and early twentieth centuries coalesced around a view that can be seen as combining the theories of moral fitness and moral sense into a new epistemological category of ethical "intuitions." It is important not to conflate "ethical intuitionism" as we are considering it here as an epistemology from the way this term is occasionally used as a framework in normative ethics (e.g. Ross 1930) or as a category in moral psychology, where we can speak of ethical "intuitions" as inchoate hunches or "folk beliefs" about certain moral matters. Ethical intuitions in the epistemological sense allegedly communicate moral knowledge to us in immediate and nondiscursive ways by tapping into properties that were eternal, irreducible, and *sui generis*. We have already examined the *metaphysical* dimension of this view in Section 3.1 when we considered metaethical non-naturalism and the famous Open Question Argument. Ethical intuitionism is, thus, the *epistemological* side of non-naturalism.

As we saw in Chapters 2 and 3, the semantics and metaphysics of non-naturalism prompted a vehement backlash by emotivists and reductionists. But the backlash was just as epistemological in spirit, as intuitionism (like its moral fitness and moral sense ancestors) became associated with imprecise and romanticized notions about what is required for a moral belief to be "self-evident." According to Roger Crisp (2002: 56), most historical usages of "self-evidence" tended to associate it with obviousness and naïve certainty. It is this sort of naiveté, for example, to which Kant seems to be responding in addressing the intuitionist epistemology of so-called commonsense philosophers such as Thomas Reid and James Beattie. Kant says that the truth of a moral proposition cannot be proved,

> by appealing to it as an oracle, when one has nothing wise to adduce in one's justification ... Seen in its true light, the argument [that ethical beliefs are obvious or straightforward] is nothing better than an appeal to the verdict of the multitude, a clamor before which the philosopher blushes, and the popular witling scornfully triumphs. (1783: 6)

Kant's worry was that attempts to justify moral beliefs merely by "commonsense" will risk begging the question, resulting in an uninformative circularity where one is justified in believing something simply because one believes that thing. Defining ethical intuitions as "self-evident" in this way seems to be guilty of an *ignotum per ignotius* fallacy—trying to derive something unknown and obscure by a process that is itself unknown and obscure.

It seems, however, that what is at the heart of intuitionism's claims of "self-evidence" is simply the idea that an intuition can be justified *noninferentially*.[7] To say that a belief is noninferential is just to say that the truth of the proposition that it is believed on the basis of is not derived in any way from the truth of any other proposition or belief. That is, a belief about a proposition whose truth is not inferred from any other belief or proposition will not by definition need to appeal to any extraneous belief. Noninferentially justified beliefs are, thus, paradigmatic examples of the sort of evidential (rather than instrumental) beliefs that we have seen in Section 6.2 are necessary for positive epistemic justification. And of course noninferential beliefs are essential to foundationalism because they are able to terminate an otherwise infinite regression of justification.[8]

Specifying intuitionism as requiring only noninferential epistemic justification, rather than needing to be generically "self-evident," helps defend the view against many common and misplaced objections. For instance, it has frequently been objected that ethical intuitionism makes possible a certain indefeasibility which could lead to close-mindedness, judgmentalism, and intolerance. If moral propositions are self-evident in the way that Kant feared, then what is to prevent one agent from insisting blindly that her particular moral beliefs, which may be at odds with others' beliefs, are correct? Of course, for the moral realist, some moral beliefs *can* be genuinely correct. But the realist should not want to be saddled with an epistemology that allows *any* moral belief to be justified just in case an individual agent thinks that it is. We want an epistemology that has the resources to allow us to criticize beliefs (even our own) no matter how firmly we hold them. But if it is sufficient for the justification of a moral belief to simply say that "the belief seems true to me," then how can we avoid a pernicious dogmatism? To put it differently, how could we ever be rationally persuaded to change our minds?

One way to address this worry is by noting that being non inferential need not involve being in any ways *obvious*. Robert Audi has offered several examples of propositions that are self-evident in the sense of being noninferential, without thereby being obvious. For instance, if one's parents never had any siblings, then one would ipso facto never have had any first cousins. This proposition is noninferential (indeed, it is necessary since first cousins are analytically dependent on the existence of uncles and aunts), but it is not obvious and may require a lot of time and reflection to recognize its truth. As Audi (1999: 291) says, "an intuition can be mistaken, and a mere prejudice can masquerade as an intuition."

Thus, the noninferential nature of ethical intuitions is compatible with the very real possibility of fallibility and error. For this reason, we can allow ethical intuitions to be justified noninferentially without thereby being unable to address dogmatic or close-minded beliefs. Indeed, for the moral realist, the most justified attitude toward our moral beliefs—even those held with the deepest conviction—is to treat them with a certain epistemic agnosticism, recognizing humbly that propositions whose truth is believed noninferentially could still ultimately be false. The self-evidence of ethical intuitionism is a thesis only about the fact that it is epistemically acceptable to hold beliefs that are not inferred from any other beliefs. It is not a thesis that all of the beliefs we do hold are true.

Intuitionism has also been objected to on the grounds that if ethical intuitions are self-evident, then why is it that so many people seem to disagree so much about them? (Recall the analogous discussion of the repercussions of *moral* disagreement for realism in §§4.1 and 4.2.) But since we have seen that intuitions do not need to be indefeasible or obvious in order to be noninferential, we can easily explain the dissensus of intuitions by noting that disagreeing parties could sometimes simply be wrong. If two parties disagree about an ethical issue, then even if both claim that their belief "just seems true," there is no guarantee that either belief *is* true. Many "self-evident" beliefs might nonetheless require a lot of time, familiarity, and reflection in order to recognize them *as* self-evident in the sense we have been unpacking. For example, sensory beliefs are typically justified as being noninferential—I am justified in believing that there is a computer in front of me because I see a computer in front of me and am in adequate lighting, etc.—but they still require that the epistemic agent bring herself into a certain perceptual vantage point in order to justifiably form her belief. For example, one's eyes must adjust to light after being in darkness in order to reliably see that there is a table in front of you, and one's olfactory palate must be cleansed by sniffing coffee beans before being able to recognize a new smell reliably.

In addition, even if there is dissensus about what strikes people as intuitive, it might be argued that this disagreement occurs at the level of general and abstract moral principles, and not at the level of particular moral duties. If ethical intuitions are exclusively particular (i.e. if we only ever intuit what is right or wrong to do in specific situations), then intuitionists can allow for disagreement at the level of general moral principles since such principles are not self-evident. Indeed, if "self-evidence" essentially means being noninferential, then general and abstract principles cannot be justified as self-evident since generalization and abstraction require inferences.[9] Thus, the self-evidence of intuitions is not threatened by the fact that people might disagree about what strikes them as evident if their disagreement is about beliefs that are not intuitions, but are instead more general and abstract moral principles. This itself strikes me as intuitive: for example, many political disagreements often seem to be primarily at the level of abstract and general commitments, and I suspect that many people who disagree vehemently over generalized political commitments may sometimes nonetheless agree on what is right or wrong in particular situations.

6.4 Moral perception

So far in this chapter, we have explored a variety of platforms in moral epistemology, and it was argued that moral realism may be best served by a foundationalist-intuitionism that allows for noninferentially justified moral beliefs to be fallible. But this will not have adequately rebutted Mackie's queerness objection unless realists can also specify the mechanism or process through which ethical intuitions are generated in the first place. Fortunately, intuitionists can leverage the same "companions in guilt" defense that we saw Sturgeon deploy against Harman in Section 6.1. According to this strategy, intuitionism needs to locate a sufficient number of other plausible epistemological processes to insulate it from the charge of objectionable uniqueness. In particular, moral realists in recent years have been interested in possible analogues between the noninferential mode of ethical intuitionism and the nature of nonmoral perceptual knowledge. Thus, specifying the conditions under which "moral perception" might be *reliable* will help articulate one way that certain types of moral beliefs can be epistemically justified.

Let us define perceptual beliefs as beliefs that are formed on the basis of sense perceptions. Perceptual beliefs are typically taken to be inherently justified simply in virtue of being based on sensory impressions, all things being equal. That is, if an epistemic agent sees that there is a table in front of her, then she will *ipso facto* be justified in believing that the proposition "There is a table in front of me" is true, provided that she satisfy certain basic *ceteris paribus* visual conditions. Thus, perceptual beliefs are "self-evident" in the way we have specified because we do not normally need to make any inferences when we believe in them.[10] Of course, even in the most reliable and reasonable epistemic conditions, a perceptual belief could still be *false*. Extreme skepticism about the external world or about the veridicality of appearances is still a logical possibility. But the point here is just that an agent's perceptual belief would be epistemically *justified*, not that it would be certain or even ultimately true. If "knowledge" is justified true belief (perhaps plus some caveat about being reliably acquired in some way), then perceptual beliefs might not qualify as full-blown knowledge even if they are justified and reliable. For these reasons, present accounts of both perceptual beliefs and ethical intuitions are intended only as accounts about how these beliefs and intuitions are epistemically justified, but we shouldn't beg any questions about whether this qualifies as full-blown "knowledge" or not.

So, can ethical intuitions be acquired and justified in a noninferential way? Lawrence Blum has offered a provocative model for how they might be noninferentially justified by analyzing them in the context of *moral perception*. In particular, Blum (1991) argues that moral perception must involve a certain form of "attention" to "morally salient features of situations." But which features are morally salient in which situations, and what does it mean to be "attentive" to these features?

First of all, Blum points out that there is a difference between understanding the features of a situation and understanding these features *as* morally relevant. Blum calls the first type of understanding "cognizance." To cognize a situation is to be perceptually aware of the features in the sensory environment. For instance, an agent adequately visually cognizes a situation if she receives sense impressions from everything in her visual field and correlates them with the appropriate ideas and concepts. So, for example, I am adequately cognizing my present situation because I am perceptually aware of all the objects and people in my immediate environment: I am sitting at a table with my computer in front of me in a coffee shop, there is a hipster with dark-rimmed glasses and skinny jeans sitting to my left, I can see a strange-looking dog sitting outside, etc. Mere cognizance of a situation is evaluatively neutral, that is, I do not see any of these features as reasons or motivations to act in any particular way—they are merely inert facts of which I am aware in my visual surroundings.

Cognizance is necessary, but not sufficient for moral perception, and moral perception is necessary, but not sufficient for moral action. To illustrate this, Blum describes three scenarios in which people are cognizant of the situation they are in, but fail to perceive the features of these situations as morally relevant. In one example, John and Joan are both riding on a subway with no available seats when another woman boards and stands in clear discomfort. Both John and Joan "see" this woman and "see" her discomfort, but only Joan "sees" these features *as* moral reasons to offer her seat. In Blum's terminology, both John and Joan are *cognizant* of the woman and her discomfort (i.e. they are perceptually aware of her), but only Joan interprets this cognitive judgment as a moral reason to help. Both John and Joan have visual perceptions, but Joan alone adds to this *moral* perception. Joan's moral perception consists of her being able to interpret her visual perception as containing a reason to act, where this reason is provided by the fact that the standing woman is in discomfort. The fact that the standing woman is in discomfort is a "morally salient" feature of the subway environment which Joan perceives, but which John does not, even though both John and Joan perceive that the woman is in discomfort. Perception of morally salient features in this way involves, in Blum's words, "distinct awareness" and "paying attention."

So, to morally perceive a situation, an agent needs to interpret the features of the situation as morally salient by being attentive to them. For the moral realist, which features of a situation are the salient or relevant ones are determined by real, evidence-independent moral values. Thus, the discomfort of the standing woman could be an instantiation or embodiment of the moral value that unnecessary suffering is morally bad, that we should help those in need, etc. Moral realism is not committed to the defense of which specific features are the morally relevant ones (although §4.3 offers such a list) just that moral relevance will be established by the fact that the features are instantiations of moral values that are causally independent of any beliefs about them and which are capable of being expressed cognitively in truth-apt propositions.[11] Features that are morally salient or relevant in this way will inherently provide reasons to act accordingly. Thus, perception of morally salient features of situations can be associated with the position of *reasons-externalism* (i.e. the view that moral knowledge provides its own justifying reasons to act independent of the contents of an agent's internal motivational set) that was defended in Section 5.2.[12] Thus, for the realist, there are objectively salient or relevant features of the subway situation that give both John and Joan reasons to give up their seat; but only Joan, because she is attentive to these features (beyond merely being cognizant of them), will recognize these reasons *as* reasons, and will form the belief that the right thing to do is to help the woman. This is not to say that Joan's moral perception necessarily provides her with *overriding* reasons to act, or that she will necessarily even be *motivated* to act in the first place. Indeed, Blum allows for motivational externalism (cf. §5.1) by describing another passenger *Ted* who both cognizes the situation and also perceives the relevant features as morally salient, but who simply doesn't *feel* like helping (Blum 1994: 33).

John McDowell (1979) articulates a very similar account of moral perception that involves "sensitivity" to moral salient features of situations. The difference between McDowell's *sensitivity* and Blum's *attentiveness*, however, seems to lie in the role that the two assign to emotional reactions. For McDowell, sensitivity to morally salient features is constituted by a disposition to act in certain ways, where dispositions to act need not have any affective dimension. Blum's attentiveness, by contrast, involves dispositions to act that require an affective dimension, so that moral perception "informs [the agent's] emotional reaction to things" and influences what she notices (Blum 1994: 43–4, n. 21). Arne Vetleson (1994) has offered a similar expression of the need for an emotive aspect to moral perception, which he takes to be a refinement of Blum's view. As he says, emotions are "active and indispensable in disclosing to us that other's weal and woe is somehow at stake in a given situation" (Vetleson 1994: 154). As both Blum and Vetleson note, this has the consequence that agents are to a certain extent held morally responsible for their emotional reactions—a point that we examined in Section 5.3.[13]

Of course, in the case of nonmoral visual perception, we are familiar with the necessary *ceteris paribus* epistemic conditions that an agent must satisfy for any beliefs formed on the basis of this perception to be justified. For example, the agent must be viewing the object that is perceived in adequate lighting conditions, from an appropriate distance and perspective, and in a situation that she reasonably believes to be veridical (e.g. not in a known virtual-reality environment, etc.). These *ceteris paribus* conditions are sufficient for sense perceptions to be justifiably translated into corresponding perceptual beliefs; but they are merely necessary conditions for translation into justified ethical intuitions because mere cognizance of a situation is not sufficient for moral perception. Moral perception requires first and foremost that the agent satisfy ordinary visual conditions of epistemic reliability— moral perceptions will not be justified if they are formed in contexts without good lighting, at too great a distance or too obtuse a visual perspective, or in situations that we have good reason to believe are not veridical. For example, my perception that someone is suffering and needs help would not be justified if I am only barely able to see that person, if I know that the person is an actor in a play whose part involves her character being in pain, etc. So, if these perceptual conditions are only necessary for moral perception, what further conditions are required for *sufficient* justified moral perception?

Blum discusses several factors that help illuminate what conditions might be additionally necessary for moral perception. In the example discussed above, John's failure to give up his seat might be explained by his being "lazy" or "self-absorbed" (Blum 1994: 33). It is important to note that this laziness and self-absorption must be interpreted as specifically *epistemic* faults. That is, John is epistemically lazy and self-absorbed by not paying attention to the standing woman's discomfort, that is, by not noticing it as morally relevant. This kind of epistemic laziness and self-absorption is different from the traits of a different individual, Ted, who perceives the discomfort as morally relevant, but who doesn't care because he is too lazy or self-absorbed. We may well be morally responsible for *epistemic* virtues (or lack thereof), but if so it is presumably to a different degree and in a different way than for *moral* traits/virtues (cf. DePaul and Zagzebski 2003).

Blum describes two additional ways in which we can fail to perceive the morally relevant features of a situation despite being cognizant of them. In another example, Blum describes Julio who works for Theresa and whose intense pain makes him ask Theresa for a break from work. Let us say that Julio's pain is a real and morally salient feature of the situation. In Blum's example, Theresa is cognizant of Julio's pain (indeed, she even talks with him about it), but she does not perceive his pain as the morally relevant factor that it is because she has a "personal resistance to acknowledging" pain as a legitimate excuse for a break from work. Blum calls this personal resistance a "bias." We should be specific, however, in characterizing the exact nature of Theresa's epistemic state. Someone can be either consciously or unconsciously biased, and someone else can be biased in a way that informs her actions and practices. It is common in antibias training (Derman-Sparks 1997; Tatum 1997) to distinguish the former instances as *bias* proper and the latter as *prejudice*, a species of bias. Thus, all prejudice involves bias (whether unconscious or conscious), but not all bias needs to lead to prejudice. In Blum's example, Theresa is consciously aware of her personal resistance to admitting that Julio's pain is a morally relevant factor (perhaps because she associates pain with weakness or because she is uncomfortable with the intimacy that recognizing another's weakness might involve), so her failure to give Julio a break is more a function of prejudice. Suffice to say, it seems we are more blameworthy for prejudices than for biases, given the comparably greater degree of control vis-à-vis the former.

In a third example, Blum describes Tim's (who is White) failure to perceive the injustice of his getting a taxi at the expense of a Black family being passed over. Tim was cognizant of the situation of the Black family being overlooked by the taxi driver, but did not initially perceive it as the morally salient feature that it was.

After some reflection at a later point, however, Tim comes to see the moral relevance of his experience with the taxi, recognizes it as an injustice, and feels bad that he did not perceive it and act on it at the time.

Blum is not explicit about what exactly goes on in Tim's reflection, and there are many possible explanations of his failure to initially perceive the moral relevance of the taxi situation. On the one hand, his inattentiveness could have been the result of a bias that caused him to overlook the plight of the Black family. Here, Tim's failure would seem to be more an instance of unconscious *bias* and less of active *prejudice* than Theresa's is, since Tim would have been moved to act if he had perceived the injustice, as opposed to Theresa, who refuses to act despite knowing that Julio is in pain. On the other hand, Tim's inattentiveness could have been the result of failing to translate an *abstract* commitment to ending racial injustice into a sensitivity to a *particular* instance of racial injustice—as, for instance, if he became convinced of the injustice of racial prejudice in a classroom or by reading a book, but had never personally encountered instances of such injustice and so was unsure how to recognize them when they actually occur. Similarly, Tim's inattentiveness could have resulted from a failure to extend his commitment about the impermissibility of another kind of injustice (maybe toward a different race or social group) to the case of the taxi driver's injustice toward the Black family.

Note that to say that the *perception* of the injustice of the Black family being passed over is noninferential is not to say that the *injustice itself* is noninferential. After all, what makes the Black family being passed over by the taxi an instance of injustice is the fact that Blacks have been systematically oppressed in the United States. The injustice of the family being passed over is derivative of a certain history and cultural state of affairs. If a taxi were to pass by a Black family in a society that did not have the same oppressive history or the same ethnic categories, then the scenario would not be one of injustice (at least not *racial* injustice—it still might be wrong for other reasons) and *a fortiori* there would be nothing morally salient for Tim to perceive or fail to perceive. But just because *what* is morally salient may be determined inferentially, this should not be confused with the fact that the *perception* of what is morally salient is noninferential.

I suspect that many of our moral perceptual failures do not fit neatly into just one of these explanations. As Blum recognizes, moral perception is not a unified or monolithic process, but "involves multifarious moral and psychological processes" (1994: 31). And failures of moral perception are presumably just as multifarious. But Blum's examples still help identify several of the factors involved in failures of moral perception, above and beyond the ordinary *ceteris paribus* conditions of nonmoral sensory perception:

- We can be epistemically lazy or self-absorbed (as John is);

- We can be prejudiced (as Theresa is); or

- We can be unconsciously biased (as Tim is), perhaps because our moral commitments are too abstract or perhaps because they are insufficiently generalized.

At any rate, this (nonexhaustive) list identifies a few specific ways in which an epistemic agent in a morally relevant situation can be cognizant of certain features, but fail to be attentive to these features as morally salient.

6.5 Summary

Moral realism requires a nonqueer epistemology capable of responding to worries about explanatory power and which situates the process of the acquisition and justification of moral beliefs in the context of other plausible epistemic domains. To address the first worry, we considered the role that scientific postulations play in explaining our observations and explored an analogous role for moral postulations. In response to the challenge regarding the acquisition of moral beliefs, we considered twentieth-century intuitionism as a possible realist platform. After surveying some of the alternative accounts of epistemic justification, such as coherentism and contextualism, it was argued that foundationalism best complements moral realism, and that a noninferential version of ethical intuitionism is the best way to understand realist foundationalism. Finally, we explored the plausibility of a perceptual model of intuitionism. Not only does appealing to a theory of moral perception help explicate moral realism, foundationalism, *and* intuitionism, it also helps sync the epistemological dimensions of realism with the motivational and metaphysical commitments of realism we examined in earlier chapters.

CHAPTER SEVEN

The applications of realism

The preceding chapters of this book have articulated the basic commitments of a robust moral realism, involving the existence of moral truths which are capable of being expressed cognitively and whose truth is determined by a correspondence to stance-independent properties. Beyond these commitments, different varieties of moral realism will arise based on other ontological, psychological, and epistemological questions. Regardless of the specific formulation of realism, as we discussed in Section 1.2, metaethical theorizing does not exist in a vacuum. It is embedded for better or worse in concrete political, anthropological, and normative contexts. The commitment to "applied metaethics" which we addressed at the outset of this book can now be tested by exploring what moral realism in general—and pluralistic moral realism in particular— might have to say about pressing first-order moral questions. In the sections that follow, we will examine how a realist might approach three separate practical issues. First, what resources might realism offer for adjudicating real-life *conflicts* between moral values and obligations? Second, what implications vis-à-vis the *toleration* of moral differences does realism suggest? Third, how might realism be leveraged to address the question of global *human rights*?

7.1 Moral dilemmas and tragedy

Previous chapters have addressed the difficulties inherent in anchoring morality to something "re-enchanting," as well as the ways

in which we often fail to perceive or act on moral truths. Another
familiar feature of the moral terrain, however, is the possibility of
moral dilemmas. The literature on moral dilemmas is large and
controversial, but for the purposes of the present discussion, let
us define a "moral dilemma" as a situation in which someone is
presented with two or more moral considerations, both of which
are equally morally obligatory, but the performance of either one
of which is mutually exclusive (given the practical realities of the
situation) with the performance of the other (cf. Gowans 1987: 3).
Many types of moral dilemmas do not seem to raise unique
issues for moral realism, for example: (1) *motivational* conflicts
between a moral consideration and a nonmoral consideration;
(2) *epistemological* conflicts in which an agent simply does not
know what are the appropriate moral considerations in a given
situation; (3) *dirty hands* conflicts in which two or more known
moral considerations are in tension, but in such a way that an agent
has recourse to a justifiable method for ranking them (a method
which, nevertheless, may countenance "collateral damage"); and,
finally, (4) what might be called *karmic* conflicts in which an agent
faces two known and mutually exclusive moral considerations
which cannot be ranked, but which also are in conflict only on
account of a previous moral error or poor decision on the part of
the agent. In contrast to these types of moral dilemmas—which
seem attributable to moral laziness, ignorance, *real politick*, and
poor judgment, respectively—many have recognized an additional
species of dilemma which is uniquely and troublingly metaethical.
Such putative dilemmas are located unnervingly in the tragic way
the world itself unfolds, such that even the most diligent, thoughtful,
and motivated agent might nonetheless find herself forced into
unavoidable wrongdoing. For these reasons, let us call these sorts
of moral dilemmas *tragic*.

One metaethical objection to the existence of tragic dilemmas
is the apparent threat that they would undermine the *raison d'être*
of first-order normative theorizing. For, if situations exist in which
an agent has no justifiable moral reason to adopt one course of
action over another, such that wrongdoing is unavoidable, then
moral theory has failed to instruct the agent about what she should
do. Michael Stocker interprets this objection as voicing the worry
about ethics becoming contaminated by a kind of "romanticism
and escapism" (Stocker 1990: 86), reflecting a more general trend

in ethics that Thomas Nagel has dubbed "the new romanticism" in metaethics (Nagel 1995: 174). As Stocker presents it, this worry combines anxieties about moral philosophy being either impractical (i.e. by telling us to pursue mutually exclusive values), incomplete (i.e. by not giving guidance about which value to pursue), or antirealist (i.e. by reducing values to culturally relative constructs in order to account for why they conflict). Earl Conee, in particular, has emphasized the first and second of these worries as sufficient grounds for rejecting the existence of tragic dilemmas, writing that if such dilemmas were real, "their possibility would cast a shroud of impenetrable obscurity over the concept of moral obligation" (in Gowans 1987: 239).

Yet, despite the potential for disrupting our theorizing, the *experience* of tragedy is nonetheless a deeply grounded feature of moral phenomenology. Think of how often highly praiseworthy individuals nonetheless insist that they "should have done more" (even if they *could not* have).[1] Indeed, we tend to find such attitudes particularly desirable and expected in our leaders (at least insofar as a given leadership role is viewed as having any kind of *moral* dimension). Something like the following scenario is hypothetical, but arguably quite representative of prevalent attitudes toward leaders' moral assessments of themselves: A military commander—on a secretive, but humanitarian reconnaissance mission—is presented with the forced and momentous choice between, on the one hand, actively sacrificing a soldier under her command who has inadvertently wandered across a foreign border; or, on the other hand, intervening to save this individual, but thereby jeopardizing the reconnaissance as well as probably instigating an international conflict which would undoubtedly lead to greater loss of life.

The commander might respond in any number of ways. She could flip a coin to decide between the two options. Or she might appeal to a normative theory to generate a justified course of action. Regardless of her decision-procedure, however, what she should *not* do is emerge from the quandary without any personal misgivings, self-recriminations, or what Williams (1965) has famously referred to as "moral remainders." For, imagine if our commander in fact succeeded in deriving (quickly!) a legitimate and plausible application of, say, the principle of utility, which dictated that she ought to sacrifice the errant soldier for the sake of preventing a much greater overall harm. Even if this makes sense of her choice to sacrifice the soldier, we still might deny that it thereby vitiates the *pro tanto* wrongness of killing an innocent person. In Stocker's words, the obligations that the commander faces—namely, to sacrifice the soldier or not to sacrifice the soldier—are "double-counted" rather than canceling out one another. Indeed, we would be morally critical of the commander's character if she evidenced no personal agony (either during her actual deliberation or after the fact) over her decision.[2] That is, it would be morally callous to cite, with unconflicted and calm self-assurance, a derivation from a principle, no matter how defensible or unavoidable a situation may be. Stocker articulates the requirement of this sort of sensitivity to tragic dilemmas by what he calls a "taxi-meter sensibility of accurately noting the cost of everything" (Stocker 1990: 16). Speaking of the sort of "admirable immorality" embodied by the agonizing commander, Stocker writes that, "for someone with such a sensibility, there would be intertwined with the pleasure of giving a present to a child a full awareness of its cost; and with the appreciation of a drive in the countryside, the cost per mile" (1990: 16).

The question of the existence of tragic dilemmas is vexing enough on its own, but it raises two special challenges for metaethics. First, how can the stance-independent properties which the realist recognizes be instantiated in such tragically impossible ways? If such dilemmas do exist, might they not be better explained by metaethical antirealism? After all, it would be unsurprising for culturally constructed institutions and norms to occasionally come into irresolvable conflicts, since these institutions and norms are understood as arising in response to contingent cultural needs. It seems far harder for a moral realist to acknowledge the existence of tragic dilemmas—for how could reality itself contain contradictions?

A second metaethical challenge raised by tragic dilemmas concerns how we respond emotionally to them. As we have seen, there seem to be situations in which we would appropriately blame people for failure to feel the full weight of a moral tragedy. Yet, as we saw in Section 5.3, one of the potential strengths of moral realism is its ability to make sense of when and why moral emotional responses are appropriate or not. So if emotional responses to tragic dilemmas—for example, guilt, blame, regret—are appropriate, then realism will need to make sense of them.

Although these are two serious challenges for realism, it's important to note that realists also have several advantages over alternative metaethics vis-à-vis tragedy. Most importantly, realism can help make sense of the feeling of *necessity* constitutive of a tragic dilemma. By contrast, it seems hard to see how antirealists could ground this necessity, since moral obligation on their view is ultimately generated by culturally relative or artificial sources. On the other hand, one of the venerable precepts of moral philosophy has been the so-called ought implies can (OIC) principle, which holds that moral responsibility ascriptions are grounded in success or failure to satisfy "ought" requirements, and that an "ought" requirement is only legitimate if it is possible for us to satisfy it. Kant famously expresses the core concept thus:

> Taken objectively, morality is in itself practical, for it is the totality of unconditionally binding laws according to which we ought to act, and once one has acknowledged the authority of its concept of duty, it would be utterly absurd to continue wanting to say that one cannot do his duty. For if that were so, then this concept would disappear from morality. (1795: 127)

OIC has a strong intuitive appeal, although several of its loopholes have been well documented (Sinnott-Armstrong 1984). At root, OIC appeals to a sense of fairness. It would be deeply unfair, so the view would have it, for morality to hold us accountable for things over which we have no deliberative control. Understood in this way, OIC is incompatible with tragic dilemmas. In a genuinely tragic dilemma there are multiple competing "ought" requirements which cannot be ranked or systematized, but each of which nevertheless generates a binding obligation. If we must choose between preserving OIC versus acknowledging the existence of tragedy, we should abandon OIC. Tragedy may be existentially uncomfortable, but given the weight of phenomenological support for it, OIC is mere wishful thinking by comparison. We have no intuitions of the reality of OIC apart from its theoretic attractiveness, whereas we have plenty of intuitive evidence for the reality of moral dilemmas which do not resolve neatly without moral stain or remainder (cf. DeLapp 2012; Greenspan 1995: 109–50; Nussbaum 1986).

Any form of moral realism can be consistent with OIC, but only pluralistic moral realism can accommodate tragedy by grounding feelings of tragic necessity in something objective. Only pluralistic realism supplies an ontology for moral properties which generate tragically incompatible "ought" requirements. Recall our discussion of potential conflicts between plural but realist values. In a trolley-type dilemma, for example, any number of basic realist values can come into conflict: we might be faced with the tragic option of saving the life of a loved one versus saving the life of a socially valuable stranger. Taking this dilemma seriously means feeling the unresolved and messy nature of the conflict. Neither option is without sacrifice and it would be morally inappropriate and callous to experience this sacrifice without some feeling of self-doubt, recrimination, or misgiving. Taking tragedy seriously phenomenologically in this way means also taking it seriously metaethically, since part of the phenomenology of tragedy is the sense that the unavoidable wrongness is grounded in some necessity. Pluralistic realism, therefore, has an explanatory and practical advantage over its alternatives since it can accommodate both the feelings of necessity (obligations are generated by stance-independent features of reality outside our control) as well as irresolvable conflict (the features of reality are ontologically plural).

A potential objection to this application of realism is that it would seem to render the scope of our obligations impossibly out of reach, resulting in crippling self-recrimination for never fully being able to do the right thing. The derivative worry here would seem to be that rejecting OIC would be morally masochistic, condemning us to a depressing and disillusioning imperfectability. And yet, despite these worries, such attitudes of self-doubt are ubiquitous in the experience of moral exemplars. Indeed, as we discussed above, we often expect and admire those attitudes in people. If we think this is psychologically unpalatable, then we should be forced to regard as pathological and misplaced the experience of those who constitute the very standard by which we measure moral goodness and rightness. Furthermore, it is not the case that tragic self-recrimination always does (let alone *must*) result in depression, disillusionment, or debilitation. Numerous studies have vindicated the positive motivational role that, for example, moral guilt can have on behavior (cf. Dovidio 1984: 391–6).

In addition, there are notable instances in which we think moral self-recrimination is appropriate, even for wrongdoing that was tragically unavoidable. Consider, for instance, the inherited racial privilege of a White individual in a society that is characterized by historic and systemic inequality against non-Whites. Even if this individual is not personally racially biased or prejudicial—indeed, even she actively condemns racial discrimination—she nonetheless benefits from her racial membership in a morally indefensible way. Racial privilege may, thus, operate in a manner akin to inheriting stolen property, but in such a way that one cannot relinquish the inheritance. In this way, the racially privileged individual is confronted with a bona fide tragic dilemma: on the one hand, she should not participate in discriminatory practices; but, on the other hand, she cannot help but participate in them. As with the commander who feels self-recrimination for her decision to cause the death of a soldier, regardless of her inability to have acted in a way that causes *no* death, so too is it appropriate that the privileged person ought to feel self-recrimination despite her not being able to avoid the harm that her privilege effects. As we might put it, the person is *morally* responsible for the benefits her racial privilege bestows upon her, even though she might not be *causally* responsible for them.

Consider how abhorrent we would regard a person who, confronted with her racial privilege, merely shrugs and says blithely, "Oh well, it is certainly a shame that there is discrimination which I benefit from; but after all, there is nothing I can do about it, so why should I feel bad?" On the contrary, recalling Stocker's injunction about "counting the cost," it is not merely morally appropriate, but obligatory that a privileged individual experience personal guilt or regret for her unavoidable complicity in such a state of affairs. Of course, this is not to suggest that merely feeling bad is *all* she ought to do in the face of her inherited inequality. She also ought to try to work toward ending the system which perpetuates the inequalities in the first place.[3] But still, we morally admire those who *feel* the tragic dilemma of racial privilege personally, and we view as escapist and inauthentic those who do not feel this way.[4]

"Counting the costs" in this way does not need to be done morosely or out of obsessive "moral fetishism" (Smith 1994: 75). It is in such a vein that Susan Wolf (1982) famously lampoons "moral saints" as being characterized by an objectionable high-handedness and moral arrogance. Yet, if we jettison OIC on the realist grounds we have been considering, we can account for the fact that actual moral exemplars are neither of these things. Rather than being morally arrogant about having satisfied all of their moral obligations, it is far more likely that exemplars would feel humbled by the fact that they are not morally perfect; and rather than being morally high-handed or holier-than-thou, we should expect exemplars instead to be enormously tolerant of the moral shortcomings of others, sensitive as they are to their own (unavoidable) shortcomings. Moreover, the sensitivity to tragic dilemmas is often embodied in the moral personality of exemplars right alongside desirable, nonmoral traits such as humor, irony, and fun-lovingness (Carbonell 2009). Contrary to Wolf's dismal portraits, the characteristics of actual exemplars include humility, solidarity with "other sinners," and an enhanced motivational capacity.

7.2 The paradox of toleration

Although realists are not social constructivists (recall §2.2), they still recognize that a large function of morality is social coordination. And even if a realist can rebut arguments about the diversity of moral opinion undermining stance-independent moral properties (§§4.1–4.3), realists must still recognize the *prima facie* persistence of this diversity. These two factors—the social coordinative function of morality and *prima facie* moral diversity—make toleration an especially vital virtue. If we want to avoid a "war of all against all," the obvious strategy seems to be to find some way to live in peace with one another. In this way, tolerance can be seen as a sort of higher order virtue of a society—one that makes possible the coexistence of other values. However, it is rare for societies that endorse some form of tolerance to surround the concept with anything more than empty platitudes and rhetorical prescriptions, altogether avoiding the tricky issues of specification and justification. As David Heyd observes, "Our firm belief in the value of tolerance is not matched by analogous theoretical certitude" (1996: 3).

Traditionally, tolerance has been closely associated with metaethical relativism. Neil Levy claims that, "The perception that relativism promotes, or is the expression of, tolerance of difference is almost certainly the single most important factor in explaining its attraction" (2002: 56). Shafer-Landau adds that one of the reasons why "most students regard moral skepticism as the default position in ethics" is because it seems to be the best justification for tolerance

(2004: 30–1). In other words, tolerance is not prescribed because antirealism is thought to be true; rather, antirealism is thought to be true as the best explanation of an antecedent commitment to tolerance. Thus, metaethical relativism seems frequently motivated by the normative concerns of dealing with moral differences. But interestingly enough, realism is also frequently motivated by the same normative concerns for tolerance.

Of course, tolerance is certainly not strictly entailed by either realism or antirealism. First, tolerance is obviously not a necessary consequence of moral realism. It is consistent with realism to think that moral knowledge justifies or even requires *not* tolerating certain moral differences. Indeed, the possibility of judgmentalism has been one of the traditional indictments of realism, with criticisms pointing to the history of genocide, cultural imperialism, and ethnocentrism that have resulted from one party claiming that it alone possesses the moral truth. Contrary to an exclusive commitment to stable social coordination, the realist may think that if some action, practice, or belief is morally required, then it is still morally required even if it produces unstable or disastrous social consequences: *amica pax, magis amica veritas* ("I love peace, but I love truth even more"). The point here is just that moral realism is conceptually compatible with intolerance.

Even if realism has historically been associated with intolerance, however, this compatibility should not be confused for an entailment. The realist can just as easily embrace tolerance since realism is a thesis about the existence of stance-independent properties, and is not necessarily committed to confidence concerning what those properties specifically are. And even if we *were* confident about specific moral values, as Shafer-Landau reminds us, "The falsity of a moral view doesn't, by itself, imply anything about what response we should make" (2004: 31).[5] In other words, Tara might feel that she is right and that Rebecca is wrong, but might nonetheless think that intervening in Rebecca's choices is none of her business. Refraining from interference can be explained in a number of ways: uncertainty about one's own position, uncertainty about another's position (which may amount to giving that person the "benefit of the doubt"), or the belief that intervention, even if morally justified, would be pragmatically counterproductive. For instance, the claim that intervention would be counterproductive is central to the argument about religious tolerance in Locke's *A Letter concerning*

Toleration (1689): we should not force others to subscribe to our religion because (a) faith must be uncoerced for it to be meaningful, (b) change is most effective when internalized, and (c) pushing someone to do something often produces greater resistance in retaliation. Similarly, in the case of Western intervention concerning foreign practices of female genital cutting (a topic to which we shall return later in this section), Ellen Gruenbaum observes that, "simplistic condemnations are not only ineffectual but can also stimulate strong defensive reactions" (2000: 25).

Furthermore, despite the traditional associations of metaethical relativism with tolerance, relativists have faced serious obstacles to adequately justifying tolerance. Specifically, it has been argued that relativism contradicts itself if it postulates tolerance as a universal value. Metaethical relativism, as we defined it in Chapter 4, is the thesis that there is no moral value independent of particular cultural practices or endorsements. This has been thought to justify tolerance, for if there is no cross-cultural criterion for what is right and wrong, then we have no business making judgments of other practices. However, realists have been suspicious of relativism's usurpation of tolerance. How can the relativist believe that tolerance is a universal value if the relativist denies the possibility of universal values in the first place? The relativist seems to be making an unjustified exception to her relativism: why is tolerance alone exempt from relativity? Why not some other or additional values? Furthermore, the position seems to self-destruct when we consider whether we ought to tolerate other actions or practices of *intolerance*. It would appear that if the metaethical relativist says *yes*, then "tolerance" has been rendered meaningless, but if she says *no*, she will have sacrificed her relativism.

Indeed, if the relativist really believes that there is no such thing as transcultural moral values, then nothing seems to prevent her from imposing her beliefs (or those of her society) upon others. Of course, the rationale for this imposition cannot be that *her* beliefs are the right ones; for such a relativist, there *are* no "right" ones (at least in the realist sense). But if there are no objectively right moral values, then *ipso facto* there are no wrong ones, and so, imposition, genocide, imperialism, etc. cannot be justifiably condemned. For this reason, it might be thought that realism can more effectively ground tolerance because for the realist societies are not the originators of moral values. Individuals, practices, and even entire cultures can be morally wrong since what is morally right is not up to us. For the realist, tolerance is checked and balanced by independent moral values: not only could tolerance itself be an independent value for the realist, but it could be further justified as a response to the large possibility of moral error.

Realists have made much of this apparent dilemma. But it does not necessarily show that metaethical relativism is *incompatible* with an endorsement of tolerance. The careful relativist will need to point out that, while tolerance cannot be justified by any transcultural criteria, it may still be true that members of a certain society ought to be tolerant of differences if commitment to tolerance is something the society values. David Wong (1984: 189) makes this point very clearly: a moral principle can be true of all agents without being universally justifiable to them. That is, while it would contradict metaethical relativism to claim that tolerance is *universally* prescribed, it is perfectly consistent to maintain that tolerance is prescribed for societies with certain moral beliefs. Of course, the relativist cannot convince another society to tolerate unless that society already has some antecedent commitment to tolerance—whether explicit, inchoate, or derivable from other moral commitments. In this way, while there may be no external (or objective) reasons for tolerance, according to the relativist, a society may still have resources *internal* to it that can ground tolerance.

Wong's move allows the metaethical relativist to justify tolerance without contradiction, but only a very restricted sort of tolerance. Specifically, tolerance will only be justifiable to societies that are already in some way committed to it. If a society has intolerant practices, the relativist can rationally motivate change if and only if these practices can be shown to be inconsistent with other commitments to tolerance. But if the society does not have these other commitments, then no amount of rational debate can persuade the practices to change.[6] Thus, relativism at best can ground tolerance as an *attitude* (of either an individual or a whole society), but not as a stance-independent property. Neither realism nor relativism entails tolerance, though both are compatible with it. But only realism is compatible with tolerance as a universal and transcultural value.

So far, we have been examining the metaethical commitments of tolerance, specifically with respect to the polarities of realism and relativism. However, there is considerable controversy as to what precisely tolerance itself *is*, independent of what ontological theory best justifies it. Different conceptions of tolerance will be yielded by distinguishing the *objects* of tolerance (i.e. who or what is to be tolerated), the *reasons* for tolerance, and the *scope* of tolerance (i.e. how much of something is to be tolerated). For example, how must we view alternative practices in order for it to appropriately be said that we tolerate them? In particular, is tolerance fundamentally an attitude, belief, or an action? That is, is there an important difference between saying "Jan *is* tolerant" and "Jan *acts* tolerantly"? Given this variety of senses of "tolerance," for the remainder of this section, it will help to distinguish three major subcategories:

1 Normative Tolerance

2 Epistemic Tolerance

3 Pluralistic Tolerance

The differences between these types of tolerance are based primarily on the *reasons* given to justify them. Normative tolerance is the view that we should not interfere with the practices of others regardless of the content of our moral knowledge. The reasons why we might not interfere, insofar as we believe in normative tolerance, might consist of any of the following: (a) indifference, (b) stoic resignation, or (c) pragmatic compromise. First, consider *indifference*: we might think that intervention with an alternative practice is not morally justified because the difference is not morally relevant or significant, that is, we are morally indifferent to it. For example, the difference between your choice to eat milk chocolate and my choice to eat dark chocolate has no moral repercussions and it would be silly, presumptuous, or even morally blameworthy for me to interfere with your chocolate eating.[7] Second, even if we view a difference as morally relevant, we might still restrain ourselves from intervention out of *stoic resignation*, that is, we might simply think that intervention would be ineffectual.[8] We might also refrain from intervention out of considerations for *pragmatic compromise*. That is, a reason for me not to interfere with you is that I in turn do not wish you to interfere with me. On a larger scale, we think that a certain degree of autonomy is the most effective or stable means to settle differences. Such a compromise has been the solution to many long-lasting historic conflicts. Thus, two parties may never substantively agree, but at least they can "agree to disagree."

Though the reasons given for noninterference may vary, the common denominator for normative tolerance is the belief that intervening is "none of my business"—that it would be rude, presumptuous, ineffectual, dangerous, or imperialistic. So, is this the sort of tolerance we should want? While normative tolerance may be better than no tolerance at all, it does not seem to capture the full moral importance of the concept. First, because normative tolerance is consistent with *both* realism and antirealism, it does not ground noninterference on anything universal or cross-cultural. Second, and more importantly, normative tolerance does not specify anything about our *attitudes* toward differences. All that normative tolerance requires is that the agent ought not to *act* in a way that interferes with another. But this is nonetheless compatible with *thinking* that another is morally inferior. This corresponds to a difference between what Williams (1996) calls "toleration as a practice" and "toleration as a value," and is particularly salient in the forms of nonintervention that cite stoic resignation or pragmatic compromise as reasons. For example, I can practice normative tolerance by not interfering with another practice—perhaps because I believe I have no choice or that interference is impractical—even though I could still *judge* the practice as morally inferior. But this kind of tolerance is of limited moral worth at best since a person may still be perniciously and wholeheartedly biased and judgmental even if she never acts on her bigotry. After all, it is possible to be a politically correct bigot, that is, believing one thing, but not voicing it. Though we do make a moral distinction between sexist actions and speech, both nonetheless reflect on the person's moral character.

Epistemic tolerance comes closer to capturing the moral importance we place on character as well as actions. Epistemic tolerance is the view that interference with another practice is not justified because of certain epistemic limitations. Limitations in this context can come in two varieties. First, we should refrain from interference if we are uncertain about the exact nature of an alternative practice, or if we are unsure of the extent to which that practice differs from our own. No moral judgments should be passed on a practice until the justifications for that practice are fully understood, where this involves (among other things) appropriate attention to "thick" accounts of the practice as well as sensitivity to the factual beliefs that underscore the practice. Second, even if we adequately understand an alternative practice as significantly different, we may still be in the dark about which one of us is morally right. Again, the realist only needs to maintain that stance-independent moral values exist, but she may (or even should) be agnostic about *what* those values are. If morality is not of our making, then it is possible that we (even whole cultures) are in moral error regardless of how confident we may be about our practices and beliefs. Thus, epistemic tolerance justifies noninterference on the basis of *humility*.

Epistemic tolerance improves upon normative tolerance by requiring something about our character, attitudes, and beliefs in addition to our actions. We still make character judgments about the person who merely "puts up with" differences, but who nonetheless persists in believing that the differences are wrong. But we don't similarly judge a person who is honestly and humbly unsure about who is right. However, even epistemic tolerance seems to morally lack something. We often want people to tolerate certain differences even if they *do* fully understand moral values. How can we accommodate this type of tolerance?

Unlike normative and epistemic tolerance, *pluralistic tolerance* recognizes that there are good reasons not to interfere with significantly different moral practices that outstrip considerations of epistemic humility, social propriety, or pragmatic *modus vivendi*. Pluralistic tolerance is the view that interference with another practice is not justified because both practices may be instantiating different and competing, but equally legitimate and real, moral values. Thus, this type of tolerance grounds noninterference in the ontological pluralism. As we explored in Section 4.3, pluralistic moral realism is the view that there is a multiplicity of irreducible stance-independent moral properties. If the difference between two practices comes down to the fact that each instantiates, or is organized around, a different but equally real moral property, then the pluralistic realist should refrain from interfering. This is because, for the pluralistic realist, both moral values are real. In other words, the point for the pluralistic realist is not just that we should refrain from interfering with another practice for pragmatic reasons (although we should), nor even out of consideration for epistemic limitations (although this is a good reason as well); rather, the pluralistic realist thinks that interference could be unjustified regardless of practical or epistemic considerations, simply because two practices both participate in moral reality, albeit in different and irreducible ways. For the pluralistic realist, the fact that the one practice instantiates a moral property does not imply that another practice, even a significantly different one, cannot also instantiate a different moral property.

Note that this does not mean that we should tolerate *every* alternative practice. Such promiscuous tolerance would obviate its moral importance. Pluralistic realism need only recognize a constrained multiplicity of fundamental moral properties. As we saw in Sections 4.2 and 4.3, findings from cultural anthropology support the existence of this kind of constraint on fundamental values. Pluralistic tolerance, therefore, is limited to noninterference only with respect to practices that legitimately instantiate one or more of these fundamental values.

To fully bring out the uniqueness of the pluralistic approach to tolerance, consider the following example: imagine a society that is composed of practices which reveal an emphasis on consequentialist properties, for example, the valuation of happiness and pleasure, the privileging of the group over the individual, etc. Ursula LeGuin provocatively describes such a society in *The Ones Who Walk away from Omelas* (1973). Omelas is a city of absolute perfection and happiness, except for the tragic fact that its prosperity mysteriously requires the extreme suffering of an innocent child, something the citizens of Omelas are aware of and are appropriately sensitive to (e.g. they are sorry, thankful, etc.). Is this perfection and happiness worth the price of such suffering? From a certain point of view, perhaps a more deontological one, many people are inclined to say *no*. They are the ones who "walk away from Omelas." However, there seem just as many balancing considerations for viewing Omelas in a positive light. After all, there really is supreme happiness for almost everyone! Were we to encounter a society such as Omelas and learn that their practices were grounded upon the suffering of an innocent, would we be morally justified in intervening?

On the one hand, assuming that our practices are fundamentally different, we might still take a *normatively* tolerant approach to Omelas, for instance, by thinking it is not our place to interfere, or that interference would be ineffective or counterproductive. Thus, normatively tolerating Omelas would amount to noninterference in *action*, even if we make moral condemnations in *belief*. Alternately, we could extend *epistemic* tolerance to Omelas if we were unsure about which value was morally right—overall happiness or individual liberty. However, if our noninterference was exclusively motivated by epistemic limitations, then the instant these limitations were removed (if they ever could be) we would lose any reason to resist judgment and intervention if we discovered that the alternative practice was morally wrong. By contrast, *pluralistic* tolerance would be able to justify noninterference regardless of practical considerations, and even in epistemically ideal situations, since Omelas is organized around a legitimate and genuine moral value, namely, consequentialism (as expressed in the tentative list of fundamental values we considered in §4.3). That is, even if *our* society privileges deontological considerations, the Utilitarian values of Omelas are still morally recognizable to us—we understand them not only as reasons or values, but also as *good* reasons and values. This does not mean that we should move to Omelas or change our society to become more Utilitarian: there are additional environmental and historical factors that may make such options practically or psychologically unfeasible and unattractive. But it would make intervention (as well as condemnation in belief) morally unjustified since the values buttressing the practices of Omelas are legitimate, even though different from our own. Again, pluralistic tolerance does not mean that we should extend noninterference to all morally different practices but only to those grounded in values recognized by pluralistic realism. For instance, pluralistic tolerance cannot be extended to a society with violent practices justified only on the basis of greed, sadism, etc. We may still have *normative* reasons to tolerate these practices, but we will not tolerate them on the grounds that they instantiate genuine moral truths.

Pluralistic realism also greatly helps explain a number of *intra*cultural moral disagreements. Consider disagreements about abortion or gun control. For instance, it could be that two parties may think they disagree, but actually do not, for example, perhaps they use the same terms in different ways. Their disagreement could also be purely factual, for example, you and I hold different positions on gun control, but only because we are aware of different facts concerning the efficacy of deterrence, the frequency of violent crimes, etc. In the terminology we utilized in Section 4.2, neither of these disagreements would be morally *fundamental*. However, we might persist in disagreeing even if we had all the same facts if our fundamental values were different, for example, you value the potential for life while I value individual rights to choose. The pluralistic realist can hold that both positions should be tolerated since both appeal to an equally real moral value. For example, although Eric may believe strongly in the sanctity of the potential life of a fetus, he can pluralistically tolerate Amy's decision to have an abortion because he understands and is sensitive to the fact that personal liberty is *also* an important and real moral value. Conversely, Amy may be pregnant and decide to have an abortion because she believes it would be financially irresponsible to raise a child; but she could still pluralistically tolerate Laura's decision to not have an abortion and raise a child, even though Laura is in the *same* financial situation, because Amy morally recognizes the validity of the values of life which underscore Laura's decision.[9]

Obviously, a complete theory of toleration will have to tackle additional questions, such as whether toleration is directed fundamentally toward social practices, individual actions, or individual agents themselves?[10] The purpose of this section was simply to explore the ways in which realists can make sense of the toleration of moral differences in substantive and constructive ways. As with the phenomenology of tragic dilemmas, accommodating toleration is an important facet of our actual ethical lives, bringing a theory like moral realism one step closer to a successful re-enchantment of morality as a meaningful region of experience.

7.3 A pluralistic realist account of human rights

As we have seen, a commitment to "applied metaethics" means that otherwise abstruse metaphysical and epistemological views about morality must have something informative to say about real-world moral issues. In the previous sections, we considered some applications of moral realism to potential conflicts between "tragically" competing moral obligations as well as the extent to which differences in moral values and practices can and should be "tolerated." In this final section, we shall explore the prospects for an applied metaethics vis-à-vis a more global topic, namely, human rights.

The conceptual analysis and history of "human rights" is an enormous domain which we need not canvas fully at present. As a minimal working definition, however, we can understand "rights" as referring to putative moral properties, the possession of which provides a reason sufficient to justify whatever corresponding action or nonaction is specified by the right. This justification is often cashed out by saying that rights grant certain "protections"—for instance, a "right to bear arms" would protect the moral permissibility of owning or carrying firearms. *Human* rights are specific types of such protections which allegedly obtain solely in virtue of being human. And because "being human" is a rather generic predicate, human rights are, thus, typically conceived as necessarily *universal* (across humans or other sentient "persons") in scope. Isaiah Berlin expresses the idea thus:

> The idea of human rights rests on the true belief that there are certain goods – freedom, justice, pursuit of happiness, honesty, love – that are in the interest of all human beings, as such, not as members of this or that nationality, religion, profession, character. . . . I think that every culture which has ever existed assumed that there exists [sic] such rights – or at least a minimum of them. (in Jahanbegloo 1992: 39)

At first glance, human rights seem like precisely the sort of things which moral realists ought to celebrate, since they purport to ensconce fundamental and cross-cultural moral values. However, on the other hand, recognizing the stance-independent reality of a domain of facts need not require thinking that those facts thereby obtain everywhere and always, for example, you may be a realist about the stance-independent existence of this book without thereby believing that this book exists everywhere. The *facticity* of a realist domain is what is universal; the *particular facts* themselves need not be. Thus, there is no conceptual requirement that a robust moral realist needs to believe that moral properties are instantiated universally, let alone that they are packaged specifically as "rights." Furthermore, the alleged universality of human rights may be equally grounded in antirealist ways. For example, Martha Nussbaum's and Amartya Sen's influential "capabilities approach" (1993) outlines a powerful framework for human rights which leverages Aristotelian understandings of the contingent features of shared human potential and teleology, but which is more properly constructivist (cf. §2.2) than robustly realist.

Despite this, moral realists still have good reason to be attracted to the idea of human rights, and vice versa: the discourse about human rights gives abstract realism a ready-made articulation of fundamental and transcultural values, and realism in turn provides human rights discourse with an account of the *source* of the alleged "inalienability" of such rights. Rights discourse is a powerful way to codify precisely the sort of moral authority and cultural independence which realists envision. However, we have also seen (in §3.4) that realism should avoid the conclusion that, in order to preserve the reality of morality, it must be divorced entirely from human sensibility. In this way, the realist might differentiate the source of human rights from their *scope* (i.e. the agents and conditions they affect) and their *justification* (i.e. how, by whom, and to whom are moral appeals legitimately made?). The source of rights might be properties which are stance-independently real, even if their scope and justification are culturally or otherwise contextually constrained.

As an example of the distinction realists ought to make between source, scope, and justification, consider the United Nations Universal Declaration of Human Rights (UDHR) which grants its protections to all humans regardless of "race, colour, sex, language, religion, political or other opinion, national or social origin, property, birth or other status" (Article 2). A realist may well insist that the source of these protections are stance-independent moral properties that transcend any particular cultural or political awareness of convention. But how are we to cash out the scope of these protections when the very categories which UDHR lists presuppose some sort of cultural input? Different cultures can have sometimes radically divergent ways of partitioning race, sex, religion, property, etc.—such that uniquely *local* knowledge and sensitivity will be necessary not only to interpret the right that is specified, but also to determine which of the identified categories apply to a particular situation or community. Other Articles of UDHR specify similar protections related to "education," "health," "family," "pleasure," and "art" . . . all of which would seem at least as culturally contested as the items above, if not more so. Does "family" mean specifically "nuclear family?" Are specific biological or sexual relationships part of the definition of "family?" And might not even "pleasure" and "health" be measured and evaluated in fundamentally different ways in cultures with different religious and metaphysical assumptions (cf. Lloyd 2009: 76–92)?

At the very least, even if the source and scope of these rights can be adjudicated in universalist terms, it will require "thick" awareness of local particularity in order to determine tactical approaches to justifying such rights to others. Not only does UDHR overgeneralize in a way the realist might find unhelpful, but it also threatens to do actual damage to cross-cultural moral dialogue. First, the self-righteous and culturally indiscriminate assertion of another's alleged violation of human rights threatens to open up the speaker to accusations of hypocrisy. Second, such moral heavy-handedness by an outsider may well push insiders to exacerbate the violation in an effort to galvanize a defensive cultural solidarity. Virginia Leary (1990), for instance, has called attention to the ways in which the neocolonialist context of early Western articulations of human rights continue to subtly impact the assessment of (and intervention in) African politics. In particular, she draws attention to the ways in which the disproportionate emphasis UDHR gives to the protection of "private property" has been used to justify Western foreign policy. This is not to say, of course, that foreign intervention on the basis of UDHR is *unjustified*—just that it may be difficult in practice to disentangle moral from economic and political motivations.

The high abstraction of most rights discourses can also gloss over thick differences in how particular practices are contextualized. Consider, for example, the current controversy surrounding various traditions of female "veiling" in many Islamic communities. For many, the wearing of a veil or "scarf" (*hijab*) has become a visceral signifier of Islamic identity, with all the connotations that it may entail, despite the number of Muslim women who do *not* wear it, not to mention the numerous non-Islamic traditions in which veiling is also celebrated.[11] In societies where secularism is more formalized, such symbols of religious identity have been targeted. For example, fully covering veils (*burqas*) were banned in public spaces by the French government in 2010–11, and even less concealing types of *hijab* continue to face controversy. Nilüfer Göle (1997) has also documented the ways in which veiling became politically amplified in modern Turkey as a result of post-Atatürk secularizing pressures, and as an expression of solidarity and resistance against perceived foreign cultural encroachment. Obviously, some veiling practices may be morally illegitimate (in a robust way which only the realist can accommodate) when, for example, they represent a means of unjust control over women's bodies or expressions, or a way of covering up (literally) other abuses. But veiling practices—no mater how aesthetically unfamiliar or "ostentatious" (to use the term popular in critical circles during the mid-1990s' heyday of the French controversy)—which instead embody merely the diversity of human clothing and ornamentation should not be lumped in with their more oppressive variations. After all, Western-style cosmetic makeup can similarly be used to cover up bruises from domestic abuses, or to reinforce unjust gender norms or insidious beauty ideals; but most often it's simply a morally neutral facet of cultural and personal expression. The tactical error in using rights discourse to diagnose the moral wrongness of oppressive veiling practices is that the overly abstract nature of such discourse threatens to conflate different veiling practices into a single monolith, often represented by its morally worst representative.

Finally, generic and platitudinous invocations of "rights" which are deaf to cultural particularities might presuppose greater moral difference than what actually obtains, and thus may fail to hear constructive local alternatives. For example, Daniel Bell (2006) has noted that the rights identified in UDHR have numerous "functional equivalents" indigenous to Asian traditions such as Confucianism. Bell explicitly rejects the suggestion that these differences are incommensurable or that they constitute some shared essence of "Asian-ness" which all and only "Asians" somehow possess.[12] His point, however, is that (without explicitly addressing the metaethical underpinnings of such issues) moral traditions such as Confucianism have rich and complex resources for addressing all the same things which UDHR would diagnose as abuses of "human rights" (e.g. political totalitarianism, infringement on individual expression or mobility, deceitful propaganda, state-sponsored genocide, etc.), but in ways which have the tactical advantage of appealing to culturally internal and familiar values.[13] Identifying similar bridges between post-Enlightenment Western ethics and Confucianism, albeit from an antirealist angle, David Wong (2006: 266–72) notes that classical Western institutions such as democracy, and traditional Asian commitments to the sanctity of shared ritual, can mutually enlighten and strengthen one another in ways that might be overlooked by focusing exclusively on the abstractions of UDHR.

We may be tempted to dismiss all these complications as a matter of mere tactics better left to politicians, sociologists, or activists.

However, for a view like moral realism to succeed in "re-enchanting" moral experience, such messy real-world applications must be taken into account when assessing the plausibility of a metaethical theory. Moral realism will insist on the cultural independence of the properties which make certain practices moral or immoral, and the pluralistic realist will go further to allow these properties to be instantiated in practically inconsistent ways. But this does not mean that realists thereby have a license to morally condemn practices *a priori* without first gathering thick culturally relative knowledge and experience. And even then, realists should be "realistic" about the pragmatic consequences of overly generalized or outsider moral diagnoses and solutions. Thus, although UDHR may accurately codify many of the moral properties realists might want to recognize, realists committed to "applied metaethics" must be sensitive about translational problems that can arise when abstract rights language differs from thick culturally relative concepts.[14]

7.4 Summary

We started this book with a consideration of a transcendental reason to be attracted to moral realism, namely, the potential to "re-enchant" morality as a sphere of meaning. This final chapter takes an important step in this direction by attempting to put moral realism—which earlier chapters unpacked metaphysically and epistemologically—into practice by exploring possible examples of "applied metaethics" in the real world. We looked first at how a view such as realism might help make sense of "moral tragedies" in which obligations and values appear to come into irresolvable conflict, such that there might be no way to avoid moral wrongdoing. We then considered the implications of realism vis-à-vis our attitudes and institutions regarding "toleration." Finally, we attempted to leverage moral realism as a framework for understanding pressing contemporary debates concerning "human rights." Although there are many additional issues to work out for a fully acceptable defense of moral realism, we have seen in the applications of this chapter a new breed of realism that is more vital, more accessible, and indeed more *realistic*.

GLOSSARY

Antirealism: the view that *moral realism* is false, whether because moral discourse is not truth-apt (see *noncognitivism*) or because there are no stance-independent truthmakers (see *metaethical relativism*).

Argument from Relativity (AFR): the argument that *metaethical relativism* is inferable on the basis of *anthropological relativism*. (§§4.1–4.3)

Cognitivism: the view that moral discourse sometimes has propositional content that can be appropriately evaluated as true or false. (§2.3)

Constructivism: the view that moral truths are constituted by the consensus of rational agreement or the perspective or judgment of an idealized spectator or divine agency. (§2.2)

Cornell Realism: a type of moral realism according to which moral properties are reducible to natural properties, but in a way that preserves moral truth; see *naturalism*. (§§3.2 and 3.3)

Correspondence Theory of Truth: the view that a proposition is true if and only if its descriptive content corresponds to some independent fact or state of affairs in the world. (§2.2)

Deflationary Theory of Truth: the view that a proposition is true in virtue of being formally expressible within a rule-governed symbolic system. (§2.2)

Dispositionalism: the metaphysical view that moral properties can be stance-independently real, but in such a way that their actualization requires the participation of the perspectives or states of affairs to which they make ineliminable reference. (§3.4)

Emotivism: a type of *noncognitivism*; the view that moral discourse does not have propositional content, but rather expresses non-truth-apt emotional responses. (§2.3)

Error Theory: a form of *antirealism* and *metaethical relativism* which diagnoses a systematic reason why morality is erroneously viewed as realist or objectivist; see *argument from relativity* and *queerness*. (§§4.1, 5.1, and 6.1)

Expressivism: a type of *noncognitivism*; the view that moral discourse does not have propositional content, but rather expresses endorsements of group norms; such endorsement can be "true" in a deflationary sense by reference to the "appropriateness" of the norms in question and the concomitant usage of the discourse about them. (§2.3)

Externalism: of *motivation*, the view that moral beliefs need not supply any concomitant motivational impetus; of *reasons*, the view that true moral beliefs could justify corresponding action even without being recognized as doing so by the actor in question. (§§5.1 and 5.2)

Fallibilism: the view that truth may be epistemologically inaccessible or unable to be adequately or objectively justified. (§§6.1 and 6.2)

Frege-Geach Problem (FGP): the argument that noncognitivist semantics do not adequately accommodate the logical structure of actual moral discourse. (§2.3)

Internalism: of *motivation*, the view that moral beliefs supply their own intrinsic motivational force; of *reasons*, the view that true moral beliefs provide justification for concomitant action in a way that will be rationally accessible to the actor. (§§5.1 and 5.2)

Intuitionism: the epistemological view that moral truths can be known a priori and justified noninferentially. (§6.3)

Moral Twin Earth Argument (MTE): a thought experiment designed to disprove naturalistic forms of moral realism (see *Cornell Realism*) by conceiving an alternate world with the same functional moral vocabulary, but denoting different physical properties. (§3.2)

Naturalism: the metaphysical view that moral properties (whether *realist* or *antirealist*) are reducible in some way to nonmoral or "natural" properties. (§§3.1–3.3)

Non-naturalism: the metaphysical view that moral properties are *sui generis*, in the sense of being irreducible to nonmoral or "natural" properties. (§§3.1–3.3)

Objectivism: the metaphysical view that the reality of moral properties requires an "absolute conception" purged of any unique perspectival content. (§3.4)

Open Question Argument (OQA): an argument against attempts to "reduce" moral predicates to nonmoral predicates by alleging the conceptual incompleteness of such reductions; often used in support of *non-naturalism*. (§3.1)

Pluralism: in *anthropology*, the descriptive view that there are differences in moral beliefs and practices (see *anthropological relativism*) (§1.1); in normative ethics, the view that moral differences should be respected or tolerated (see *normative relativism*) (§§4.3 and 7.2); in *metaethical relativism*, the view that even though there are no transcultural moral values, nonetheless acceptable moralities are subject to naturalistic constraints (§4.3); in *realism*, the view that there are multiple, irreducible, and potentially irreconcilable moral values which are all equally stance-independent. (§§1.3 and 4.3)

Queerness: in *epistemology*, the objection to realism on the grounds that it cannot explain the acquisition and justification of moral knowledge in ways consonant with other familiar modalities and processes (§6.1); in *metaphysics*, the objection to realism on the grounds that it would necessitate a suspiciously unique form of *internalism*. (§5.1)

Realism: the view that moral discourse expresses truth-apt propositions (see *cognitivism*) which can sometimes be true as determined by *correspondence* to stance-independent properties.

Relativism: in *epistemology*, the view that truth varies according to the perspective or context of justification; in *anthropology*, the view that, as a matter of descriptive fact, there are differences in moral beliefs and practices; in normative ethics, the view that differences in moral beliefs and practices should be respected or tolerated; in metaethics, the view that there are no transcultural truthmakers for moral propositions. (§§4.1–4.3)

Retributive Emotion: an emotional response to a moral assessment of another (e.g. blame, praise) or one's self (e.g. guilt, pride, shame, regret). (§§5.3 and 7.1)

Supervenience: a relationship between different types of properties, such that any variation in the base property must be isomorphic with a corresponding variation in the supervenient property. (§3.2)

Tragic Dilemma: an alleged conflict between two or more moral values in which there is no singular or definitive way to rank or systematize the values, and in which the obligatory force of each value remains intact. (§7.1)

NOTES

Chapter 1

1 As I will be using this term, "antirealism" is simply the negation of "realism," regardless of whatever more specific form that negation takes. Other usages of this nomenclature vary widely. Sometimes "antirealism" refers specifically to the sort of moral "error theorists" we shall consider in Section 4.1. Sometimes "antirealism" is contrasted with "irrealism," where the former refers to the rejection of realism on the basis of "noncognitivism" (see §2.3) and the latter refers to the rejection of realism on the basis of the nonexistence of truthmakers for moral propositions. I will use "antirealism" as a generic category for all of these nonrealist positions, including noncognitivism, error theory, relativism, nihilism, fictionalism et al.
2 For an overview of these trends, see the Pew Research Center's "Forum on Religion and Public Life" (www.pewforum.org).
3 Again, this is not to say that there weren't atheists per se in premodern times. The point is just that Atheism as a recognized ism or category is a relatively modern option.
4 Although see Taylor (2007) for ways in which Taylor's view departs from Weber's own understanding of the process and outcome of secular modernity.

Chapter 2

1 Although, for the sake of stylistic ease, I will speak frequently about "human" conception, experience, sensibility, etc., this should not be taken as a denial that there might be legitimate and recognizable moralities within nonhuman entities, cf. DeLapp (2011) for a discussion of the conceptual constraints on our capacity to think of morality in nonanthropocentric ways.
2 Of course, if we *never* agree about morality, we might worry that this could be because there is simply nothing to agree about. But this

would be an objection to the truth or plausibility of moral realism, not to its characterization or coherence as a possible metaethical position, which is the present focus of our discussion. The objection from disagreement will be revisited in §§4.1–4.3.

3   Note that, in suggesting that gravitation, entropy, and natural selection are not "created," we need not make the stronger (and dubious) claim that the *laws* which measure, express, and predict these phenomena are not themselves created. In this sense, as empirical generalizations, laws require lawmakers (i.e. those who make the generalizations) in a trivial way.

4   Here I use the word "robust" in the sense identified by Brock and Mares (2007: 11) in their comparative study of the way "realism" is understood across different philosophical debates. A position is "robustly" realist if it affirms not merely the "existence" (generic with respect to any modality) of a certain entity or domain of entities, but specifically the existential independence of that entity or domain of entities (which Brock and Mares take as a necessary condition for any bona fide realist view).

5   The correspondence theory of truth has been a hallmark of traditional Western philosophy, cf. Plato (*Cratylus* 385b2), Aristotle (*Metaphysics* 1011b25), and Aquinas (*Summa Theologiae* Q16).

6   Shafer-Landau (2003: 30–3) similarly notes that deflationary theories of truth typically appeal to "*contextualist*" semantics, where a sentence can be true in one context, but false in another. The problem with this, argues Shafer-Landau, is that it cannot resist antirealism. If the whole reason why people go in for an alternate theory of truth is so that they can preserve some type of stable and robust (albeit, not stance-independent) moral truth, the deflationary theory has backfired on them. (Note, however, that this needn't mean that contextualism is not still plausible phenomenologically or epistemologically.)

7   Precisely what sort of mental entity is supposed to take the place of beliefs in moral judgment is a matter of contention even among noncognitivists: "emotivists" such as C. L. Stevenson (1944) and A. J. Ayer (1952) think moral language expresses emotions or feelings, "prescriptivists" such as R. M. Hare (1952) think it expresses proattitudes and desires for others to similarly express, and "norm-expressivists" such as Allan Gibbard (1990) think it expresses the endorsement of norms that are universal in form.

8   Non-belief-states can, however, be correspondently true or false in a mind-*dependent* way. That is, propositions expressing emotions, feelings, attitudes, or endorsements may be true if they correspond to what state the speaker is actually in; if they do not correspond in this way (e.g. if I actually dislike something, but

lie and say that I like it), then such propositions would be false. The point is just that such truth and falsity is not determined by correspondence to anything mind-independent. And since mind-independent correspondence is a necessary feature of moral realism, noncognitivism cannot be realist.

9　Lewis (1944) also notes that, even if noncognitivism is not descriptively accurate for a vast majority of the history of ethics, it might, under conditions of modernist disenchantment, become accurate as our moral intuitions evolve.

10　Cf. Schueler (1988) for an analysis of FGP specific to moral realism.

11　Blackburn (1984) exploits this refinement to articulate his "quasi-realism." According to Blackburn, whereas the first premise directly expresses an endorsement, the conditionality of the second premise instead involves a metaexpression, namely, the expression of a disposition to express an endorsement. For a more recent deployment of the same strategy on behalf of noncognitivism, see Kalderon (2008).

Chapter 3

1　See also Moore's distinction between "good" and "*the* good," the latter being acceptably transparent to definition (1903: 8).

2　See Regan (1986) for a more detailed account of the generally positive assessments of OQA by Moore's peer group, especially by the members of the artsy Bloomsbury Group.

3　This might not be true. Robert Audi (1999, 2004) has suggested that propositions may be necessary, a priori, or otherwise analytic without thereby being "obvious"—consider the case of knowing that my grandmother's sister's son is my first cousin once-removed; this is tautologically true, though it is not immediately apparent to many people (cf. §6.2).

4　We must say "except in a trivial way" because, for instance, normative statements *do* follow validly from necessarily false or logically inconsistent premises (*ex falso quodlibet*); they can also be validly disjoined to a non-normative conclusion that follows from a non-normative premise (cf. Prior 1960).

5　Pigden (1991) has called these views examples of "sociological naturalism" and adds to the list Anscombe (1958), MacIntyre (1981), and Lovibond (1983). Anscombe and MacIntyre, however, maintain agnosticism about realism, and Lovibond explicitly calls herself a realist.

6　Much of these naturalistic realisms are epistemological in focus, and we will revisit these aspects in Section 6.1.

7 Cf. Putnam's (1967) own appeal to the ways in which a property might have "multiple realizability" vis-à-vis a supervenient bases.

8 By contrast, we might distinguish a merely "methodological" form of ethical naturalism which simply requires that the formation of ethical and metaethical theories be informed (and to some extent constrained) by the available information of the sciences, remaining agnostic about any ontological property identities (Flanagan 2006; Tropman 2008).

9 Cf. Foucault (1969), Rorty (1989), and Longino (1990) for similar diagnoses of the subtle ways in which social and political "webs of power" can distort the notion of scientific progress or objectivity.

10 Or at least against the *absolutist* realist. See Section 4.3 for the distinction between absolutist versus pluralistic moral realisms.

11 In fact, it is plausible to say that ethics *has* converged greatly. After all, the notion of human rights seems increasingly universal and international (cf. §7.3). Of course, it might be argued that this convergence is more a result of globalization than any progression toward moral truth. And perhaps it is. But a similar objection could be made about much scientific convergence.

12 Of course, it will matter here what we mean by a "law." At least in the context of "natural sciences" like physics, a law is typically thought to be an empirical generalization which, among other things, is *universal* in scope. However, this might make it difficult to ever construct biological laws, given the *particularity* of environmental and historical factors involved. Of course, biologists could always redefine "law" in a way more congenial to their discipline (cf. Rosenberg 1994), but then so could ethicists.

13 Nor is it clear that moral realists need to be committed to the view, commonly called "motivational internalism," according to which moral judgments intrinsically supply motivation to act (see §5.1).

14 Despite arguing that these distinctions collapse, Shafer-Landau himself thinks that ethics and science ultimately can be differentiated epistemologically, namely, on the basis of the apriority of the former. Indeed, Sylvester (1990) has argued that Moore's own understanding of non-naturalism might have been essentially epistemological. We shall return to the question of the role of apriority in ethics in Sections 6.3 and 6.4.

15 Williams also unpacks his notion of objectivity as requiring that absolute conceptions be purged of "our perspective and its peculiarities" (1985: 138–9). Smart (1963: 151) similarly maintains that absolute conceptions cannot be in any way "anthropocentric."

16 The "moral functionalism" of Jackson and Pettit (see §3.2), by contrast, bypasses realist ontology in favor of a purely functional analysis. For Jackson and Pettit, realists don't need to say what moral

properties *are*, just what they *do*. Or, more strongly, moral properties for the functionalist are *nothing more than* the roles they play.

17 Note that Mackie himself anticipated the morality-color analogy (1977: 19–20), which shouldn't come as a surprise, given his work on Locke's and Hume's accounts of secondary qualities.

18 McDowell's dispositional view of color can be traced to Locke's claim that secondary qualities are "relational" though not "resembling." See Bennett (1971: 10–11) and Langton (1998: 43–7) for defenses of this interpretation of Locke.

19 Dispositional theories of color are defended by Peacocke (1984) and Johnston (1992), and also jibe with Aristotle's claim that it is wrong to suppose that "nothing is pale or dark without sight . . . for in a way [this] is correct, but in a way incorrect" (*DeAnima* 3.2.426a; cf. *Metaphysics* 4.5.1010b).

20 David Lewis has also defended a dispositionalist account of moral value that attempts to address this putative disanalogy—which Lewis (optimistically) calls "the only disturbing aspect of the dispositional theory" (1989: 88–9). To accommodate this disanalogy, Lewis concedes that values are ultimately contingent, not necessary (recall our consideration of this possibility in §3.2). Lewis's version of dispositionalism, however, is not robustly realist since, on his account, values are reduced (both coextensively and cointensively) to facts about human psychology. Lewis himself calls this "realism, loosely speaking," but not realism in the sense of stance-independent correspondence to features of the external world. Indeed, if values can be reduced merely to facts about our psychology, then it is not even clear that this "loose realism" even needs to be cognitivist.

Chapter 4

1 Levy (2002: 20) favors "descriptive relativism." Gewirth (1994) prefers "cultural pluralism." Descriptive relativism has also been historically known as "cultural relativism" in anthropology. Sumner (1906) and Rachels (1978) also use "cultural relativism," but not in a purely descriptive way. Their use is more akin to what we shall call "metaethical relativism" below. Moody-Adams (1997) helpfully makes the position as explicit as possible by calling it "descriptive cultural relativism." Wong (1984: 48–67) has also expressed the view as "environmental relativism."

2 Mackie is not alone in his armchair speculation: Wellman (1975: 213) provides a list of other philosophers who make similar assumptions. In addition, the apparent ubiquity of moral dispute might stem

in many cases from an "availability bias," that is, mistakenly generalizing about a subject simply on the basis of a single, but more cognitively available example. Thus, moral dispute could appear commonplace only because when people are asked to think of moral issues they tend to focus on the few highly visible "big ticket" items (e.g. abortion, euthanasia, war) furnished by mainstream political debate. Availability bias is an extremely well-confirmed finding in cognitive science (Kahneman 1982).

3   Neither would the mere fact of consensus ensure that moral beliefs are true (*pace* the constructivist alternative to realism which we considered in §2.2). Agreement can arise from a lack of exposure to alternatives, from brainwashing, socialization, or force.

4   Similar distinctions between moral obligations and what is merely demanded by convention have even been found in young children (cf. Nichols 2003).

5   Note that I am not claiming that the converse is true, namely that more educated or wealthier individuals are thereby better moral authorities (and certainly not that they are thereby morally better people!). The point is simply that poverty and a lack of education arguably disqualify certain disagreements from the stemming from the requisite epistemic positioning that would be needed to warrant relativism abductively.

6   It is often forgotten that Kohlberg himself noted the relativism of undergraduates and even provided an intermediate stage (stage 4.5) for them that represented healthy development, even though it appeared to be moving backward.

7   We may highlight the fact that even Malinowski (taken by many as a paragon of rigorous objectivity) admitted to extreme personal bias in his posthumously published *Diary* (Geertz 1983: 56).

8   Although, as Appiah (2010) has convincingly argued, the actual tipping points for moral reforms to become full cultural revolutions often requires additional mechanisms, such as conceptions of individual, class, or national "honor."

9   I use the term "cutting" here rather than the more connotative terms "circumcision" or "mutilation" so as not to beg any questions about its moral permissibility. The Arabic words most often used to refer to the practice are *sunna* ("tradition") and *tahur* ("purification," which is also applied to male circumcision).

10 And we should not forget that similar practices existed in nineteenth-century America as "cures" for masturbation, nymphomania, and female hysteria. It is worth noting, though, that these practices were condemned even among contemporaries. Furthermore, such condemnation, while often taking a moral tone, was often made on the bases of (perceived) "facts" about anatomy and psychology.

11 An attempt to codify Gilligan's alternative "moral voice" into a full-fledged normative theory can be found in Nel Noddings's (1984) formulation of an "ethics of care."

12 Thus, Markus and Kitayama (1991) observe that Japanese respondents identify "social harmony" as a fundamental value distinct from justice. See also Kasulis (2002) for discussions of Japanese versus American values implicit in child rearing.

13 Similarly, Haidt (2004) has collated fundamental values according to four "modules": suffering, hierarchy, reciprocity, and purity. That is, different cultural practices or individual moral commitments seem generally to be reducible to some combination or privileging of these four values. Shweder (1993) has also identified a remarkably similar list of fundamental values: autonomy (including justice, rights, freedom), community (including social roles, peace), and divinity (including sanctity, purity).

14 For example, it might be that the value of fulfilling social role expectations ultimately is due to the fact that such roles are voluntarily assumed, in which value (3) might be reducible to value (2); or it might be that the value of role expectations has more to do with the fact that fulfilling these expectations brings about a better overall state of affairs, making value (3) reducible to value (1). Likewise, it might be possible to reduce aspects of the value of fidelity to the value of producing overall utility if certain sophisticated versions of *rule*-consequentialism are thought to be plausible.

15 Furthermore, pluralistic realism is not committed to multiplying *kinds* of entity, but merely the number of entities that fall under the same kind (viz. moral value). Of course, one could object that *any* moral values are an unparsimonious addition to our ontology, but this would be an objection to moral realism in general, and not unique to pluralistic realism.

16 In this way, pluralism might provide at the ontological level an explanation of "particularism" at the normative level (cf. Hooker and Little 2000).

Chapter 5

1 Smith (1994) calls this weak version of motivational internalism the "practicality requirement" of moral judgment and attempts to defend it against objections by Brink (1989). Both Smith and Brink's views will be discussed in more length below.

2 For a more detailed textual analysis of Plato's sometimes shifting views concerning ignorance and deliberate evil, see Penner (1971). This usage of the phrase "Socratic paradox" was popularized by

Santas (1964). See also Irwin (1977) for a classic discussion of this issue.

3 In this way, most of the Sentimental writers also affirmed some form of *reasons internalism*, which we will explore in Section 5.2.

4 Further discussion of the ought-implies-can principle will be provided in Section 7.1.

5 Unless, of course, "friend" itself is stipulated in a normatively loaded way—as in Plato's *Republic* (ff. 332–6) and Aristotle's *Nicomachean Ethics* (ff. 1156a27–1157a1).

6 It should be noted that neither Stocker nor Baron themselves use the *de re/de dicto* terminology, preferring to speak of "acting from inclination" versus "acting from duty." Stocker also notably distinguishes acting *from* duty (which he thinks is repugnant, insincere, and potentially arrogant) and acting *for* duty (which he thinks is morally acceptable and indicative of personal inclination).

7 Presumably, Shafer-Landau is referring only to moral demands and obligations that are fundamental in some sense. After all, there are many moral demands which arise only in specific situations, for example, my keeping a promise to you is only obligatory, given that I have made such a promise. What Shafer-Landau must mean is that what is universal about such obligations is that promises must be kept anywhere and always *whenever they are made*.

8 One source of hesitancy might be that differentiating moral demands as requiring a uniquely generalized scope rules out *tout court* any possibility of "moral particularism," that is, the view that fundamental moral obligations are expressed not in abstract or universal propositions, but instead must be sensitive to particular features of specific agents, social roles and positions, and environmental considerations. For example, instead of the generalized obligation "Do not lie," particularism might furnish obligations such as "It would be wrong for Edward to lie to Jin." Moral realism itself, though, is agnostic about particularism versus universalism, and so I will not directly consider this debate in this chapter. For a more comprehensive overview of the particularism debate, see Hooker and Little (2000).

9 Traditional perceptual psychology has suggested an interesting parallel to this idea that realist moral values might supply their own inherent justifying reasons for action. J. J. Gibson (1979) has argued in favor of the idea of "objective affordances." An "affordance" is a property of an object or a feature of one's immediate perceptual environment that indicates how to interact with that object or feature. For example, according to Gibson, a door handle "affords" the possibility of turning it to open the door. Gibson envisioned

affordances as objective, belief-independent properties or features which refer to all "action possibilities" in an environment (and which depend on the contingent features and capacities of agents), but which do not necessarily require agents to recognize them as possibilities. This parallel to perceptual psychology should be kept in mind during the discussion of a perceptual model of moral epistemology in Section 6.4.

10 I adopt this terminology while dodging the debate about whether retributive emotions, on the one hand, necessarily involve hatred, the concomitant desire for retaliation, or for the object of the retribution to suffer (cf. Duff 1986); or whether, on the other hand, we can make sense of retributive emotions which are, as it were, impersonal, for example, "hating the sin, but not the sinner" (cf. Holroyd 2010).

11 I say "moral guilt" to distinguish it from idiosyncratic or theory-indexed usages of the term (e.g. "guilt" in psychoanalysis), and from legal or procedural notions of guilt (as when, for example, a defendant is found guilty by a jury even if she might be wrongly convicted, and thus morally innocent).

12 It might sound implausible to claim that someone *should* experience an emotion, since it is not clear that emotions are the sorts of things over which we have cognitive or deliberative control. Regardless of this issue, however, all I mean is that we would properly view an agent as lacking something if she fails to experience the appropriate emotion; a claim I take to be compatible with the psychological question of whether or not we can actually deliberatively control our emotions.

13 Of course, it is important to note that Greenspan's own brand of this sort of emotion-informed realism—which she calls "social artifact realism"—is less ontologically robust than the view I have presented here. According to Greenspan, the developmental, motivational, and phenomenological status of moral emotions envisions a morality which is "dependent on minds for its existence and purpose and therefore at least to some extent for its form" (1995: 89). Morality, for Greenspan, is, therefore, tantamount to a social artifact; and other familiar social artifacts, such as tables and chairs, have a persistent belief-independent existence and "deserve a place in the fabric of the world" (*ibid.*). Yet, while the social artifact analogy might allow Greenspan to preserve the nonmalleability and normative authority (i.e. external justificatory reasons) of morality, the fact that chairs and tables are created by humans would seem to render her view more of a constructivist account, rather than a type of robust realism proper. See Section 2.2 for discussion of the constructivist alternative to realism.

Chapter 6

1 Recall that we explored a similar strategy of appealing to a critical mass of "companions in guilt" in Chapters 3 and 4.

2 Of course, it is not Sturgeon's point (nor is it our point in this chapter) to defend the connection between character and action. Sturgeon is focused just on what role our beliefs in the interrelatedness between character and action play, not that these beliefs are true. Indeed, Harman's (1998) diagnosis of the "fundamental attribution error," according to which we project more stability to character than the social-psychological evidence warrants, may be viewed as criticizing this very assumption. See also Doris (2002) for a comprehensive presentation of this strategy and literature. Moreover, note that Sturgeon only claims that belief in realist moral properties *partly* explains why we believe Hitler and the hoodlums are depraved, not that it does all the explanatory work all by itself, or even that it always features in every single explanation. Given Harman's suspicion of *any* explanatory role, however, even a partial explanatory role is all that Sturgeon needs.

3 Actually, it seems more natural to me to say that the *truth* of the statement is what is relative to contrast classes, that is, it is just plain *false* that skyscrapers are big compared to galaxies. This suggests that truth and justification might be largely intertwined. At any rate, neither type of relativity needs threaten moral realism, which is a claim only that the features (i.e. values) that serve as truthmakers for moral propositions are nonrelative.

4 For example, Audi (2004) defines epistemic justification as involving, among other things, *understanding*, where understanding a belief requires not only being "conscious" of it or "reflecting" on it, but also the ability to be articulated, reported, or proved to others. In this way, ethical intuitions for Audi must be understood in addition to being merely self-evident for them to be justified. Indeed, Audi goes so far as to say that not even the logical necessity of a belief would thereby justify if it is not reportable, etc.

5 Coherentism has been most notably applied to *moral* justification by Brink (1989), Sayre-McCord (1985), and Timmons (1990). Sinnott-Armstrong (1996) also notes that coherentism has deep roots in John Rawls's (1971) notion of "narrow reflective equilibrium."

6 Important proponents of this view include Gauthier (1986) and Reiman (1990). We can also consider as ancestors of the view anyone in the social contract tradition (including Rawls).

7 Audi (1999) seems to endorse this characterization by defining self-evidence as "providing its own justification." Stratton-Lake

(2002: 18) defines self-evidence as "knowable on the basis of an understanding of it," and Scanlon (1998) similarly describes allegedly self-evident propositions as "independently credible." In a more recent work, Audi (2004) explicitly associates self-evidence with being noninferential, although he thinks this is only a necessary and not a sufficient condition of self-evidence. Shafer-Landau (2003) also defines self-evidence in a similar way, as "sufficient to justify believing it given the conditions of adequate understanding and attentive consideration." Both Audi and Shafer-Landau agree that self-evidence involves being noninferential, but they disagree about whether or not this is sufficient for epistemic justification. For Audi, justification requires "understanding" as well as being publicly defensible. For Shafer-Landau, understanding is already built into the definition of self-evidence (such that self-evidence automatically entails justification) and justification does not need to be publicly defendable.

8 Note that in calling intuitions noninferential we need not imply that they are necessarily believed on their own basis: as we will suggest in Section 6.3, intuitions may be epistemically justified if and only if they are believed on the basis of perceptual experiences that satisfy certain *ceteris paribus* conditions. Note also that to say that an intuition or basic belief is essentially noninferential is not to say that it must be *exclusively* noninferential, that is, to say that a proposition is noninferential is just to say that it does not *need* inferential support or evidence to justify believing it. It might still be independently justified inferentially—it's just that such inferential justification is not necessarily required for it to be justifiably believed.

9 This is not to say that general and abstract principles and rules cannot be epistemically justified in other ways; the point is just that they will not be justified noninferentially on the basis of corresponding perceptual experiences since generalities and abstractions are not directly perceived, although they may be induced from particular perceptual beliefs. In this way, general moral beliefs are prone to even greater threats of fallibility and defeasibility since there is more room for them to be erroneously formed.

10 Again, this is one way reason why I prefer to speak of "noninferential" beliefs rather than "self-evident" beliefs, as "self-evidence" often carries the connotation that a belief is justified all by itself. On the model of justification I am offering, a belief ("intuition") will only be justified noninferentially if it is believed on the basis of the requisite perceptual experiences. Note also that many phenomenological beliefs—for example, that I am in pain right now—are similarly noninferential. I do not need to deduce or induct the fact that I am in pain by referencing any extraneous beliefs or propositions.

11 Blum himself is explicitly agnostic about the metaethical commitments of moral perception and whether the moral salience or relevance of features of situations is fixed by realist values or by other antirealist factors (1994: 34, n. 8). Although Blum *does* say that John "misses something of the *moral reality* confronting him" (1994: 33, my italics), he seems to mean this only in Iris Murdoch's (1970) sense of morality being concerned with other people's subjectivities.

12 Blum's own position is somewhat less explicit, although he does say that perception of morally salient features of situations "provide reasons for action" (1994: 32–3).

13 Vetleson himself seems to take his view to endorse some version of metaethical relativism. However, moral realism is compatible with admitting the ineliminable role of emotions in moral perceptions so long as neither emotional reactions nor cognitive judgments *constitute* moral values. That is, emotional dispositions may affect our ability to perceive the morally relevant features of situations, but (at least for the realist) they do not affect the existence of these morally relevant features.

Chapter 7

1 Hale (1991) leverages this observation as an argument against the normative category of supererogation (i.e. those actions which are allegedly good to do, but not blameworthy not to do). Although Hale does not address tragic dilemmas as such, his argument is that we have good metaphilosophical reason to avert to the reported phenomenology of our avowed moral experts, and that these experts experience their "ought" requirements as obligatory rather than supererogatory—even in cases where they might not be able to physically perform what they believe is morally required of them.

2 My own view is that the *personal* nature is essential to this requirement to agonize: the commander must feel the agony as part of her own decision, and not merely regret impersonally that the world around her is such as it is (DeLapp 2012).

3 Indeed, feeling morally responsible for tragically unavoidable racial privilege seems to be importantly connected with an increased motivation to act against racial injustice. For example, in a series of recent studies by Amodio (2007), White participants who had self-identified with moral concern for racial injustice were falsely told that brain-imagery nonetheless detected racial biases in them. Yet, rather than succumbing to morose defeatism or blithely shrugging the excuse that "ought implies can," they tended instead to volunteer for prejudice-reducing activities with increased celerity.

4   Even more strongly, such self-recrimination might even be a *necessary* condition for moral praise vis-à-vis racial injustice: I think there would still be something morally objectionable about the privileged person who happily volunteers to participate in all sorts of antiracist activities, who abhors racial inequality, and who can identify racial prejudice and bias with remarkable accuracy, but who self-righteously refuses to acknowledge her own personal privilege, viewing that as a problem for "other, less enlightened" people.

5   Of course, while this may be logically consistent, we also feel that moral views should sometimes be accompanied by *conviction*. We are justifiably suspicious of someone who claims to believe in the rightness of something, but who never stands up in its defense; or someone who claims to believe in the impermissibility of something, but does not try to act to stop it. An adequate theory of tolerance needs to take seriously the importance of moral conviction. The view of *pluralistic tolerance* I discuss below is an attempt to reconcile these two commitments.

6   Of course, practices and beliefs can be changed for nonrational reasons. Practitioners can be killed, silenced, or otherwise persuaded. See Appiah (2010) for a historical analysis of the role that "honor" has played in stimulated "moral revolutions" when "morality itself" was insufficient.

7   Perhaps this sort of normative tolerance cannot be properly called "tolerance" at all, but something more akin to "allowance." This is because, as several writers on tolerance have emphasized, tolerance *proper* requires something that the tolerater views as mistaken, wrong, or undesirable in some way. Cohen writes that, "Some negative response is necessary for our lack of interference to count as toleration" (2004: 70). And Williams calls our attention to the fact that calling as an act of "tolerance" something that should be morally indifferent can be self-righteous or condescending: "If I and others in the neighborhood said that we were *tolerating* the homosexual relations of the couple next door, our attitude would be thought less than liberal" (1996: 20).

8   Again, this form of normative tolerance does not fully capture all the moral weight that "tolerance" is imbued with in social-political discussions, but it is still a possible reason given for nonintervention with an alternate practice. Accordingly, we might call this type of normative tolerance "endurance" since, as Cohen says, "One endures what one (believes one) has to; one tolerates what one (believes one) should" (2004: 70).

9   "Tolerance" might not be the proper word for the noninterference supported by pluralistic realism. As indicated above, "tolerance" seems to connote an alternative that one judges *negatively* in

some way. Indeed, part of the "difficulty" of tolerance, according to Williams, is that "it seems to be at once necessary and impossible . . . Toleration, we may say, is required only for the intolerable. That is its basic problem" (1996: 18). If tolerance proper requires viewing an alternative negatively, then the response of the pluralistic realist to moral conflict cannot properly be called tolerance since the pluralistic realist does *not* judge the alternatives negatively; they are morally valid. Accordingly, the psychology of pluralistic tolerance might be better reflected by words such as "acceptance"— or even "celebration" and "embracing"—all of which connote a more active and supportive approach to legitimate moral difference.

10 Heyd has argued that by distinguishing actions from agents, we can educate children to tolerate others even while morally judging (and perhaps intervening with) actions and practices: "There is no contradiction between judging an action as wrong and yet appreciating or respecting its agent" (2003: 199). Specifically, Heyd thinks that this distinction between actions and agents can be achieved by a "perceptual shift" similar to the epistemology we examined in Section 6.4.

11 El Guindi (1999) draws attention to different versions of the practice in different Christian communities throughout history, Greco-Roman variations, and even widespread *male* practices of veiling— problematizing the narrow view of veiling which abstract rights discourse can too often engender.

12 Bell notes that not only have Western commentators been guilty of such essentialist stereotypes, but also that Asian leaders themselves have often cultivated a similar "politics of difference" in order to justify divergent economic or political agendas.

13 For this reason, Bell (2006: 84–117) argues that locally positioned advocacy groups (which are often staffed by cultural insiders knowledgeable about facts on the ground) may often be better at effecting moral change than large international nongovernmental organizations.

14 Kwon (2009: 108) has undertaken a comparative study of intercultural translations of UDHR and found that, while translational accuracy is preserved at an abstract level, nonetheless "cognitive processes derived from distinct semantic structures result in unique mappings of text as a whole, creating the possibility to differently understand the translated document that is supposed to convey the same meaning as the original text." See also Angle (2002) for an analysis of the modern coinage of the Chinese neologism quanli权利as an attempt to translate the English "rights."

BIBLIOGRAPHY

Adams, R. M. (1979). "Divine command metaethics modified again," *Journal of Religious Ethics* 7: 66–79.

Altham, J. E. J. (1986). "The legacy of emotivism," in McDonald, G. and Wright, C. (eds), *Fact, Science, and Morality*. Oxford: Blackwell Publishing, pp. 275–88.

Amodio, D. M., Devin, P. G., and Harmon-Jones, E. (2007). "A dynamic model of guilt: implications for motivation and self-regulation in the context of prejudice," *Psychological Science* 18: 524–30.

Angle, Stephen. (2002). *Human Rights and Chinese Thought: A Cross-cultural Inquiry*. Cambridge: Cambridge University Press.

Anscombe, Elizabeth. (1957). *Intention*. Ithaca: Cornell University Press.

—(1958). "Modern moral philosophy," *Philosophy* 33 (124): 1–19.

Appiah, K. A. (2006). *Cosmopolitanism: Ethics in a World of Strangers*. New York: W. W. Norton & Co.

—(2010). *The Honor Code: How Moral Revolutions Happen*. New York: W. W. Norton & Co.

Audi, Robert. (1999). "Moral knowledge and ethical pluralism," in Greco, J. and Sosa, E. (eds), *The Blackwell Guide to Epistemology*. Oxford: Blackwell Publishing, pp. 271–302.

—(2004). *The Good in the Right*. Princeton: Princeton University Press.

Augustine, Saint. (1961). *Confessions*, trans. Pine-Coffin. London: Penguin Classics.

Ayer, A. J. (1952). *Language, Truth, and Logic*. New York: Dover Books.

Baron, Marcia. (1995). *Kantian Ethics Almost without Apology*. Ithaca: Cornell University Press.

Bell, Daniel. (2006). *Beyond Liberal Democracy: Political Thinking for an East Asian Context*. Princeton: Princeton University Press.

Benedict, Ruth. (1934). "Anthropology and the abnormal," *The Journal of General Psychology* 10: 59–82.

Bennett, Jonathan. (1971). *Locke, Berkeley, Hume: Central Themes*. Oxford: Oxford University Press.

Berlin, Brent and Kay, Paul. (1969). *Basic Color Terms*. Berkeley: University of California Press.

Blackburn, Simon. (1984). *Spreading the Word*. Oxford: Oxford University Press.

—(1993). *Essays in Quasi-Realism*. Oxford: Oxford University Press.

Blair, Richard. (1995). "A cognitive developmental approach to morality: investigating the psychopath," *Cognition* 57: 1–29.

Blum, Lawrence. (1991). "Moral perception and particularity," *Ethics* 101 (4): 701–25.

—(1994). *Moral Perception and Particularity*. Cambridge: Cambridge University Press.

Boas, Franz. (1911). *The Mind of Primitive Man*. New York: The Macmillan Company.

Boyd, Richard. (1988). "How to be a moral realist," in Sayre-McCord, G. (ed.), *Essays on Moral Realism*. Cornell University Press, pp. 181–228.

Brink, David. (1989). *Moral Realism and the Foundations of Ethics*. Cambridge: Cambridge University Press.

Brock, Stuart and Mares, Edwin. (2007). *Realism and Anti-Realism*. Montreal: McGill-Queen's University Press.

Carbonell, Vanessa. (2009). "What moral saints look like," *Canadian Journal of Philosophy* 39 (3): 371–98.

Chomsky, Noam. (1965). *Aspects of the Theory of Syntax*. Cambridge: MIT Press.

Cohen, Andrew. (2004). "What toleration is," *Ethics* 115 (1): 68–95.

Cohen, Jonathan. (2009). *The Red and the Real: An Essay on Color Ontology*. Oxford: Oxford University Press.

Crisp, Roger. (2002). "Sidgwick and the boundaries of intuitionism," in Stratton-Lake, P. (ed.), *Ethical Intuitionism: Re-evaluations*. Oxford: Oxford University Press, pp. 56–75.

Damasio, Antonio. (1995). *Descartes' Error*. New York: HarperCollins Publishers.

Dancy, Jonathan. (2000). *Practical Reality*. Oxford: Oxford University Press.

Darwall, Stephen, Gibbard, Allan, and Railton, Peter. (1992). "Toward *fin de siecle* ethics: some trends," *Philosophical Review* 101 (1): 115–89.

Darwin, Charles. (1859). *The Origin of Species*. Reprinted in New York: Bantam Classic Books, 1999.

Davidson, Donald. (1974). "On the very idea of a conceptual scheme," *Proceedings and Addresses of the American Philosophical Association* 47: 5–20.

DeLapp, Kevin. (2011). "The view from somewhere: anthropocentrism in metaethics," in Boddice, R. (ed.), *Anthropocentrism: Humans, Animals, Environments*. Leiden: Brill Publishers, pp. 37–57.

—(2012). "Giving responsibility a guilt-trip: virtue, tragedy, and privilege," *Philosophica* 85: 1–32.

DePaul, Michael and Zagzebski, Linda (eds) (2003). *Intellectual Virtue.* Oxford: Oxford University Press.

Derman-Sparks, Louise. (1997). *Teaching/Learning Anti-Racism.* New York: Teachers College Press.

Doris, J. M. (2002). *Lack of Character: Personality and Moral Behavior.* New York: Cambridge University Press.

Dovidio, J. F. (1984). "Helping behavior and altruism: an empirical and conceptual overview," *Advances in Experimental Social Psychology* 17: 361–427.

Duff, R. A. (1986). *Trials and Punishments.* Cambridge: Cambridge University Press.

Duhem, Pierre. (1914). *The Aim and Structure of Physical Theory,* trans. Wiener. Princeton: Princeton University Press, 1954.

El Guindi, Fadwa. (1999). *Veil: Modesty, Privacy and Resistance.* New York: Berg Publishers.

Engberg-Pederson, Troels. (1995). "Justice at a distance – less foundational, more naturalistic," in Heinaman, R. (ed.), *Aristotle and Moral Realism.* Boulder: Westview Press, pp. 48–60.

Firth, Roderick. (1952). "Ethical absolutism and the ideal observer theory," *Philosophy and Phenomenological Research* 12: 317–45.

Flanagan, Owen. (2006). "Varieties of naturalism," in Simpson, Z. and Clayton, P. (eds), *The Oxford Handbook of Religion and Science.* Oxford: Oxford University Press, pp. 430–52.

Foot, Philippa. (1972). "Morality as a system of hypothetical imperatives," *The Philosophical Review* 81 (3): 305–16.

Foucault, Michel. (1969). *The Archaeology of Knowledge.* Reprinted in New York: Harper and Row Publishers, 1972.

Gansberg, Martin. (1964). "Thirty-eight who saw murder didn't call the police," *New York Times*, March 27.

Gauthier, David. (1986). *Morals by Agreement.* Oxford: Oxford University Press.

Geach, Peter. (1965). "Assertion," *Philosophical Review* 74: 449–65.

Geertz, Clifford. (1983). *Local Knowledge: Further Essays in Interpretative Anthropology.* New York: Basic Books.

Gewirth, Alan. (1994). "Is cultural pluralism relevant to moral knowledge?" *Social Philosophy and Policy* 11 (1): 22–43.

Gibbard, Allan. (1990). *Wise Choices, Apt Feelings.* Cambridge: Harvard University Press.

—(2003). *Thinking How to Live.* Cambridge: Harvard University Press.

Gibson, J. J. (1979). *The Ecological Approach to Visual Perception.* Hillsdale: Erlbaum Publishers.

Gilligan, Carol. (1982). *In a Different Voice.* Cambridge: Harvard University Press.

Göle, Nilüfer. (1997). *The Forbidden Modern: Civilization and Veiling.* Ann Arbor: University of Michigan Press.

Gould, S. J. (1981). *The Mismeasure of Man.* New York: W. W. Norton & Co.

Gowans, Christopher (ed.) (1987). *Moral Dilemmas.* New York: Oxford University Press.

Greenspan, Patricia. (1995). *Practical Guilt: Moral Dilemmas, Emotions, and Social Needs.* New York: Oxford University Press.

Grice, Paul. (1957). "Meaning," *The Philosophical Review* 66: 377–88.

Gruenbaum, Ellen. (2000). *The Female Circumcision Controversy: An Anthropological Perspective.* Philadelphia: University of Pennsylvania Press.

Habermas, Jürgen. (1990). *Moral Consciousness and Communicative Action.* Cambridge: MIT Press.

Haidt, Jonathan and Craig, Joseph. (2004). "Intuitive ethics: how innately prepared intuitions generate culturally variable virtues," *Daedalus* 133 (4): 55–66.

Haidt, Jonathan, Koller, Silvia Helena, and Dias, Maria. (1993). "Affect, culture, and morality, or is it wrong to eat your dog?" *Journal of Personality and Social Psychology* 65: 613–28.

Hale, Jacob [Susan]. (1991). "Against supererogation," *American Philosophical Quarterly* 28 (4): 273–85.

Hancock, Roger. (1960). "The refutation of naturalism in Moore and Hare," *Journal of Philosophy* 57 (10): 326–34.

Hare, R. M. (1952). *The Language of Morals.* Oxford: Oxford University Press.

— (1995). "A new kind of ethical naturalism," *Midwest Studies in Philosophy* 20 (1): 340–56.

Harman, Gilbert. (1975). "Moral relativism defended," in Harman, G. (ed.), *Explaining Value.* Oxford: Oxford University Press, 2000, pp. 3–19.

— (1977). *The Nature of Morality.* New York: Oxford University Press.

— (1985). "Is there a single true morality?" in Harman, G. (ed.), *Explaining Value.* New York: Oxford University Press, 2000, pp. 77–102.

— (1998). "Moral philosophy meets social psychology: virtue ethics and the fundamental attribution error," in Harman, G. (ed.), *Explaining Value.* Oxford: Oxford University Press, 2000, pp. 165–80.

Heyd, David (ed.) (1996). *Toleration: An Elusive Virtue.* Princeton: Princeton University Press.

— (2003). "Education to toleration," in McKinnon, C. and Castiglione, D. (eds), *The Culture of Toleration in Diverse Societies.* Philadelphia: University of Pennsylvania Press, pp. 196–208.

Holroyd, Jules. (2010). "The retributive emotions: passions and pains of punishment," *Philosophical Papers* 39 (3): 343–71.

Hooker, Brad and Little, Margaret. (2000). *Moral Particularism*. Oxford: Oxford University Press.

Horgan, Terence and Timmons, Mark. (1991). "New wave moral realism meets moral twin earth," *Journal of Philosophical Research* 16: 447–65.

—(1992). "Troubles for new wave moral semantics: the 'open question argument' revived," *Philosophical Papers* 21 (3): 153–75.

Hume, David. (1740). *A Treatise of Human Nature* (2nd edn), Nidditch, P. H. (ed.) Oxford: Oxford University Press, 1978.

—(1751). *An Enquiry Concerning the Principles of Morals*, Schneewind, J. B. (ed.). Indianapolis: Hackett Publishing, 1983.

Hutchinson, Brian. (2001). *G. E. Moore's Ethical Theory*. Cambridge: Cambridge University Press.

Irwin, Terence. (1977). *Plato's Moral Theory*. Oxford: Oxford University Press.

Jahanbegloo, Ramin. (1992). *Conversations with Isaiah Berlin*. London: Peter Halban Publishing.

James, William. (1891). "The moral philosopher and the moral life," *The Will to Believe and Other Essays in Popular Philosophy*. Reprinted in New York: Dover Publishing, 1956, pp. 184–215.

Johnston, Mark. (1989). "Dispositional theories of value," *Proceedings of the Aristotelian Society*, Suppl. Vol. 63: 139–74.

—(1992). "How to speak of the colors," *Philosophical Studies* 68 (3): 221–63.

Joyce, Richard. (2001). *The Myth of Morality*. Cambridge: Cambridge University Press.

Kahneman, Daniel, Slovic, Paul, and Tversky, Amos. (1982). *Judgment Under Uncertainties: Heuristics and Biases*. New York: Cambridge University Press.

Kalderon, Mark. (2005). *Moral Fictionalism*. Oxford: Oxford University Press.

—(2008). "Moral fictionalism, the Frege-Geach problem, and reasonable inference," *Analysis* 68: 133–43.

Kant, Immanuel. (1783). *Prolegomena to Any Future Metaphysics*, trans. Hatfield. Cambridge: Cambridge University Press, 2004.

—(1788). *Critique of Practical Reason*, trans. Gregor. Cambridge: Cambridge University Press, 1997.

—(1795). *Perpetual Peace*, trans. Humphrey. Indianapolis: Hackett Publishing, 1983.

Kasulis, Thomas. (2002). *Intimacy or Integrity: Philosophy and Cultural Difference*. Honolulu: University of Hawai'i Press.

Kellert, Stephen, Longino, Helen, and Waters, C. Kenneth. (2006). *Scientific Pluralism*. Minneapolis: University of Minnesota Press.

Kim, Jaegwon. (1993). *Supervenience and Mind: Selected Philosophical Essays*. Cambridge: Cambridge University Press.

King, Martin Luther King Jr. (1963). "Letter from Birmingham Jail," in Washington, J. (ed.), *I Have a Dream: Writings and Speeches That Changed The World*. San Francisco: HarperCollins, 1992.

King, Timothy. (2005). "Human color perception, cognitions, and culture: why 'red' is always 'red'," *The Society for Imaging Science and Technology* 20 (1): 1–7.

Kohlberg, Lawrence. (1971). *From Is to Ought: How to Commit the Naturalistic Fallacy and Get away with It in the Study of Moral Development*. New York: Academic Press.

Korsgaard, Christine. (1996). *Creating the Kingdom of Ends*. Cambridge: Cambridge University Press.

Kraemer, Erik. (1991). "On the moral twin earth challenge to new-wave moral realism," *Journal of Philosophical Research* 16: 467–72.

Kramer, Matthew. (2009). *Moral Realism as a Moral Doctrine*. Oxford: Wiley-Blackwell Publishers.

Kuhn, Thomas. (1962). *The Structure of Scientific Revolutions*. Chicago: University of Chicago Press.

Kwon, Kyounghee, Barnett, George, and Chen, Hao. (2009). "Assessing cultural differences in translations: a semantic network analysis of the Universal Declaration of Human Rights," *Journal of International and Intercultural Communication* 2 (2): 107–38.

Langton, Rae. (1998). *Kantian Humility*. Oxford: Oxford University Press.

Laurence, Stephen, Margolis, Eric, and Dawson, Angus. (1999). "Moral realism and twin earth," *Facta Philosophica* 1: 135–65.

Leary, Virginia. (1990). "The effect of western perspectives on international human rights," in An-Na'im, A. A. and Deng, F. M. (eds), *Human Rights in Africa: Cross-cultural Perspectives*. Washington: The Brookings Institute, pp. 15–30.

LeGuin, Ursula. (1973). "The ones who walk away from Omelas," *New Dimensions* 3: 1–8.

Levy, Neil. (2002). *Moral Relativism: A Short Introduction*. Oxford: Oneworld Publications.

Lewis, C. S. (1944). *The Abolition of Man*. Reprinted in San Francisco: Harper Books, 2001.

Lewis, David. (1989). "Dispositional theories of value," *Proceedings of the Aristotelian Society* 63: 113–37.

Lloyd, G. E. R. (2009). *Disciplines in the Making*. Oxford: Oxford University Press.

Locke, John. (1689). *A Letter Concerning Toleration*. Reprinted in Indianapolis: Hackett Publishing, 1983.

Longino, Helen. (1990). *Science as Social Knowledge: Values and Objectivity in Scientific Inquiry*. Princeton: Princeton University Press.

Lovibond, Sabina. (1983). *Realism and Imagination in Ethics*. Minneapolis: University of Minnesota Press.

MacIntyre, Alasdair. (1981). *After Virtue*. Notre Dame: University of Notre Dame Press.

Mackie, J. L. (1977). *Ethics: Inventing Right and Wrong*. London: Penguin Books.

Malinowski, Bronisław. (1922). *Argonauts of the Western Pacific*. Reprinted in Long Grove: Waveland Press, 1984.

Markus, Hazel and Kitayama, Shinobu. (1991). "Culture and the Self: Implications for Cognition, Emotion and Motivation," *Psychological Review* 98 (2): 224–53.

McDowell, John. (1978). "Are moral requirements hypothetical imperatives?" *Proceedings of the Aristotelian Society*, Suppl. Vol. 52: 13–29.

—(1979). "Virtue and reason," *The Monist* 62: 331–50.

—(1985). "Values and secondary qualities," Sayre-McCord, G. (ed.), *Essays on Moral Realism*. Reprinted in Cornell: Cornell University Press, 1988, pp. 166–80.

McNaughton, David. (1988). *Moral Vision*. Oxford: Blackwell Publishers.

Milgram, Stanley. (1974). *Obedience to Authority*. New York: Harper and Row Publishers.

Mill, John Stuart. (1869). *The Subjection of Women*. Reprinted in Indianapolis: Hackett Publishing, 1988.

Miller, J. G. and Bersoff, D. M. (1992). "Culture and moral judgment: how are conflicts between justice and interpersonal responsibilities resolved?" *Journal of Personality and Social Psychology* 62: 541–54.

Moody-Adams, Michele. (1997). *Fieldwork in Familiar Places*. Cambridge: Harvard University Press.

Moore, G. E. (1903). *Principia Ethica* (2nd edn). Cambridge: Cambridge University Press. Reprinted in Amherst: Prometheus Books, 1988.

Murdoch, Iris. (1970). *The Sovereignty of Good*. London: Routledge & Kegan Paul.

Nagel, Thomas. (1970). *The Possibility of Altruism*. Oxford: Oxford University Press.

—(1986). *The View from Nowhere*. Oxford: Oxford University Press.

—(1995). *Other Minds*. New York: Oxford University Press.

Neu, Jerome. (2000). *A Tear is an Intellectual Thing: The Meanings of Emotion*. Oxford: Oxford University Press.

Nichols, Shaun. (2004). "After objectivity: an empirical study of moral judgment," *Philosophical Psychology* 17: 3–26.

Nichols, Shaun and Folds-Bennett, Trisha. (2003). "Are children moral objectivists? Children's judgments about moral and response-dependent properties," *Cognition* 90: B23–B32.

Noddings, Nel. (1984). *Caring: A Feminine Approach to Ethics and Moral Education*. Berkeley: University of California Press.

Nucci, Larry. (2001). *Education in the Moral Domain*. Cambridge: Cambridge University Press.

Nussbaum, Martha. (1986). *The Fragility of Goodness*. Cambridge: Cambridge University Press.

—(1997). *Cultivating Humanity*. Cambridge: Harvard University Press.

Nussbaum, M. C. and Sen, A. K. (eds) (1993). *The Quality of Life*. Oxford: Oxford University Press.

Peacocke, Christopher. (1984). "Colour concepts and colour experience," *Synthese* 58: 365–82.

Penner, Terry. (1971). "Thought and desire in Plato," in Vlastos, G. (ed.), *Plato II: Ethics, Politics, and Philosophy of Art and Religion*. Garden City: Doubleday Anchor Books.

Pettit, Philip and Jackson, Frank. (1995). "Moral functionalism and moral motivation," *Philosophical Quarterly* 45 (178): 20–40.

Pettit, Philip and Smith, Michael. (1993). "Practical unreason," *Mind* 102 (405): 53–79.

Piaget, Jean. (1932). *The Moral Development of the Child*. London: Kegan Paul, Trench, Trubner and Co.

Pigden, Charles. (1991). "Naturalism," in Singer, P. (ed.), *A Companion to Ethics*. Oxford: Blackwell Publishers.

Platts, Mark. (1991). *Moral Realities: An Essay in Philosophical Psychology*. London: Routledge Publishers.

Price, Richard. (1757). *A Review of the Principal Questions in Morals*. Selby-Bigge, L. A. (ed.), *British Moralists*, Vol. 2. Reprinted in Oxford: Clarendon Press, 1897: 105–84.

Prior, A. N. (1960). "The autonomy of ethics," *Australasian Journal of Philosophy* 38 (3): 199–206.

Putnam, Hilary. (1967). "Psychological predicates," in Capitan, W. H. and Merrill, D. D. (eds), *Art, Mind, and Religion*. Pittsburgh: University of Pittsburgh Press.

—(1973). "Meaning and reference," *Journal of Philosophy* 70 (19): 699–711.

—(1975). "The meaning of 'meaning'," in *Philosophical Papers*, Vol. 2: *Mind, Language, and Reality*. Cambridge: Cambridge University Press, pp. 215–71.

—(1981). *Reason, Truth, and History*. Cambridge: Cambridge University Press.

Rachels, James. (1978). *Elements of Moral Philosophy*. New York: McGraw-Hill.

Railton, Peter. (1986). "Moral realism," *Philosophical Review* 95 (2): 163–207.

——(1998). "Aesthetic value, moral value, and the ambitions of naturalism," in Levinson, J. (ed.), *Aesthetics and Ethics*. Cambridge: Cambridge University Press, pp. 59–105.

Ramsey, Frank. (1927). "Facts and propositions," *Proceedings of the Aristotelian Society* 7 (1): 153–70.

Rawls, John. (1971). *A Theory of Justice*. Cambridge: Harvard University Press.

Reiman, Jeffrey. (1990). *Justice and Modern Moral Philosophy*. New Haven: Yale University Press.

Regan, Donald. (2003). "How to be a Moorean," *Ethics* 113 (3): 651–77.

Regan, Tom. (1986). *Bloomsbury's Prophet: G.E. Moore and the Development of His Moral Philosophy*. Philadelphia: Temple University Press.

Rescher, Nicholas. (1993). *Pluralism: Against the Demand for Consensus*. Oxford: Clarendon Press.

Rorty, Richard. (1989). *Contingency, Irony, and Solidarity*. Cambridge: Cambridge University Press.

Rosaldo, Renato. (1989). *Culture and Truth: The Remaking of Social Analysis*. Boston: Beacon Press.

Rosati, Connie. (2003). "Agency and the open question argument," *Ethics* 113 (3): 490–527.

Rosenberg, Alex. (1994). *Instrumental Biology or the Disunity of Science*. Chicago: University of Chicago Press.

Ross, W. D. (1930). *The Right and the Good*. Oxford: Oxford University Press.

Rottschaefer, William. (1999). "Moral learning and moral realism: how empirical psychology illuminates issues in moral ontology," *Behavior and Philosophy* 27 (1): 19–49.

Said, Edward. (1978). *Orientalism*. New York: Vintage Books.

Santas, Gerasimos. (1964). "The Socratic paradoxes," *Philosophical Review* 73: 147–64.

Sarkissian, Hagop, Park, John, Tien, David, Wright, Jennifer, and Knobe, Joshua. (2011). "Folk moral relativism," *Mind and Language* 26 (4): 482–505.

Sayre-McCord, Geoffrey. (1985). "Coherence and models for moral theorizing," *Pacific Philosophical Quarterly* 66: 170–90.

——(ed.) (1988). *Essays on Moral Realism*. Ithaca: Cornell University Press.

Scanlon, Thomas. (1996). "The difficulty of tolerance," in Heyd, D. (ed.), *Toleration: An Elusive Virtue*. Princeton: Princeton University Press, pp. 226–40.

——(1998). *What We Owe to Each Other*. Harvard: Harvard University Press.

Schroeder, Mark. (2005). "Realism and reduction: the quest for robustness," *Philosophers' Imprint* 5 (1): 1–18.

Schueler, G. F. (1988). "Modus ponens and moral realism," *Ethics* 98 (3): 492–500.

Schwartz, Robert. (2006). *Visual Versions*. London: MIT Press.

Selby-Bigge, L. A. (1897a). *British Moralists*, Vol. 1. Oxford: Oxford University Press.

—(1897b). *British Moralists*, Vol. 2. Oxford: Oxford University Press.

Shafer-Landau, Russ. (2003). *Moral Realism: A Defence*. Oxford: Oxford University Press.

—(2004). *Whatever Happened to Good and Evil?* Oxford: Oxford University Press.

Shaftesbury, Earl, Anthony Ashley Cooper. (1699). *Inquiry concerning Virtue or Merit*. Selby-Bigge, L. A. (ed.), *British Moralists*, Vol. 1. Reprinted in Oxford: Clarendon Press, 1897: 1–67.

Shah, Timothy and Toft, Monica. (2006). "Why God is winning," *Foreign Policy* 155: 39–43.

Sharpe, L. T. (1999). *Color Vision: From Genes to Perception*. Cambridge: Cambridge University Press.

Shweder, Richard and Haidt, Jonathan. (1993). "The future of moral psychology: truth, intuition, and the pluralist way," *Psychological Science* 4 (6): 360–5.

Sinnott-Armstrong, Walter. (1984). "'Ought' conversationally implies 'can'," *Philosophical Review* 93 (2): 249–61.

Sinnott-Armstrong, Walter and Timmons, Mark (eds) (1996). *Moral Knowledge?* Oxford: Oxford University Press.

Smart, J. J. C. (1963). *Philosophy and Scientific Realism*. London: Routledge Publishers.

Smith, Michael. (1994). *The Moral Problem*. Malden: Blackwell Publishing.

Sosa, Ernest. (1991). *Knowledge in Perspective*. Cambridge: Cambridge University Press.

Stevenson, C. L. (1944). *Ethics and Language*. New Haven: Yale University Press.

Stocker, Michael. (1976). *Plural and Conflicting Values*. Oxford: Clarendon Press.

— (1990). *Plural and Conflicting Values*. Oxford: Oxford University Press.

Stratton-Lake, Philip (ed.) (2002). *Ethical Intuitionism: Re-Evaluations*. Oxford: Oxford University Press.

Stroud, Barry. (1996). "The charm of naturalism," *Proceedings and Addresses of the American Philosophical Association* 70 (2): 43–55.

—(2000). *The Quest for Reality: Subjectivism and the Metaphysics of Colour*. Oxford: Oxford University Press.

Sturgeon, Nicholas. (1985). "Moral explanations," in Sayre-McCord, G. (ed.), *Essays on Moral Realism*. Ithaca: Cornell University Press, 1988, pp. 229–55.

Sumner, W. G. (1906). *Folkways*. Boston: Guinn Publishers.

Sylvester, Robert. (1990). *The Moral Philosophy of G.E. Moore*. Philadelphia: Temple University Press.

Tännsjö, Torbjörn. (1990). *Moral Realism*. Savage: Rowman and Littlefield Publishers.

Tatum, Beverly. (1997). *Why Are All the Black Kids Sitting Together in the Cafeteria?* New York: Basic Books.

Taylor, Charles. (1989). *Sources of the Self*. Cambridge: Harvard University Press.

—(2007). *A Secular Age*. Cambridge: Harvard University Press.

Timmons, Mark. (1990). "On the epistemic status of considered moral judgments," *The Southern Journal of Philosophy*, 1990 Spindel supplement on moral epistemology, 29: 97–129.

—(1996). "A contextualist moral epistemology," in Sinnott-Armstrong, W. and Timmons, M. (eds), *Moral Knowledge?* Oxford: Oxford University Press, pp. 293–325.

Tropman, Elizabeth. (2008). "Naturalism and the new moral intuitionism," *Journal of Philosophical Research* 33: 163–84.

Tylor, E. B. (1871). *Primitive Culture: Researches into the Development of Mythology, Philosophy, Religion, Language, Art and Custom*. Reprinted in New York: Gordon Press, 1976.

Vetleson, A. J. (1994). *Perception, Empathy, and Judgment*. University Park: University of Pennsylvania Press.

Waldron, Jeremy. (2003). "Toleration and reasonableness," in McKinnon, C. and Castiglione, D. (eds), *The Culture of Toleration in Diverse Societies*. Manchester: Manchester University Press, pp. 13–37.

Weber, Max. (1948). *Essays in Sociology*, Gerth, H. H. and Mills, C. W. (eds). Reprinted in London: Routledge 2004.

Wellman, Carl. (1975). "Ethical disagreement and objective truth," *American Philosophical Quarterly* 12 (3): 211–21.

Wiggins, David. (1976). "Truth, invention, and the meaning of life," Wiggins, *Needs, Values, Truth*. Reprinted in Oxford: Oxford University Press, 1987, pp. 87–138.

Williams, Bernard. (1965). "Ethical consistency," *Proceedings of the Aristotelian Society* 39: 103–24.

—(1981). *Moral Luck*. Cambridge: Cambridge University Press.

—(1985). *Ethics and the Limits of Philosophy*. Cambridge: Harvard University Press.

—(1996). "Toleration: an impossible virtue?" in Heyd, D. (ed.), *Toleration: An Elusive Virtue*. Princeton: Princeton University Press, pp. 18–27.

Wolf, Susan. (1982). "Moral saints," *Journal of Philosophy* 79 (8): 419–39.

—(1992). "Two levels of pluralism," *Ethics* 102 (4): 785–92.

Wong, David. (1984). *Moral Relativity*. Berkeley: University of California Press.

—(2006). *Natural Moralities: A Defense of Pluralistic Relativism*. Oxford: Oxford University Press.

Wright, Crispin. (1992). *Truth and Objectivity*. Cambridge: Harvard University Press.

INDEX